LIGHTWEIGHT CAMPING
A Four Seasons Source Book

to John Latimer with thanks

LIGHTWEIGHT CAMPING

A Four Seasons Source Book

by Michael J. Hatton

Thompson Educational Publishing, Inc.

Requests for permission to make copies of any part of the work should be mailed to the publisher. Additional copies may be obtained from Thompson Educational Publishing, Inc. Tel. (416) 766-2763 / Fax (416) 766-0398

Cataloguing in Publication Data

Hatton, Michael J. (Michael John), 1948-
    Lightweight camping

Includes bibliographical references and index.
ISBN 1-55077-003-9

1. Outdoor recreation.   2. Camping - Canada.
3. Camping - United States.   I. Title.

GV191.7.H37 1992   796.54   C92-093848-5

Photo Credits
Photos on pages x, 174, 186 by Drew Danniels; pages 20 and 76 by Joe Kaczmarczyk; pages 96 and 114 by Adam Saperstein; and pages 237, 243, 246, 254, 261, 264, 265, and 269 by Terry Skrien. All other photos are by the author.

1 2 3 4 5 97 96 95 94 93 92

Printed in the United States of America.

Table of Contents

Acknowledgements

Many people provided assistance and support in the development of this book. To them I extend my genuine appreciation.

At the risk of omitting someone I would like to thank Clara Hatton—unflagging proofreader; Drew Danniels—a wilderness traveller extraordinaire; Gino Ferri—my survival guru; Jack Gryfe—specialist in medicine and humour; Pamela Hanft—English specialist; Carol Kalbfleisch—another language authority; Doug Leonard—emergency care specialist; Bill Lorimer—medical master; Carol Marchalleck—ready typist; Don McClement—artist and philosopher; Bill Mills—equipment authority; Adam Saperstein—a fine person to share a tent and canoe with; Terry Skrien—purveyor of fine wilderness routes on every continent; and Gerry Weisberg—wilderness gourmet.

I owe a special debt to Christine, my best buddy and favourite wilderness travel partner.

Selected North American Routes

Taking a break on the Chilkoot Trail.

1

Why Go Camping?

The wild places are where we began.
When they end, so do we. — *David Brower*

Increasingly, or so it seems, large numbers of North American city dwellers choose to spend a part of their lives away from the conveniences associated with urban life. For some this means spending a day or two hiking in a nearby conservation area. For others it means spending three or four months, or even a year or more, away from the electrical appliances, central heating, automobiles, radios, and televisions that have become the "necessities" of modern life. Why do they do it? Probably for the same, simple reasons that men and women have always explored wild and unknown areas—exploration, challenge, sport, adventure, duty, science and simple wanderlust. Exploration and adventure motivated Europeans to explore North America and, over a period of several hundred years, document the rivers, lakes and trails that became the "highways" for travel throughout the continent.

Many of the original wilderness routes have been lost to civilization. The Hudson, St. Lawrence, and Mississippi rivers were once wild and untamed. Now they run thick with industrial waste. There are, however, many rivers and trails that remain largely untouched. Some are small while others are grand; some are isolated while others are relatively accessible. In fact, many of the northern trails, rivers and lakes explored by Hearne, Franklin, Richardson, Rae, Back, and more recently by Pike, Hanbury, and Tyrell, remain isolated from the modern world. These routes and their more modest counterparts attract more and more outdoor enthusiasts every year.

TECHNOLOGY AND CAMPING

Although many untracked areas, large and small, remain largely unspoiled, the manner in which they are explored and enjoyed has changed dramatically. Technological developments have affected the camping scene just as forcefully as they have affected our homes, workplaces, and urban recreational activities.

As recently as the early 1970s many, if not most, lightweight campers slept in canvas tents. Few of these tents had floors and most leaked profusely whenever anyone or anything inadvertently touched the canvas walls. Bugs entered easily and the tents were often little more than windbreaks. Nowadays, tents seem to be almost hermetically sealed. Velcro, zippers, tabs and grommets combine with double walls, vestibules, shock-corded poles, and free-standing capability to make instant lodging available in almost any outdoor locale or situation. But not only tents have been affected. New materials and production techniques have transformed clothing, sleeping bags, canoes, pack frames, stoves, and just about every other item used by lightweight campers during the last twenty years. The net effect of these changes has been to make camping safer and more pleasant than it was for earlier campers. The actual physical activity, walking or canoeing, is basically as it always was, but the creature comforts and the acceptable margins for error have been modified by better and stronger equipment.

It is interesting to compare the experience of today's explorers with that of earlier travellers. When George Back set out to trace the route of the river that now bears his name he had to spend a winter on Great Slave Lake in order to be in place early enough in the spring to both explore the river and return to the relative safety of Fort Reliance before winter arrived. These days, canoeists can fly from any major city in North America, connect through Edmonton to Yellowknife, then take a charter that will set them, their canoes and other gear down at almost any central arctic location, *all within the same day.* At the conclusion of their trip, these same canoeists may eat a hurried breakfast while hunkered behind a makeshift windbreak near the Arctic Ocean and enjoy a late dinner in Los Angeles or Toronto.

When David Hanbury spent a year and a half travelling through the central arctic he had little more than some basic supplies, including his rifles and ammunition. He had no food drops, no resupply points. In late fall, with the thermometer falling close to −40°, the point where the fahrenheit and celsius scales meet, he described the situation: "We were in a bad way for meat now. We had none left, and the dogs had starved three nights already." On the same trip he noted: " ... we started next morning, August 29th, at 2.30, for I was determined to reach the foot of the lake before the wind sprang up and stopped us. Breakfast did not cause us delay for we had none." Extreme hunger, and sometimes starvation, was a common occurrence among early explorers, as were long, arduous travel days. It was not possible to carry enough food, so hunting and bartering were expected to fill the dinner plate on most expeditions. Today's wilderness trips depend heavily on a variety of dried foods, high protein nourishment, and other long-lasting lightweight edibles. Living off the land is virtually unheard of, in part because of the attendant uncertainty.

Using paddles to portage a 40 kilo (90 lb.) Royalex canoe.

While technology has made wilderness travel safer, more than any other single factor, technology has also made possible the large influx of campers into wild and semi-wild regions throughout the world. Places that were once inaccessible without in-depth planning and long term commitment, including discomfort, privation, and physical danger, are now visited regularly by some who are no better prepared than if they were going for a stroll through an urban park. From the summer of 1834, when Back fought his way down and back up the Great Fish River, until the late 1960s, only a handful of adventurers ever repeated Back's journey. Now the river, or at least parts of it, is travelled every summer. And the same is true for trails, rivers and lakes throughout the world. Where once only the most intrepid were willing to venture, hundreds if not thousands now test themselves.

Technology has increased comfort, reduced risk, and made many regions easily accessible, but it has also made it possible for thousands of inexperienced and often ill equipped light-weight campers to penetrate the wilderness. The dangers in this tendency are obvious. Without proper preparation, including skill development, planning, and provisioning, novice canoeists and backpackers are a danger to themselves and others. A theme running through this book is: *prepare, practice, and always err on the side of caution.* Technology has made lightweight camping safer, but not free from danger. In fact, the advantages achieved through technology can provide a false sense of security. Know your equipment, know your skill level and, most of all, exercise good judgement.

CAMPING TIP

When camping, there is no substitute for good judgement.

Tarps provide quick protection from rain and sun.

HOW IT STARTS

Many canoeing and backpacking enthusiasts, particularly those with years of experience, were first exposed to the sport as children. Consequently, for thousands of campers, it was as summer campers, Scouts, Guides and cottagers that they discovered a lifelong love and appreciation for the natural world. For folks such as these, camping is simply an extension of an activity that was quite natural to them in their youth. Many friendships that began in childhood continue because of a common interest in canoeing and backpacking. The background of people on wilderness trips is often diverse: young, old, professional and blue collar come together because they share a sense of adventure, challenge and love for the outdoors, often developed in childhood. For such campers, who have grown up in a tradition of camping, finding partners and updating skills are quite natural. They read outdoor magazines, attend presentations, survey national parks in the off season and generally spend time talking, planning and dreaming about the next trip; wilderness travel isn't a question of "if," it's a question of "where" and "when."

Others lack childhood memories of camping—discovering camping only in adulthood. Their interest in wilderness travel may have developed through participation in an outers club at college or university, a vacation that exposed them to a national park or other wild place, or simply through reading one of the journals written by early explorers. Still others are just coming to the sport now. The motivating factor for them might be a morning of cross country skiing, an invitation to go canoeing at a friend's cottage, or getting turned on to bird watching during spring migration. Whatever the reason, more and more city dwellers are enjoying natural areas of the world.

For those new to the sport, finding the right partners, selecting an appropriate route, accumulating the necessary equipment, and actually setting off on the first big trip can be difficult. In most cases, making connections with others is the toughest challenge, but there are a variety of ways to accomplish this. Taking a wilderness course, such as canoeing, backpacking or survival, offered by a local board of education or a community or junior college can help. Volunteer work at a local conservation area, park or nature reserve is another approach. Bulletin boards in local outdoor stores are also good places to connect with groups or individuals looking for partners. It is always advisable to complete a short trip—two or three days—with people you have just met before tackling anything more adventurous. Personality

CAMPING TIP

Finding compatible camping partners is critical to the success of any trip.

conflicts, as well as different skill levels and goals, are difficult to assess when pouring over maps in the comfort of someone's basement. Know your partners well before you leave home.

TAKING CHILDREN

Lightweight camping with children can be a delight or it can be a disaster. With proper planning and preparation children will almost certainly have a fantastic outdoor experience that will help instill values related to teamwork, cooperation, self-reliance, independence, hard work, and an appreciation and love for the natural world. They will want to do it again and again. My goal when taking children camping is to ensure that they have fun. If the trip isn't fun, you shouldn't be surprised if children don't want to repeat it.

I clearly recall one of my first canoe trips. In mid afternoon, after having paddled for five or six hours, the leader in the stern of the canoe where I was assigned began to splash me, while simultaneously yelling at me to paddle harder. He continued doing this for the next two hours, until we finally made camp for the night. I was eight years old. To this day I remember thinking and feeling that I was paddling just about as hard as I could. How could he expect more? Did he feel the way I felt? I doubt it. When I began leading trips with young kids, I remembered how I felt on that day. My rule with kids in a canoe is simple: you can paddle or not paddle as you wish, but please don't paddle backwards! I encourage them to paddle, I praise their paddling, and I attempt to subtly maximize their paddling effort when I need it most, but I never punish a child based on paddling performance. Similarly, when backpacking with kids, it is important to be realistic about how much a child can carry and over what distance. I believe every child should have a paddle when canoeing and every child should carry some gear when backpacking, but the basic rule remains the same: fun comes first. Come to think of it, that's the same rule I apply to myself!

The question of how old children should be before you take them on a wilderness trip is difficult to answer. It depends in large part on the child, and, to at least some degree, upon the parents or leaders and the type of trip. I know some parents who have taken four and five year old children on trips lasting several weeks. I find that three or four days when they reach the age of six or seven is plenty. A trip of that length is much easier to control.

Fishing for walleye below Hell's Gate on the Missinaibi River.

Before taking any child on a wilderness trip you need to consider carefully how well the child will follow instructions, how easily the child is distracted and, if you are canoeing, how long the child will be able to sit in a confined space. Another critical issue to address is your degree of patience. Children will be slower, clumsier, and more easily distracted when in the outdoors. There is much to see and do, and so much of it is new. Considerable patience is required. If you are highly tolerant and the children are able to listen carefully and follow instructions then wilderness trips are possible at an earlier age. In any event, every child needs to be carefully coached ahead of time. You need to discuss what to do in all those "what if" situations, such as what if the canoe tips; what if someone gets lost on the trail; what if an animal comes into the campsite; what if black flies or mosquitoes get into the tent at night; and so on. Swimming ability is another important variable to consider. Planned well, a trip with children can be the best kind.

THE ENVIRONMENT

Not so long ago, most wilderness campers expressed little concern for the natural environment. It was considered perfectly acceptable to cut down trees in order to make a tripod from which to hang the tent. It was commonly accepted that digging trenches around the tent was the best way to ensure that rain wouldn't encroach into a sleeping area. No one seemed disturbed by the large fire rings common at popular campsite areas on trails, and garbage was often left at campsites or even dumped in the water. Such attitudes are no longer appropriate.

How well today's campers protect the natural environment will determine what parts, if any, of our wilderness areas remain for our children and our children's children to explore during the twenty-first century. In most designated wilderness areas, there is a carry-in and carry-out policy. Campers are expected to leave nothing behind. Some parks go further, banning all bottles and, in a few cases, wood fires. In these areas campers are expected to empty the contents of bottles into plastic containers or to look for alternative foods. Instead of wood fires, stoves are required unless campers go fireless. The number of areas where strict regulations are in force is increasing, but the ultimate value of these restrictions will always depend on the goodwill, if not good sense, of all canoeists and backpackers. Strict enforcement is not possible, so self-regulation is required. Campers must accept responsibility for policing their own actions. This means teaching children by example, and not being afraid to constructively comment on the environmental behaviour of others in your party.

Disposal of cooking and human waste is a neglected topic in many camping books. This has fostered outdated ideas, a general lack of awareness, and very often an attitude of indifference. Inappropriate treatment of waste can attract animals, pollute the soil and water, and despoil campsites. The importance of the subject merits its inclusion in the first chapter of this book. Foodstuffs, scraps, leftovers and cooking waste must be carried out, burned, or securely buried far enough from the water table to prevent it leaching into the system. The specific approach will depend on the area and the type of use it receives. Appropriate disposal of human waste is even more important, both for personal enjoyment of the outdoors and for the environmental concerns that relate to it. A major cause of *giardia* is human fecal waste. Basically, this means that there are many people who don't have the good sense and commitment necessary to avoid destroying sections of wilderness simply because they are unable to deal with the disposal of human waste in the outdoors. The required approach is pretty simple—*human waste should be buried far from any water source.* Typically, this means at least 50 metres (160 feet) from lakes, rivers, and any high water marks, as well as at least 1 metre (3 feet) above the water table. Feces are buried in order to prevent disease being spread by people, storm run-off, or animals, including flying insects. One reason we are struggling with the problem of *giardia* and other waste associated problems is that few of us were taught as children what to do when faced with the need to defecate in the woods. If you camp with children, make sure they understand what is expected and how to go about it. You will probably discover that they find the subject much easier to deal with than do most adults. For a comprehensive treatment of the subject see Kathleen Meyer's book noted in the suggested reading at the end of this chapter.

FOCUS OF THIS BOOK

This book's primary goal is to provide a broad reference source for a host of information and ideas related to lightweight camping. Consequently, you will find that the following chapters deal with various issues that are often the subject material for single books. In providing this scope I have necessarily not given great depth to some topics. For this reason, every chapter concludes with suggested reading that will allow those with specific and detailed interests to investigate them further.

Chapter Two examines insulation, fabrics and materials common to lightweight camping clothing and gear. Chapter Three reviews and evaluates equipment. Together, these two chapters provide a detailed overview and critique of designs and new materials that have affected the construction and manufacture of outdoor clothing and basic camping gear during the last two decades.

Chapter Four focuses on wilderness travel, examining the effective use of topographical maps in conjunction with orienteering compasses. Chapter Five describes basic dietary issues of interest to lightweight campers and includes menu suggestions for backpacking and canoeing. Although prevention is always the best cure, problems can crop up and accidents do occur. For this reason, Chapter Six reviews a variety of survival tips and techniques, and Chapter Seven provides an overview of wilderness emergency care procedures.

Chapters Eight and Nine focus on equipment and techniques for canoeing, backpacking, snowshoeing and cross country skiing. Chapter Ten highlights a variety of very special hiking, cycling, canoeing, snowshoeing, and cross-country routes that are particularly special for their history, geography, wildlife, or beauty.

See you on the trail!

ENVIRONMENTAL TIP

Deet based bug repellants are the most effective. However, Avon's Skin So Soft lotion and Ben Gay are good, earth-friendly alternatives.

SUGGESTED READINGS

- Back, G. (1836). *Captain Back's Journal: Narrative of the Arctic Land Expedition to the Mouth of the Great Fish River and Along the Shores of the Arctic Ocean in the Years 1833, 1834, and 1835.* London: John Murray.

- Douglas, G. (1914). *Lands Forlorn: A Story of an Expedition to Hearne's Coppermine River.* New York: The Knickerbocker Press.

- Downes, P. (1943). *Sleeping Island.* New York: Coward-McCann.

- Gordon, P., and Choquette, F. (1990). *Nowhere to Grow but Up: A Guide to Tree Planting.* Toronto: Plot Publishing.

- Hanbury, D. (1904). *Sport and Travel in the Northland of Canada.* London: Edward Arnold.

- Hubbard, L. (1909). *A Woman's Way through Unknown Labrador: An Account of the Exploration of the Nascaupee and George Rivers.* New York: Doubleday, Page & Company.

- Mowat, F. (1973). *Tundra.* Toronto: McClelland & Stewart Ltd.

- Meyer, K. (1989). *How to Shit in the Woods.* Berkeley, California: Ten Speed Press.

- Pike, W. (1892). *The Barren Ground of Northern Canada.* London: MacMillan and Co.

- Russel, F.(1898). *Explorations in the Far North.* Iowa City, Iowa: State University of Iowa.

- Russel, M. (1986). *The Blessings of a Good, Thick Skirt: Women Travellers and their World.* London: Collins.

- Seton, E. T. (1911). *The Arctic Prairies: A Canoe Journey of 2,000 Miles in Search of Caribou; Being the Account of a Voyage to the Region North of Aylmer Lake.* New York: Charles Scribner's Sons.

- Tyrell, J. W. (1908). *Across the Sub-Arctics of Canada* (3rd Ed.). Toronto: William Briggs.

- Wallace, D. (1905). *The Lure of the Labrador Wild: The Story of the Exploring Expedition Conducted by Leonidas Hubbard, Jr.* (5th Ed.). New York: Fleming H. Revell Co.

- Wallace, D. (1907). *The Long Labrador Trail.* New York: The Outing Publishing Company

- Whitney, C. (1896). *On snowshoes to the barren grounds: Twenty-eight hundred miles after musk-oxen and wood-bison.* New York: Harper & Brothers Publishers.

Setting up camp quickly before a snowstorm.

Several layers of wool clothing and a thick-walled
snow shelter make for a comfortable night's sleep

2
Insulation and Clothing

A good camper knows that it is more important to be ingenious than to be a genius.

Pierre Trudeau

S ummer campers in the Canadian Barrens often experience severe winter blizzards. And anyone who has hiked in the Scottish highlands has probably been surprised by sudden summer storms bringing brutal weather conditions. Complacency in the summer months can leave us dangerously unprepared for unexpected weather changes. Unanticipated cold weather is a constant danger for the unwary. Understanding the basics of insulation and heat loss is one of the most important lessons anyone who spends time outdoors can learn. This chapter examines how heat loss occurs, how to minimize it, and the characteristics and qualities of camping fabrics and clothing that enable us to guard against it.

HEAT LOSS

The ways in which the human body loses heat can be classified according to five types: radiation, conduction, convection, evaporation, and respiration. Understanding the ways in which body heat may be lost is the first step towards control and prevention.

The body *radiates* heat directly away from the core, most severely at exposed areas such as the face, hands, and neck. For exposed areas, the greater the differential between air temperature and skin temperature, the greater the rate of heat transfer. If the skin and the air are at the same temperature, the heat loss through radiation is minimized.

Conduction takes place when heat moves away from the body in a similar fashion to the way in which electricity moves along a

IN THIS CHAPTER
- **Heat Loss**
- **Insulation**
- **Fabrics and Insulators**
- **Manufacturing Quality**
- **Clothing**
- **A Few Words about Kits**

wire. If you sit on a rock in the dead of winter wearing only a pair of jeans, heat will be transferred directly from your body into the rock. Again, the greater the temperature differential, the faster the rate of heat transfer.

Heat loss through *convection* occurs when the wind blows cold air against the body. Air molecules quickly absorb body heat and are immediately replaced by new, cold air molecules which then absorb more body heat. If the body is not exposed to the wind, the air molecules do not get replaced as quickly. So, as the air molecules absorb body heat, the temperature differential between the molecules and the body decreases, resulting in diminished heat loss. In a vigorous wind, the air molecules are constantly being replaced; therefore, the temperature differential is not reduced. For this reason, campers in cold weather conditions should always minimize exposure to the wind. There is a common fallacy that, for significant heat loss to take place through convection, winds must be strong, something in the order of 30–40 kilometres per hour (18–24 miles per hour). The truth is that a wind of only 10–15 kilometres per hour (6–9 miles per hour) can result in significant heat loss under borderline conditions.

Heat loss through *evaporation* takes place as sweat dries on skin. If you don't sweat, heat loss by evaporation is minimal. Body heat loss through *respiration* is particularly noticeable in the winter, when cold, dry air goes into the lungs, and warmer, moist air comes out. Covering your mouth with a scarf may reduce the heat loss, but the scarf soon becomes quite uncomfortable since the water vapour condenses and freezes. The frozen scarf is solid evidence of water loss and shows why it is important to drink plenty of fluids when camping in cold weather conditions.

CLOTHING TIP

The goal is to balance heat production and heat loss.

Heat results from normal life processes. In other words, if we are alive, we produce heat. Heat results from food digestion and exercise. Our goal should be to reach a balance between heat loss and heat production, preferably without sweating. The wise camper is aware of all the ways to gain and lose heat and always works towards an equilibrium state.

INSULATION

The function of insulation is to minimize heat loss. Surrounding your body with one or more layers of material between your skin and the great outdoors creates a barrier that slows down the rate at which body heat dissipates. If heat passes through the material slowly, then little body heat is lost. The slower the heat

Managing Heat Loss

The rules for reducing heat loss are simple and obvious:	In hot weather, the rules are simply reversed:
1. Minimize the amount of exposed body surface. This means wearing gloves, hat or balaclava, and a scarf.	1. Maximize the amount of exposed body surface, providing you are not directly exposing it to an object warmer than your body.
2. Don't sit, lean on or touch cold surfaces unless you have a good insulator between your body and the object.	2. Eat cold foods, soak your hands and feet in cool water, and sit on rocks, moss, or earth that are in shaded areas.
3. Minimize the exposure of your body to the wind.	3. Maximize the exposure of your body to the wind.
4. Avoid sweating.	4. Sweating should be automatic.
5. Drink plenty of warm liquids.	5. Drink plenty of cool liquids.

loss, the better the insulator. Therefore, one measure of the quality of insulation is the degree to which it impedes heat transfer. With regard to clothing, superior insulation occurs with material that traps and holds air in tiny spaces within the fabric. Trapped air is a very good insulator.

The trapped air phenomenon is often referred to as layering or as the *layering principle* of dressing for the outdoors. Several layers of clothing will also trap air between the materials, whereas one thick article of clothing only traps air within the garment itself. In addition, under changing conditions, several thin layers of clothing can be manipulated. If your body is too hot, one layer of clothing can be removed. When you stop for a rest, and your body starts to cool off, it's time to add a layer or two. Wearing only one thick piece of clothing is an all or nothing proposition.

Water is a good conductor of heat; therefore, sweating will quickly extract heat from the body, particularly in cold weather. Sweating also creates a secondary problem. The water effects a structural change in many types of insulators, making them less effective. It is important to try to avoid sweating, not simply because it speeds heat loss from the body, but also because sweating reduces the insulating effectiveness of many types of clothing.

A cup of tea and a high protein snack help keep the cold at bay.

Wearing a windproof shell over layered clothing reduces the effect of wind on the body's supply of heat. If the weather is cold and wet, the shell should also be water resistant or waterproof. This will both reduce the effect of water on heat loss and enhance the insulation of clothing.

Your body also produces moisture from within by producing and emitting water vapour as part of the normal body process. This water vapour can build up and condense on your clothing, particularly if you are wearing an outer shell that is waterproof. This is why insulation needs to be vented. A waterproof shell, designed for rain protection, will also prevent water vapour that comes off the body from exiting. On a nice sunny day water vapour has little problem exiting through layered clothing. However, this is not necessarily true when camping in wet or cold conditions, particularly if you are wearing waterproof clothing. Under these conditions it is even more important to vent the water vapour given off by the body. Tips include wearing clothing that is loose at the bottom, minimizing perspiration by moving slowly, and not allowing the body to overheat.

CLOTHING TIP

Waterproof shells need to be vented, otherwise you will feel as if it rained inside your jacket!

In summary, the purpose of insulation is to prevent excessive heat loss from the body. Good insulators often make use of trapped air in small compartments of the fabric. The greater the thickness of the insulator, and the less air movement or transfer, the greater the insulation value. Trapped air is a good insulator for campers since it is light and costs nothing. Layered clothing creates additional dead air space between the layers. In addition, the layering technique can be used to help balance heat loss and

Staying Warm	
1. Minimize heat transfer by trapping air molecules. The best insulators work in this way.	3. Keep your clothing dry.
2. Use the layering principle whenever practical; it is effective and low cost.	4. Make sure your clothing can breathe, so water vapour doesn't get trapped. In wet weather, this is more difficult, but also more important.

heat production. Sweaters can be put on at rest points on the trail, then taken off just before starting again. Windproof and rainproof shells are excellent for preventing heat loss under windy and rainy conditions. However, it is also important that you properly vent your clothing to ensure that water vapour from your body evaporates, thereby keeping clothing dry and snug.

FABRICS AND INSULATORS

This section of the chapter examines a variety of fabrics that are typically used in the production of camping clothing, focusing especially on some of the synthetic materials developed during the last two decades. If you know something about materials currently used in making camping clothes and gear, you will spend your money more wisely.

Although *cotton* is an old standby, it is not a great insulator. If cotton gets wet, it provides almost no insulation. When wet it simply becomes cold, clammy and whisks heat away from the body. Cotton also takes a very long time to dry. The advantage of cotton is that it breathes extremely well. Water vapour loves to skip right through the material. Yet, if you wear a non-breathable fabric outside cotton, the "breathability" of the cotton disappears and the material absorbs perspiration and becomes dripping wet. Cotton is very comfortable next to skin, few people are allergic to it since it is a natural fabric, and it expands slightly when wet.

Traditionally, *wool* has been a frequently used material for outdoor clothing. Its most important quality is that, when wet, wool retains a good deal of its ability to insulate. Wool is warm. This is because it effectively traps air molecules and absorbs very little water. Wool also breathes well; it can be worn even in hot weather. Wool pants, shirts, jackets, hats, mitts and other wool articles have been and still are very popular. Another very attractive advantage of wool is its cost. Compared to some "high-tech" materials, wool is inexpensive. Campers on a tight budget might consider visiting an army surplus store, purchasing a set of wool clothes, and wearing them until them until they fall apart. Some people find wool very abrasive; it chafes the skin, and creates burn-like sores. This is worse in warm weather, of course. While some people can wear woollen underwear quite comfortably, others wouldn't last a day in it. My advice is to wear wool if you can. It's cheap and effective.

Nylon is a strong fabric. But since it is quite thin, nylon is not effective, by itself, for trapping air. Nylon often serves as a shell or encloses insulation materials. *Ripstop nylon*, a variation of ordinary nylon, has an extra thread woven into it. This helps prevent runs when individual threads break. For camping clothes and gear, ripstop nylon is *de rigueur. Taffeta* and *cordura* are heavier nylon materials and more abrasion resistant than lightweight ripstop nylon. Usually, *oxford* and *duck* are progressively heavier cotton fabrics; however, the terms oxford and duck also describe some heavy, abrasion-resistant nylons. Another fabric often used for camping clothes is *60/40 cloth*. It makes use of the strength of nylon and the breathability of cotton. The horizontal threads are nylon (40%) and the vertical threads (60%) are cotton. Some vertical shrinkage will take place. Another variation is *65/35 cloth*. It combines 65% polyester and 35% cotton, coiled together then woven. Finally, *80/20 cloth* uses the same materials in different proportions.

Manufacturers sometimes coat fabrics to enhance their water repellency. *K-Kote*[TM], produced by Kenyon Industries, is a common urethane coating used to coat fabrics and seams. On the plus side, heavily coated fabrics keep the rain out. But coated fabrics don't allow water vapour to exit, and they add weight to the garment. By comparison, some newer fabrics do a pretty good job of incorporating water-resistance with breathability.

Well-known breathable and waterproof fabrics include *Helly Tech*[TM], *Entrant*[TM], *Nature-Tex*[TM], *Dermoflex*[TM], *H2 No*[TM], and *Ultrex*[TM]. The best known and generally accepted leader in the field is *Gore-Tex*[TM] (a registered trademark belonging to W. L. Gore and Associates). Gore-Tex fabric is made from polytetrafluoroethylene, an extremely porous material. These pores are minutely small—approximately 9 billion per square inch. The pores are too small for water drops to pass through, but large enough for water vapour. Gore-Tex is not a coating or a laminate, as are most of the waterproof and breathable fabrics; it is a membrane sandwiched between fabrics. Before the introduction of Gore-Tex,

Fabric Comparison Table

Material	Water Entry Pressure (*p.s.i.*)	Moisture Vapour Transmission Rate (Grams M²/24 hr.)	Windproofness (CFM x 1,000)
Gore-Tex™	65.0	11,250	0
Helly Tech™	4.2	4,040	67
Entrant™	5.0	2,500	8
Ultrex™	3.3	1,754	26
H₂ No Storm™	19.0	1,620	0
K-Kote™ *	39.7	500	**
60/40 Cloth *	0.5	5,200	**

* For comparison purposes.
** Not tested.

The first column in the Fabric Comparison Table notes the air pressure required to force water drops through the fabric. The higher the number, the greater the "waterproofness." The moisture vapour column notes the rate at which the water vapour will pass through the fabric. The higher the number the more breathable the fabric. In the last column, the lower the number the more windproof the fabric.

NOTE: With the exception of the figures for K-Kote and 60/40 cloth, this data was taken from the *Gore-Tech Answer Book*, published by W.L. Gore, 1990.

waterproof and breathable fabrics were mutually exclusive. Now it is possible to have one shell for both sunny and rainy weather.

When Gore-Tex fabric was first introduced, there was a tendency for the small pores to become clogged with oils. Gore introduced a new and refined Gore-Tex in 1979 to overcome this problem. Later, in response to marketplace concerns, Gore moved from being a fabric supplier to a licenser. Now, every manufacturer using Gore-Tex fabric must meet Gore's production standards. (As a result, you can't buy Gore-Tex fabric in kit form.) The manufacturer checks Gore garments to ensure that the product meets high standards and that leaks don't occur because of poor design or sewing.

The figures in the Fabric Comparison Table show that Gore-Tex fabric combines waterproofness and extremely good water vapour transmission *when compared to other waterproof/breathable fabrics*. This, along with the Gore-Tex guarantee, is why many outdoor enthusiasts describe Gore-Tex as the Cadillac of waterproof and breathable fabrics. There is, however, an impor-

CLOTHING TIP

Gore-Tex is considered by many to be the Cadillac of waterproof and breathable fabrics.

Wool hats and spray covers help keep these canoeists warm on a windy, overcast day in the central arctic.

tant qualification. Your comfort level will be influenced to a much greater degree by how you dress, what activities you undertake, and how you treat your clothes and your body, than by whether you purchase a Gore-Tex or Helly Tech jacket. Carrying a heavy canoe across a long and difficult portage during a rainstorm is going to produce more sweat than can be easily and readily transmitted through any fabric. The ideal is to pace your activities, move slowly, vent your clothes, and wear waterproof and breathable fabrics when appropriate. Technique and high-tech clothes should be combined.

The technology of waterproof and breathable fabrics can make life on the trail more pleasant, but it requires understanding and effort on your part. Many campers spend a lot of money on a new Helly Tech or Gore-Tex outfit only to discover that they still sweat, and end up being uncomfortable. These fabrics are not a panacea, just a tool. As with other tools, you have to understand and work with their limitations. Gore-Tex fabric continues to be used in the construction of more and more camping clothes and gear, including tents, sleeping bags and even boots. High cost and licensing requirements are drawbacks that have prevented wider adoption of Gore-Tex.

These new high-tech, waterproof and breathable fabrics may be windproof but they don't do a great job as insulators. One of the best pure insulators, and the most traditional, is *down*. Down is the undercoating of waterfowl (tiny little fluffs of feathery material). Most commercially used down comes from ducks and geese raised for the poultry market in Asia. Down has no quills,

How To Wash A Down-Filled Article

First, try to keep the article as clean as possible. This reduces the number of times it has to be cleaned, thereby increasing its life. When it's time to wash your down sleeping bag or jacket, soak it thoroughly in warm water with a non-detergent soap such as Ivory. Specialty camping stores sell prepared cleaning detergent for down. After soaking the item fully, hand wash it, being careful not to put too much stress on the seams and other weak areas. After gentle washing, rinse the garment completely. If soap remains in the material, the down will not regain its natural loft as much as it otherwise would. After rinsing the article, dry it in an automatic dryer on the cool setting. Add a running shoe to the dryer to break up the clumps of down, and a small towel or wash cloth to absorb excess moisture. The drying procedure takes a while.

just plumes, from which many soft fluffy hairs emanate. These hairs interweave with each other, and their surface area forms the thousands upon thousands of dead air spaces that act as insulators. Water vapour has little difficulty escaping through the dead air spaces unless the down is enclosed by a non-breathable fabric. In that event, the water vapour will build up over time, condense, and collapse the down. Once down has collapsed, the dead air spaces are gone and its effectiveness as an insulator is almost completely destroyed. Down is an excellent insulator because of its light weight, compressibility, and high lofting ability. (The loft is the thickness of the insulator. All other things being equal, the greater the thickness, the better the insulation.)

As the saying goes, "quality just isn't what it used to be." The market for down has changed and so have the standards. Good quality down of the 1990s doesn't loft to nearly the same degree, by weight, as good quality down of the 1960s. And, the supply of quality down is likely to continue to diminish. Although it's still possible to get very high lofting down, you now have to pay a much higher price for it. Be sure to check the quality of the down, and its loft, before investing in any down product. The lofting ability of the down is more important than what type of bird it came from. Beware of labels that state "100% Down" since it is impossible to separate the feathers from the down completely.

There are two major drawbacks to down. The first is its high cost. The second is that down will lose most of its loft, and therefore its insulation value, when wet. To make down articles

Candles can be used to provide heat and light inside a snow shelter.

retain their lofting abilities as long as possible, one should avoid storing them for long periods in stuff bags, using them as cushions, or allowing them to get unnecessarily dirty.

Synthetic insulators have made great inroads on the camping scene during the last two decades. Dupont produces and markets a synthetic insulator under the trademark *Hollowfil II*™ and another one under the trademark *Quallowfil*™. These products act as insulators in clothing, sleeping bags, and duvets. Quallowfil is the better of the two products. Dupont describes it as a modern alternative to down. In truth, both Hollowfil II and Quallowfil are bulky, heavier, and less compact than down. However, they are considerably less expensive, can be easily washed, are non-allergenic, and lose little of their insulation value when wet. This last point is the most important. For wet and cold weather camping on a budget, Quallowfil is a good choice. Celanese markets a synthetic material, under the trademark *Polarguard*™, that is similar in insulation value and character to the Dupont products.

These synthetic insulators are polyesters—petrochemicals converted into thin fibres. The Dupont products consist of hollow fibres, while Polarguard has long continuous filament fibres. Dupont claims that the hollow fibres create more insulation per weight and that, since they treat the resin used to stabilize the fibres with silicone, there is less friction, shifting, and consequent cold spots. According to Celanese, Polarguard batting doesn't shift because of its continuous filament fibres. This characteristic is particularly important for good quality sleeping bags, and is mainly why some sleeping bag manufacturers and wholesale buyers prefer Polarguard. It also supports the conviction held by some wholesale buyers that Polarguard sleeping bags are more durable than other bags constructed with similar synthetic insulators. I have slept in sleeping bags with Hollowfil II insulation and in bags with Polarguard insulation, and have found that both kept me warm and comfortable. My impression is that the most important differences are in the manufacture of the garment or gear, such as the quality of the fabric, number of stitches per centimetre, or type of seam used.

Another synthetic widely used in outdoor clothing is *Thinsulate*™, a registered trademark of 3M Company. Thinsulate makes use of microfibres many times smaller than the fibres found in conventional polyesters. The result is more trapped air and greater insulation. According to the company, a given thickness of Thinsulate is about twice as efficient as the same thickness of Polarguard or Hollowfil II. Along with the standard advantages of synthetics, Thinsulate reduces much of the bulk normally associated with synthetics. The price of Thinsulate is usually somewhere between down and Quallowfil. Not to be outdone by 3M's Thinsulate, Dupont has a competing product—*Thermolite*™. Dupont claims that the size of the fibres in Thermolite are the same length as the wave length of the body's radiant heat. Supposedly, this helps minimize heat loss. For practical purposes, Thermolite and Thinsulate are comparable. Both are "thin" insulation materials that lose very little insulative value when wet.

To make matters just a little more confusing, there is another, quite different insulator product edging its way into the clothing and equipment market—*Primaloft*™. Primaloft was developed because of the U.S. Army's interest in finding a down equivalent that would retain its loft when wet. Albany International markets the product.Compared to other synthetics, Primaloft is a much more realistic down equivalent. It combines the high warmth to weight ratio found in down, with extremely low water absorption. After Primaloft was immersed in water for twenty minutes, one test showed it gained only 6% of its weight, compared to 159% for down. Even more surprising are test results that show Primaloft slightly better in the heat retention category than equal amounts of down.

INSULATION TIP

Primaloft doesn't lose its loft when wet, and some tests suggest it retains heat better than down.

Over the last few years, polyester based synthetic fleece has had a tremendous influence on the outdoor clothing market. Most high-quality synthetic fleece comes from Malden Mills in the United States. Initially priced high, synthetic fleece is now fairly inexpensive and widely available. It is very warm, absorbs very little moisture, and is quick drying. One of the best known designers and marketers of synthetic fleece products is Patagonia. Their fleece products, marketed as *Synchilla*™ pile, are among the best, and their prices tend to reflect that positioning. Many other companies make good fleece products and most campers include a fleece-lined jacket or shell in their stuff bags. If you get cold on a rainy day, find yourself cooling off too quickly as the sun sets on the barrens, or simply like to cosy up with a piece of soft, comfortable fabric at night, consider fleece products.

MANUFACTURING QUALITY

We have already mentioned in this chapter, but it bears repeating, that the quality of the manufacturing process may be more important than the specific fabrics used. Three important things to look at before purchasing any garment or piece of gear are the seams, the quality of the stitching, and the type of zippers.

Figure 2-1
Lap Felled Seam

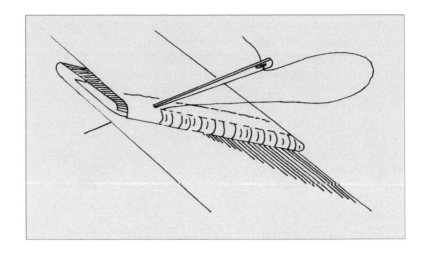

Seams vary considerably, but a good, common seam is the lap felled (see Fig. 2–1). It is strong, durable, and usually reflects a manufacturer who is proud of the product. When considering a purchase, check the ends of the seams to make sure each is finished evenly and straight, and that there is no material left hanging. Stitching should be regular and consistent.

Zippers may be either metal or synthetic, the latter being more common. Coil zippers have the advantage over cast tooth zippers in that they are self-healing. On the other hand, coil zippers are not as strong as metal and each time a coil zipper breaks open, it loses some strength. Good strong zippers are imperative. I have had more equipment problems related to zippers than any other specific feature of my clothing and gear. In particular, tents and sleeping bags often seem to suffer from inadequate zippers. During bug season or in cold weather, a broken zipper can have drastic consequences.

In summary, there are a host of different fabrics designed to provide protection from the wind and rain and transmit water vapour away from the body. Insulation traps dead air and thus reduces heat loss. Down is the best natural insulator, providing it stays dry. Besides down, there are many synthetics that are highly effective insulators. Much of the discussion in this chapter has centred on so-called high-tech fabrics. Not surprisingly, these products are expensive. Therefore, it is appropriate to conclude this section by stressing that you don't need the latest fabrics and insulators to enjoy the outdoors. Wool clothing, a coated rain jacket, and sturdy boots will hold you in good stead for most trips. Often, it is the most inexperienced people on the trail or the river who have the most expensive clothing and gear. The old-timers are the ones dressed in army surplus clothes. High-tech fabrics and insulators are effective and helpful, but they are not essential for a great camping experience.

CLOTHING TIP

Wool is often the best choice for outdoor clothing.

CLOTHING

With outdoor clothing and camping gear, it is important to understand the purpose that the particular item has been designed to serve, its strengths and limitations, and then to appropriately match clothing and gear to the specific needs of your budget and the particular trip. It is important that you carry the right type of clothing and equipment, don't under use it, or end up disappointed by its failure, if and when you stretch the material beyond its design.

Socks come in a variety of shapes, sizes and materials. The most popular are mid-calf 100% wool, largely because of the inherent properties of wool. As discussed earlier, wool absorbs very little moisture, compared to cotton, and is faster drying. As an insulator, wool is better than cotton, nylon or orlon. Nylon, as a component (10–20%) of wool socks, adds strength and helps the socks to retain their shape. *Spandex* is sometimes used to give stretch to the sock. For camping socks, the amount of spandex need not exceed 5% of the total material. *Orlon* is found in many of the wick dry socks. This type of sock is designed to wick moisture away from the foot, leaving it comfortable and dry. Some users report that Orlon also seems to wick away heat; consequently, the feet get cold quickly. *Silk socks* are preferred by some campers because they reduce friction and allow moisture to pass through to an outer sock. Silk socks may be a good alternative for people who find wool too rough for wearing next to the skin. Wearing two pair of socks is often a good idea, providing your boot has been sized accordingly. The extra layer provides more insulation (remember the layer theory), and two pairs of socks will allow for greater movement between the boot and foot thereby reducing the likelihood of blisters.

Underwear is available in a variety of fabrics and designs. In summer, many people find that wool worn next to the skin, particularly in the area of the hips and inner thighs, is too rough. For this reason, and the problem of cleanliness, cotton boxer shorts are often the preferred choice in warm weather conditions. Cotton boxer shorts absorb moisture, they can be easily washed, and they don't chafe the skin. In colder conditions, long cotton underwear is problematic. Though comfortable, cotton

Bug hats make life much easier in the barrens.

Good fitting boots and Vibram soles make it much easier to traverse scree slopes like this one in Dena National Park.

longjohns are very difficult to dry. Therefore, in the winter, wool longjohns are preferred, providing you can put up with the roughness. Fishnet underwear used to be popular, but is becoming much harder to find. In part, this is because of increased competition from synthetics. The advantage of fishnet underwear is that pockets of air are created next to the skin. Water vapour can easily move into these pockets, instead of being trapped in the garment itself, and the trapped air acts as a good insulator. Silk underwear, though difficult to find, has a strong following. It has a good feel to it, breathes extremely well, and, with proper care, spun silk underwear will last a very long time. However, with the development of more and more synthetics, it probably won't be long before silk underwear is a collector's item.

In terms of synthetics, waterproof *polypropylene underwear* has become quite popular. Because the material is waterproof, water vapour passes through the underwear, often driven by body heat, to the outside layers of clothing. *Lifa*™ is one of the best known brands of polypropylene underwear. Disadvantages of polypropylene underwear include its tendency to retain body odour and the fact that it is hard to wash. Polypropylene is hard to wash because it won't absorb any water, so body oils, salt and other foreign substances can't be rinsed away. If you tend to have more than an average problem with body odour, you may prefer to stay away from polypropylene products. If washed, polypropylene should be dried on a cool cycle since it tends to cook at high temperatures. *Chlorofibre*™ and *Capilene*™ are different from polypropylene. These polyester synthetics have been treated to wick moisture away from the body by lifting and dispersing or spreading the water vapour throughout the fabric. Polyesters are normally water-repellent (not waterproof); however, Chlorofibre and Capilene, have had their surfaces treated to make them hydrophillic (water-loving). This results in a core material that remains dry, and a surface area that attracts water and carries or wicks it away from the body. These polyester synthetics are softer and easier to wash than polypropylene. And, by contrast, polypropylene has virtually no wicking ability since it is waterproof. Both polypropylene and polyester synthetics are good insulators, often used for cold weather camping. Most manufacturers using these materials offer several different thicknesses. I recommend polypropylene. The latest polypropylene products are excellent, and I have not found the washing and odour problems to be critical.

CLOTHING TIP

Wool underwear is warm, but most campers find it too rough on the skin for summer use.

When the wind cooperates, rain ponchos can be rigged to work as sails.

Blue jeans or other denim type **pants** are not recommended for serious outdoor activities. They don't insulate well, are hard to dry, soak up too much moisture, and often bind in strategic areas. Still, blue jeans are very popular and many campers manage to make do with them. For reasons already mentioned, wool is a far better pant material for camping. Though not always as stylish as blue jeans, wool pants are abrasion resistant, excellent insofar as their insulative value is concerned, and they dry quickly. For those who find wool too irritating to wear next to the skin, *orlon whipcord* is an excellent alternative. As with socks, blends of different materials are popular among pant manufacturers. Consequently, 60/40 cloth, 85% wool/15% nylon, 62% polyester/33% cotton/5% spandex, and 65/35 cloth are often used for the construction of rugged pants. When examining blends, remember that nylon adds strength but takes away insulative value, spandex adds stretch, cotton provides a nice texture next to the skin, wool acts as an excellent insulator, and so on. Knowing the strengths and weaknesses of the individual fabrics will allow you to buy wisely.

Knickers are those funny looking pants cut off just below the knees. They are designed to permit greater freedom of movement in the lower leg. However, it is unlikely that one or even two layers of socks, plus long underwear, will provide the same degree of insulative value on a windy day as a windproof full-length pant. Knickers provide the freedom of movement required by cross-county skiers, but are not the best clothing for sitting around a campfire, sawing wood, or cooking a meal.

Shirts come in 100% wool and 100% cotton varieties, as well as all the blends and combinations found in other articles of clothing. Again, understanding the strengths of the various fabrics allows for an informed choice. On trips where both hot, sunny days and cool nights are likely to be encountered—in other words, most trips—one wool (or primarily wool) shirt and one synthetic or cotton shirt is a good combination. I recommend staying with long sleeve shirts to maximize protection from the sun and bugs.

Sweaters are ideal items for making use of the layering approach to outdoor clothing. They are readily available in wool, and, if two sweaters are combined with fishnet underwear, two shirts, and outerwear, they offer many combinations to suit the weather. Make sure the sweaters are roomy in order to fit over shirts, and that they can be combined, with one worn over the other. Many people swear by the old "oiled" wool sweaters.

Figure 2-2
A good vest will be cut low on
the body and include a collar

In cold weather conditions, a **vest**, in addition to a sweater, can be helpful. Differences between vests and sweaters include the fact that most vests are made from synthetics (though some wool vests are still available, and these are often of very high quality) and vests do not have sleeves. In fact, the lack of sleeves is what makes the garment a vest instead of a sweater. Down vests used to be very popular until just a few years ago; however, with the increase in down prices, synthetics have taken over most of the market. Many people complain that vests don't protect the arms, but this is not what a vest is supposed to do. The vest is designed to give added protection to the vital organs, not the arms. A high collar and low cut extending to the rump will increase the effectiveness of the vest. Look for an insulation tube running behind the zipper. This will reduce the likelihood of a cold spot running up the front of your body. Buttons may create unwanted openings.

Gaiters (see Fig. 2–3) are made from heavy cotton, 60/40 cloth, nylon, duck or other abrasion resistant material. Gaiters are designed to provide protection from snow or brush by covering the leg area from below the ankles on the outside of the boot, to midcalf or slightly higher. **Anklets** are mini-gaiters that only come

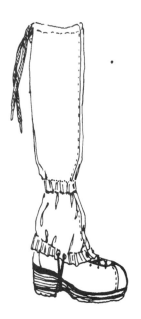

Figure 2-3
Gaiters provide additional
protection, particularly while
cross-country skiing.

up to the top of the ankle. Gaiters and anklets should be water repellant and mildew resistant. They are excellent for ski touring or snowshoeing. It should be noted that, if you are handy with a sewing machine, gaiters are very easy to make. Borrow a pair from a friend and make a pattern.

Boots are one of the most important items you will buy. For snowshoeing and cross-country skiing, boots are very specialized. For this reason, specific details on footwear for winter travel are described in Chapter Nine. This section focuses on footwear for hiking and, to a lesser extent, canoeing. Whether you plan to do simple day hiking, moderate backpacking, or take part in strenuous expeditions, footwear selection should focus on comfort and durability. A pair of boots that fit well and are comfortable can easily make the difference between a good trip and a horror show. Unfortunately, there is no rule or set of rules that make boot buying straightforward. It is not unusual for people to spend lots of money on top-of-the-line boots, only to find that the fit of the boots never developed properly, as the salesperson said it would. Once you have chosen an activity, the fit of the boot must be the basic consideration. This means first determining if you will be using your boots for easy walking, summer day hikes, backpacking in the Rockies, or challenging Everest, then looking for a comfortable fit within the boot types designed for that activity. It's always wise to make the rounds of several specialty camping stores in order to try on a variety of boots.

Most people need and buy either trailshoes for day walks, or trailboots for backpacking. Trailboots come in various weights designed to correspond to the weight of the wearer, weight of the loads carried, and type of trail hiked. Make it clear to the salesperson what type of activity you intend. Also, take the socks you plan to wear on the trail to the store. This is the only way to get a feeling for the sock and boot in combination. And, don't be afraid to walk around in the boots for twenty minutes or longer in order find out if they really are comfortable. A good store will encourage this, and may suggest you take the boots home and wear them indoors for a few days to check the comfort level. Try kicking a post or wall stud to see if your toe contacts the front of the boot. It shouldn't, or else you will find your toes bruised after travelling downhill. Your heel should not lift up without the boot as you walk, or blisters on the heel will turn out to be a constant source of irritation for you. The soles of the boot should be flexible. Most trail boots use *Vibram*™ soles. Vibram has a reputation as one of the best non-slip soles available. Look for the

Vibram name on the sole of the boot. Some boots have tight scree collars around the ankle. If the collar pushes on or grabs at your tendon, it will cause painful injury after several hours of wearing. The scree collars are designed to keep pebbles and other debris out of the boot, but if tendonitis is the result you may find it necessary to cut the collar off. Lengths and widths of trailboots will vary from manufacturer to manufacturer, and except for the few general considerations cited above you should purchase trail boots by trying them on, checking for comfort, and asking friends for recommendations. Be sure to break-in your boots before you begin a serious trip. The easiest way to do this is to wear the boots for half an hour of shopping, an hour of gardening two days later, and so on.

Figure 2-4
If a boot is uncomfortable, all its other virtues are negated.

For canoe tripping, look for a boot that is comfortable, supports the ankle on portages, and dries out reasonably quickly. It seems there is no overwelmingly preferred style or type. I have seen mid-calf, waterproof, rubber boots used in the barrens, neoprene booties used in glacial runoff rivers, high-cut running shoes used for wading and running fast-flowing whitewater rivers in southern Ontario, and standard workboots used for all of these occasions. I prefer a workboot, simply because it gives a reasonable degree of ankle support and never seems to wear out. However, the downside of workboots is the drying time they require. Because weight is not as critical on a canoe trip as it is while backpacking, I occasionally pack a pair of sneakers to wear instead of my workboots when I know that my feet are going to be in and out of the water all day long.

Anoraks (see Fig. 2-5), also referred to as **mountain jackets**, complement the layer system of dressing. They provide a windproof, roomy outer layer that is easy to slip on and off. Features to look for in a good anorak include adjustable velcro cuffs, an inner drawstring to tighten the jacket at the waist, many pockets both inside and outside, front zipper *and* buttons with overlapping material, a low cut back that reaches the upper thighs, roominess, and windproofness. To check for windproofness, gather some of the fabric tightly across your mouth and try to blow through it. Most anoraks are water-repellent rather than waterproof. This is because an anorak that doesn't breathe would be very uncomfortable. However, the advent of Gore-Tex, Helly Tech, Ultrex, and other waterproof/breathables has resulted in a class of anorak that is more waterproof than traditional breathable fabrics such as 60/40 cloth, and is still breathable. The cost differential between a traditional 60/40 cloth anorak and a high-

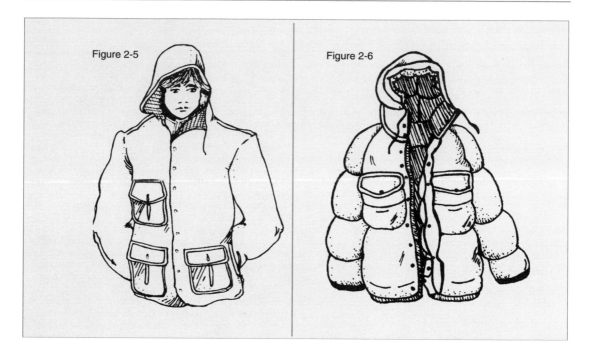

Figure 2-5

Figure 2-6

Figure 2-5
Anorak or Mountain jacket

Figure 2-6
Parkas should be designed to provide protection under extreme conditions.

tech waterproof/breathable anorak is considerable. I do not recommend zipperless anoraks, the ones that you have to slip over your head. You can't vent them as easily, and they are a pain to get on and off in wet weather.

Traditionally, **rainwear** for hiking and canoeing has been made from coated fabrics such as K-Kote fabric or Bukflex. For the most part, campers accepted the fact that in rainy weather you would have to endure the dampness caused by perspiration in order to avoid the outright soaking you would get from the rain. Once again, however, waterproof/breathables, such as Gore-Tex, Helly Tech, Ultrex and the like, have changed this picture. Now, it is possible to have an anorak that serves as protection in sunny and rainy conditions. As the cost of Gore-Tex and other waterproof/breathables has dropped, their use has increased quite dramatically. **Rain pants** and **wind pants** have changed in the same way. Not so long ago, most were made from coated fabrics. Now, many campers have switched to waterproof/breathable fabrics or coatings. It is worth noting, however, that rain and wind pants are particularly susceptible to abrasion, dirt, and oil stains, which can clog the tiny pores that make high-tech fabrics breathable. Thus, they require special care and cannot be treated as roughly as the older coated pants often were. It is worth noting that effective raingear is one of the most important pieces of clothing that a camper has. In good weather, rainwear may appear to be a bothersome extra. However, when the bad weather appears, good rainwear is critical. It allows you the flexibility to continue to travel in relative warmth and comfort. Even if you only have a few dollars to spend, consider investing in a good rain jacket and rain pants. This does not, however, mean that you must have the latest Gore-Tex or Helly Tech top-of-the-line outfit. A coated, waterproof jacket and rain pants combination will, with care, work well under most conditions.

Cagoules are long poncho type coverings that are designed to work as both rain jackets and pants. Many people find that they tend to drag in the mud, drip from the bottom onto pant legs, and fly up at inconvenient times. Cagoules are not recommended for serious canoeing or hiking.

Insulated Parkas (see Fig. 2-6) can be an alternative to the layering approach to dressing. Instead of several layers, a high quality insulated parka can do a good job. Parkas are also standard issue for cold weather camping and for expedition use. With features that include zippers, buttons, breathability, lightweight insulation, water repellency, and roominess, a good parka makes life quite comfortable, even in bad conditions. As with vests, synthetics have taken over a significant proportion of the parka market. Many features described earlier should be considered when purchasing an insulated parka. These include pockets, drawstrings, high collar, hood, and long cut. The methods used to hold the insulation in place inside the parka are similar to those used in sleeping bags (see Chapter Three). When buying a parka, many campers will purchase more parka than is actually required. Remember, you don't need to get an Everest parka unless you really plan to go to Everest. Don't let an unethical or uninformed salesperson convince you that the top-of-the-line is the best. The one that suits the conditions under which you will be camping is precisely what you need, no more and no less. For most camping, you can probably make do with an anorak and some sweaters. The primary use for a parka is for protection in extremely cold conditions or while performing outdoor jobs that involve very little movement.

A **hat** is a necessity, both in summer and winter. The value of a sunhat on hot summer day cannot be overestimated. Novices often believe that a hat is an optional item. Unfortunately, the result of being hatless can be heat exhaustion or heat stroke. During the winter, when the weather is cold, windy, or wet, the smart camper knows that a great deal of body heat can be radiated

CLOTHING TIP

Effective raingear may be your most important clothing.

Figure 2-7
A balaclava will give
additional protection to the
head, face, and neck

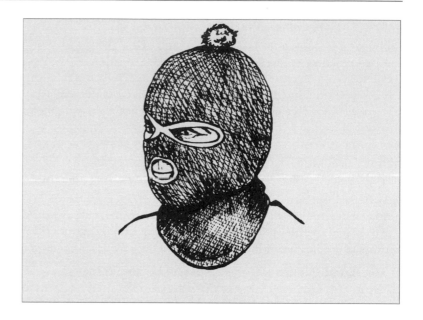

off an exposed head. This occurs in part because the blood
vessels in the head are very close to the surface of the skin, and,
when the head is exposed, constriction of the blood vessels does
not occur, as happens in other areas of the body. Virtually any
type of hat can help keep heat locked in, but the old standby,
wool, is one of the best. Wool hats that roll down to become face
masks, known as **balaclavas** (see Fig 2-7), are very useful for the
winter camper. Wool watch caps are also very good and, on a
cold winter night, can be combined with the hood of a sleeping
bag to provide excellent protection for your head. Scarves also
play an important role in winter camping. They protect the throat
and face. **Bandannas** provide needed summertime protection
for the neck and, in some cases, the ears. Bandannas can also be
used as sweatbands and, in a pinch, for moving hot pots around
the kitchen area.

    Gloves can be quite advantageous around the campfire during
the summer or winter. I have also found wool and leather gloves
to be quite handy when paddling under cold weather conditions,
and I have used light cotton gloves on the barrens when the
mosquitoes have been thick enough to completely cover any area
of exposed flesh. **Mittens** are the choice of most winter campers.
They are warmer than gloves and easier to dry. Many winter
campers wear a pair of wool inner mitts and a bulky pair of leather
outer mitts that are long enough to reach up to and engulf the
parka or anorak sleeve. This helps prevent snow from going up

Gravel bars are good campsites, providing the water level doesn't rise overnight.

the jacket sleeve. During the winter, at least one pair of backup inner wool mitts should be carried.

A FEW WORDS ABOUT KITS

During the last few years, the market for "make it yourself" camping equipment and clothing kits has developed into something more than a cottage industry. The reasons for the increase include the opportunity to save money, the enjoyment of creating your own garments, better quality, and the ability to get precisely what you want. By purchasing a kit, for either clothing or equipment, you have removed the major cost of production—labour. The savings can be as much as 30-50%. If the kit is bought directly from a manufacturer, the retail mark-up is also saved.

If you are considering buying a kit, don't overlook the fact that in order to save money you will need to work quite hard on a kit. Usually, the time required to complete the kit will require an amateur sewer to work for less than minimum wage. Therefore, the rationale for purchasing a kit should not be based on saving money since in most cases you would be better off to work at some job you are familiar with and then use your wages to hire an expert sewer to put the kit together. I recommend kits only if you believe you will get some satisfaction from making the clothing or equipment yourself.

The kit maker gets an opportunity to produce a superior product that reflects his own creative abilities. Seams can be doubly reinforced, backstitched and seared. It's difficult to buy that standard of quality. Embroidery and applique adorn many completed kit products. Kit makers are also adept at repairing and maintaining their clothing and equipment.

When purchasing a kit it is important to look for an inherently good design based on the criteria previously discussed, item by item. Fabrics and other materials should be of high quality, and appropriate for the task they are to serve. Are the instructions adequate and easy to follow? Can the item be sewn on a regular sewing machine or is a heavy duty model required? Does the manufacturer answer questions after you have bought the kit? These are important questions, and there is little doubt that, as the kit field becomes more competitive, manufacturers will have to increase their services to remain competitive.

SUMMARY

First, proper fitting, comfortable footwear is paramount to an enjoyable outdoor experience. It is easy to become wrapped up in issues such as split grain versus full grain, steel shank versus free soles, and speed laces versus eyelets; however, if the boot doesn't fit, all its so called virtues are useless. Second, the choice of clothing should depend on the outing, personal preferences, budget, and availability. Third, the principles are simple. Stay warm through the use of layering and effective insulation, don't sweat, and allow water vapour coming off the body in the form of perspiration to exit.

Some campers choose to wear their clothes while sleeping, the idea being to supplement the insulative properties of the sleeping bag. In order for this concept to work best, the clothes must be dry. Clothes that have been worn during the day will most likely be wet from perspiration. If worn to bed, the dampness in these clothes will sap body heat, though the clothes themselves will probably be dry by morning. In cold weather camping, I carry a set of separate sleeping clothes. I put them on at night and take them off in the morning. Wearing clothes to bed in the summer, early fall, or late spring is usually not necessary unless the sleeping bag is of very low quality.

Finally, as noted earlier, it isn't necessary to spend a great deal of money on high-tech clothing in order to have a good time in the outdoors. Simple clothes, with the accent on wool, will be a solid base for an enjoyable experience under most conditions.

ADDITIONAL SOURCES

Catalogues from various manufacturers and retailers make for enjoyable and informative reading.

- Albany International, Primaloft Division
  P.O. Box 1907, Albany, New York, U.S.A. 12201
  (for information on Primaloft)

- Celanese Corporation, Fibres Division
  P.O. Box 6170, Station A, Montreal, P.Q., Canada H3C 3K8
  (for information on Polarguard)

- Dupont Fibrefill Marketing Division
  Centre Road Building
  Wilmington, D.C., U.S.A. 19898
  (for information on Hollowfil II, Quallowfil, and Thermolite)

- Mountain Equipment Co-op
  1655 W. 3rd Avenue
  Vancouver, B.C., Canada V6J 1K1
  (for a general catalogue of outdoor clothing and gear)

- Quaberg Rubber Company
  P.O. Box 155B
  North Brockfield, Mass., U.S.A. 01535
  (for information on Vibram)

- Patagonia Inc.
  1609 Babcock St. P.O. Box 8900
  Bozeman, Montana, U.S.A. 59715
  (for information on Patagonia products)

- W. L. Gore
  P.O. Box 1220, Rt. 213
  North Elkton, M.D., U.S.A. 21921
  (for information on Gore-Tex)

Carry a small whetstone on your trips and you will never have to suffer from a dull knife.

3
Equipment

It's hard for the modern generation to understand Thoreau, who lived beside a pond but didn't own water skis or a snorkel.

Bill Vaughn

This chapter describes and evaluates a variety of camping equipment on the market. Some of the equipment examined is quite esoteric; however, as in the last chapter, the reader must determine his or her own needs and evaluate equipment accordingly. When shopping for gear, remember that the most expensive equipment has likely been designed for extreme conditions. Unless you are planning a polar expedition, moderately priced equipment should suit your needs.

SLEEPING BAGS

A sleeping bag is designed to retain heat. By doing this, the bag will keep a person warm and comfortable during times of retreat, either at night in order to sleep or at other times to simply rest or wait out a storm. Sleeping bags surround the body with insulation. Insulation is required, in part, because the body generates less heat at rest and, under most conditions, fewer clothes are worn while sleeping. As discussed previously, insulation may be natural material such as down or feathers, a synthetic, or a combination of natural and synthetic materials. It is worthwhile noting that older or inexpensive bags may make use of synthetics that are largely waste material and do not have the properties described in last chapter's discussion on high-tech synthetic insulators. Check the "Do Not Remove" tag for a description of the fill used in the product.

Different techniques have been used to rate the effectiveness or minimum temperature rating of sleeping bags. For example, some manufacturers have used charts that equate a certain loft (thickness) to a minimum temperature rating. This approach is

Old style canvas tents require tent poles to be cut from saplings at each campsite. This practice is no longer environmentally acceptable.

EQUIPMENT TIP

Choose a sleeping bag that has been manufactured by an established company—one that has been in business for at least two years.

based on the principle that thickness is the prime factor in determining the calibre of the insulation. It assumes that the air is deadened or held fixed, no matter what the insulating material may be. This approach is not entirely satisfactory since it fails to take into account factors such as humidity, wind velocity, metabolism, shape of the bag and clothing worn to bed. Other manufacturers rate bags according to the weight of the fill. As well as not taking into account the factors noted above, this method also falls short in that it does not distinguish between different size bags. Most reputable manufacturers rate their bags using a range. They take a number of different factors into consideration, including loft and weight of the fill. If a bag is rated at 0° to 10° Celsius (32° to 58° Fahrenheit), and you are a cold sleeper, don't expect to be comfortable in the bag when the temperature dips below 10° Celsius (58° Fahrenheit). On the other hand, if you are a warm sleeper, you might be able to use this bag even in temperatures slightly below freezing. Virtually all temperature ratings for sleeping bags are based on the assumption that the sleeper is in a windproof tent at a fairly low altitude. If you have any doubts when purchasing a bag, choose the one that has been made by a manufacturer who has been in business for more than two seasons. If you are a particularly cold sleeper, and don't want to purchase an expedition bag for spring and fall camping, take an extra set of clothes to wear while you sleep and be sure to use an insulating pad beneath the sleeping bag.

Internal differences in sleeping bag construction are important. These differences are a good indicator of the quality of the bag. Virtually all good quality bags being produced for today's market use ripstop nylon to hold the insulation. However, the way in which the insulation is held in pockets or baffles differs significantly (see Fig. 3–1). The sewn through method is used to hold polyester insulation in place or prevent down from slipping to one end. The major problem with the sewn through method is that it creates cold spots where the only protection is the seam itself. Sewn through bags are inexpensive, and appropriate for campers on a very restricted budget who are planning summer trips only. The straight box method is produced by sewing strips of material between the two layers of fabric. Used primarily in down bags, it can result in cold spots if the sleeping position is not perfectly horizontal. A slight improvement on the straight box method is slant box construction. A further refinement is the overlapping "V" construction. It assures equal distribution of insulation. The offset double quilt method is used in the construc-

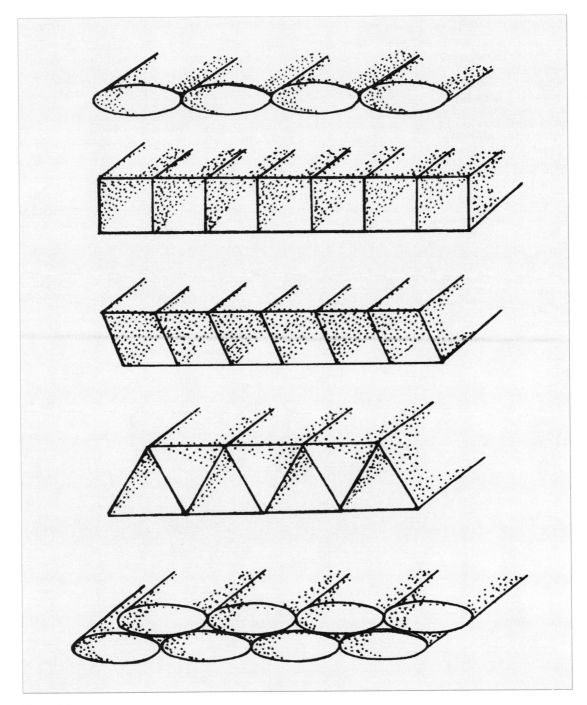

Figure 3-1
Baffle construction

CAMPING TIP

When the weather turns cold, sleep with your boot insoles inside your sleeping bag. In the morning, when you slip your boots on, your toes will thank you.

tion of synthetic bags and down parkas. It eliminates the problem of cold spots sometimes found in sewn through bags.

Prior to purchasing a sleeping bag, it is important to examine the stitching. Unevenly spaced stitches, improperly finished ends, and crooked seams are indications of shoddy work. If poor stitching is combined with intricate baffles, such as the box or slant box construction, it is unlikely that the retaining walls will stand up to rough treatment. As a result, the insulation will not be held in place. Too few stitches indicates that the manufacturer is cutting corners, while too many stitches will result in weak seams. Three or four stitches to the centimetre (7 to 10 stitches to the inch) is a good average. All seams should be reinforced at points of stress.

Good quality sleeping bags will be differentially cut. This means that the inner shell of the sleeping bag will have a smaller circumference than the outer shell. This prevents the inner and outer layers pushing against each other; thereby reducing the effectiveness of the insulation.

Many of the better sleeping bags come with a choice of right or left handed zippers. This allows you to join two bags together. It is important to be able to open the zipper from both the inside and outside. Three season, and winter sleeping bags, normally come equipped with a draft tube, also called a zipper baffle. This is a long thin insulated baffle that runs inside the bag along the full length of the zipper. Without a draft tube, tremendous heat will be lost through this cold spot and the zipper itself could cause considerable discomfort. Winter bags also come equipped with a hood that has drawstrings. These drawstrings permit you to close the bag right around your face. Check the end of the bag to see if the manufacturer has included a circular baffle area where the feet will be located. On a summer weight bag an end baffle may not be necessary; however, in the winter it is often the feet that suffer first.

Bags come in a variety of shapes, usually reflecting the season they are designed for. The rectangular shape, satisfactory for summer use, is inexpensive and easy to air out. Mummy shapes and contoured bags are better for cold weather use. They tend to be more expensive, and stuff smaller. The stuffed size will vary according to the type of insulation used.

Down sleeping bags can be dry cleaned. However, the dry cleaner should be reminded that down products must be treated gently. Check to see that the dry cleaner uses the Stoddart Method for cleaning. It is the most appropriate for down products. After

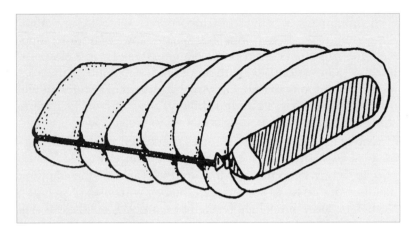

Figure 3-2
Quality sleeping bags will usually be differentially cut and have a zipper baffle.

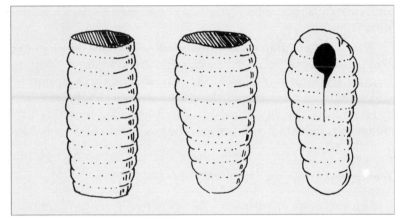

Figure 3-3
Sleeping Bag shapes—rectangular, barrel, mummy

dry cleaning, down bags must be aired out for at least 3–4 days. Using a dry cleaned down bag without first airing it out can be fatal. Hand washing is an alternative to dry cleaning. For instructions on this, see the section dealing with down as an insulator in the previous chapter. Polyester bags can easily be machine washed in a front loader (one without an agitator). Use a gentle action and no bleach.

A good way to protect your bag and reduce the number of times you will need to clean it is to use a sleeping bag liner. This will keep the bag cleaner, make it last longer, reduce your dry cleaning bills, and any concerns you might have over lending the bag will be diminished. You can make yourself a bag liner by folding an old sheet in two, cutting the sheet, if necessary, to the contour of the bag, and sewing up one end and the open side. During hot spells, a sleeping bag liner gives you the option of sleeping on top of the bag with just the liner as a covering.

EQUIPMENT TIP

Never leave a down sleeping bag stored in a stuff bag.

Sleeping bags, whether they incorporate synthetic or natural fill, should never be left in a stuff bag for long periods of time. Sleeping bags are best stored by hanging them up in a closet or, if that is not possible, laying them out flat so that the fill material has an opportunity to fully loft. Any bag stored in a stuff bag will quickly begin to lose its lofting ability. The seams will be unduly stressed and synthetic batting will tend to break down.

One of the biggest single worries purchasers of sleeping bags have is, "will I be warm enough? " This concern causes some people to buy sleeping bags that are too warm for the camping that they do. Better to supplement the bag with a set of sleeping clothes or more munchies (remember, a good, solid meal will help generate a lot of heat), than to buy the expedition model simply because you might have one or two cold nights sometime next winter.

When winter camping it is important to get into the sleeping bag before you are cold. It is asking an awful lot for a sleeping bag to warm your body up since it has no inherent heat producing capabilities. As noted earlier, the sleeping bag is simply designed to retain heat. The wise camper recognizes and accepts this fact. If you are cold when you get into the bag, the fault does not lie with the bag.

SLEEPING PADS

EQUIPMENT TIP

Closed-cell foam pads are far superior to open-cell foam pads.

The use of sleeping pads, placed between the ground and sleeping bags, has increased dramatically during the last few years. For backpackers and canoeists, the ground pad provides added insulation from the cold, and cushy padding for a more relaxed sleep. Most serious backpackers pack a sleeping pad, even on short trips. For canoeists, ground pads are still in the optional category, though if you are travelling either very early or very late in the season they are recommended.

Open-cell foam pads are soft and springy; however, they soak up moisture and tend to rip and fall apart at the most inopportune times. *Ensolite*™, *Airolite*™, *Evazote*™ and *Volarfoam*™ are examples of commercially produced closed-cell foam pads. In contrast with open-cell pads, closed-cell pads don't absorb water. Some closed-cell pads will remain flexible to approximately –40° Celsius (–40° Fahrenheit). Closed-cell 3/8 inch pads are good to –10° Celsius (14° Fahrenheit), below which 1/2 inch should be used. The Cadillac of sleeping pads is the *Therma-A-Rest*™ pad. With an open-cell construction that suppresses convection heat loss, the Therma-A-Rest pad self-inflates when the valve is opened, except under extremely cold conditions (at which time, do not put your lips around the valve). Disadvantages to the Therm-A-Rest include the high price and increased weight. Most of these pads are available in different lengths. The shortest will run from the shoulders to the hips, while the longer ones run from the head to the toes. In most cases, dead winter being an exception, you can get away with a short pad by putting some clothing under your head and resting your feet on your boots.

TENTS

A tent should provide a warm, dry, comfortable environment, safe from the elements and psychologically pleasing. It is a home away from home, much more than just a shelter. Anyone who has spent a day or two waiting out a storm will confirm these thoughts. I strongly believe that the size of your tent should be adequate to provide an opportunity for comfortable living. Many poorly designed two person tents provide minimal sleeping space, and unless you are lying down you have to change your clothes outside. The same is true of three and four person tents. Would you want to spend two days in such a tent? When purchasing a tent, imagine yourself in it for a few days at a stretch. Is the colour warm and pleasing? Does it have pockets and hangers for items such as flashlights and toothbrushes? Does it have a vestibule for storage?

Tents used to be made of canvas or Egyptian cotton. Nowadays most tents are constructed of ripstop nylon. This material is strong, light, and durable. The least expensive tents are single wall, coated tents (see Fig. 3-4). These tents are based on the principle that a single waterproof nylon sheet, fully encasing the occupants, will provide adequate protection. While the theory may appear sound, the problem of venting water vapour is difficult to overcome. In a single wall tent, it is very hard to vent the water vapour, and, as a result, the camper is likely to end up with a puddle on the floor during dry weather, and almost certainly with a small lake if things are wet outside.

Double wall construction (see Fig. 3-5), where the tent is surrounded by a coated fly, helps solve the venting problem. As a result, double wall tents are *de rigueur* for serious backpackers and canoe trippers. With double wall construction, it is common for the bottom of the tent and a few inches of the lower walls to be constructed of coated, waterproof nylon. The rest of the inner walls are breathable fabric, either nylon or mosquito netting. This inner tent is surrounded by a coated fly, leaving a 6 to 10 cm. (2 to

Tunnel tents like this one are designed to withstand severe weather conditions.

EQUIPMENT TIP

Single wall, coated nylon tents are inadequate for serious camping.

Figure 3-4
In a single-wall, waterproof tent it is difficult to vent water vapour.

Figure 3-5
A double-walled tent has a breathable inner wall and a waterproof fly.

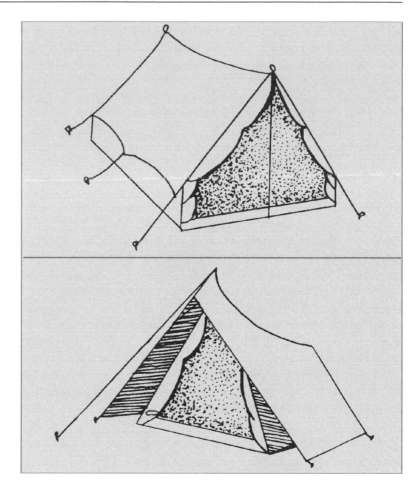

4 inch) gap between the walls. Water vapour passes through the breathable inner wall and condenses on the inner side of the outside wall or fly. The water vapour then dissipates into the air. Most tent flys are detachable.

Tent characteristics, from shape to colour, are almost infinitely variable. For this reason, it is best to clearly determine your needs and the conditions under which you will be using the tent *before* shopping. Are you planning to do a few trips during the summer? Or, will you be out during mid-winter? Will you be carrying the tent on a bike trip, or will you be using it primarily for canoe camping? Do you want to have the option of inviting someone to share the tent space with you, or do you plan on sleeping solo? If you don't consider these issues before you visit the store, you may find the salesperson discusses aspects not relevant to your needs.

Dome tents stand up well during high winds.

Figure 3-6
It is important to evaluate a tent on the basis of usable space

As with sleeping bags, there is a tendency to purchase more tent than you actually need. You will see lots more expedition tents in the outdoors than there are expeditions taking place, and while it is important to have some strength and durability in reserve, don't be tempted to waste money on the super deluxe Everest model.

Tent design has been the subject of much discussion. "A" frame tents are one of the most common designs. They are reasonably easy to construct, set up quickly, and are fairly sturdy in strong winds. Ridge vents are normally found at the top of the doors, adding to the ease with which water vapour may be drawn off. If this type of tent suits your needs, compare several "A" frames to examine the ease of set-up. Then, try to determine how easy it would be to knock one down. Some of these tents are self-supporting and do not require stakes to pitch them.

The fly of the tent should overhang the inner wall at all points, and it is preferable if the floor has no seams. All seams, whether they are on the floor or sides of the tent, should be sealed with K-Kote or a similar product. If this is not done at the factory, it probably just means that the manufacturer is giving you a chance to save a few dollars by doing it yourself at home. Stakes should be strong and durable. If they are a bright in colour, they will be harder to lose. I always recommend taking a few extra, even though some types are guaranteed to be indestructible. Vestibules provide for storage and a cooking area, particularly important for the backpacker. A raised lip on the door of the tent helps prevent dirt or snow from being kicked inside.

As with other gear, check the tent seams for evenness, reinforced corners, and stitches per centimetre. "A" frame tents should have a generous catenary cut. This means that the peak, running from end to end, should be a gentle arc rather than a straight line. This characteristic will reduce wind flap and help spread stress.

A variety of tent designs other than "A" frames are available and worth consideration. Hexagons, box tents, ovals and geodesic domes are a few of them. I am particularly fond of dome tents, ever since I spent a night in one during a gale. I emerged in the morning to find a number of "A" frames and other designs shredded, while my dome, though bent a little, seemed little the worse for wear.

Tunnel entrances are typically found in expedition tents. The tunnel is usually incorporated to provide a second exit/access in the event of emergency. Two tunnel tents can often be adjoined, making for row housing during stormy periods. Very few tents are designed for cooking, and to attempt to light a stove inside a tent is extremely dangerous. Fumes can build up in the confined area of a tent and explode, or carbon monoxide, which is odourless, can slowly suffocate the inhabitants. Every year there are stories of campers who died using a stove to heat a tent.

It is important when comparing and evaluating tents to determine the usable space, not simply the total space. Generally speaking, reputable manufacturers produce tents at prices relative to the quality. It is advisable to avoid the bargain basement models. These tents will not last. The good news is that strong, well built, durable tents have fallen in price during the past few years, and price increases will likely continue to lag behind inflation well into the foreseeable future.

TENTING TIP

Brightly coloured tent stakes rarely get left behind when packing up your camp.

On a final note, it's worth remembering that the free-standing capability of a tent can be particularly helpful if you are camping on rock, but any non-staked tent will blow away if left to its own devices. I recall one instance of this happening while I was eating dinner on a sand spit near the mouth of the Albany River in northern Ontario. After putting the first spoonful of a big spaghetti dinner into my mouth, I glanced around to see my Eureka "A" frame rolling over and over, just like a lopsided ball, towards the river. Putting my dinner down, I raced towards the tent, adrenalin pumping. If the tent became damaged or destroyed, my home was essentially lost. Bugs, cold, and wet weather would be future companions, each and every night. The lesson was simple: with a free standing tent, always use stakes or tie lines to secure it. Never leave the tent pitched but unsecured. On the Albany I saved the tent, but returned to the spit to find my spaghetti dinner covered in sand.

STOVES

In many of the less travelled areas of the world, open fires are used for cooking and warmth. In well travelled areas, including much of the United States, open fires are not permitted. The sheer numbers of campers and the fragile nature of the environment demand the use of stoves. Stoves are also commonly used in the barrens and in other areas or conditions where an open fire may not be practical. There is little doubt that the use of stoves will continue to grow as concern for the environment increases.

There are four main fuels used in lightweight stoves: white gas, kerosene, butane, and propane. The most popular is white gas. It is inexpensive, readily available, and burns well under most conditions. Kerosene is readily available, but is sometimes difficult to ignite in cold weather. Butane and propane are usually sold in disposable cartridges, a form that causes concern among some environmentalists. As well, butane and propane are more expensive than either kerosene or white gas. Butane has the additional disadvantage of not vaporizing at low temperatures.

As well as fuel type, stoves vary in terms of the size of the burner area, size of fuel tank, priming methods, weight, simmering ability, boiling times and the rate of fuel use. All these factors are significant, but even more important is the need to be able to comfortably operate the stove under difficult conditions. A stove that appears to be easy to operate during an in-store demonstration may be a very different kettle of fish during a rain storm in the late fall. One of the best ways to choose a stove is to borrow

Figure 3-7
Seva Stove

a couple of different models and go with the one you find easiest to operate. Don't take someone else's word that a particular type of stove is easy to operate; test it yourself. Over time, stoves take on individual characteristics. One stove may need a little tap before it is lit, another may work only if you never fill it beyond the 3/4 mark. Just because someone else can make it look easy, doesn't mean you will.

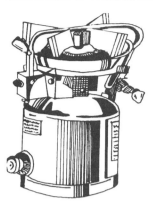

Figure 3-8
Coleman Pocket II Stove

Almost all white gas and kerosene stoves require priming. This is the art of heating and pressurizing the vaporizing chamber so that the gas emerges as a burning vapour, not as liquid. The *Svea 123R* stove is a very simple white gas stove (see Fig. 3–7). Though popular for decades, it has always had a reputation for being a little cantankerous, particularly in cold weather. The fuel tank on the Svea is filled from the top. Simply unscrew the nut, and pour the gas in. There is a priming cup at the base of the stove stem, also referred to as a spirit cup. Priming pressurizes the fuel so that it comes up the stem in vapour form. The standard priming technique with a Svea is to fill the priming cup with fuel and ignite it. This pre-burning will heat and pressurize the fuel in the stem. During this process the stove regulating key—this is the control that permits more, or less, fuel to flow up the stem—is in the off position. As the primer fire dies down, you turn the regulating key on in order to open up the stem and permit additional fuel to be pre-heated and pressurized. Thus, as fuel burns, more is being pre-heated. The burning fuel also warms the fuel container. This helps increase the pressure and force more gas up the stem—at least that's the theory. Most people find they have to light the Svea burner with a second match, after sufficient pressure has been built up in the stove. Others claim that the Svea can be preheated and pressurized by simply cupping the fuel tank in warm hands or by removing the fuel tank cap and blowing into the tank itself. These people have warmer hands and more hot air than I ever expect to have.

In cold weather conditions, priming becomes increasingly difficult with virtually all stoves. Insulating the stove from the ground will help, but in many situations you will have to continue to pressurize the stove as you are cooking. This problem prompted the company that makes Svea stoves to market an accessory pump that allows you to re-pressurize the stove as you cook. Most other lightweight stoves have pumps built into the design, or they make use of butane and propane sold in pressurized containers.

CAMPING TIP

In cold weather, slip a small piece of foam pad under your stove to help insulate it from the ground.

Carry a small grill and you will find it much easier to organize your pots over the campfire.

The *Coleman Pocket II* is quite a bit different than the Svea (see Fig. 3–8). The Coleman fuel tank is larger, the burner area is wider and more stable, and the priming pump is built into the tank. It is one of the simplest stoves to operate. I particularly like the fact that the directions are printed on the side of the tank. From a backpacker's point of view, the greatest disadvantages to this stove are its size and weight. The stove is primed with 15 or 20 quick strokes of the pump, after which the regulator is turned to the pre-heat position. At this stage, providing you have pumped the stove sufficiently, you will hear the gas escaping in vapour form. A match will set it alight, and as the stove warms up the regulator is turned until a clear blue flame is present. If the stove starts to lose its pressure and heat because the fuel level is low or because it's very cold, simply give the pump a few strokes and the stove should come back to life. Ease of operation and relatively low price make the Coleman lightweight stoves popular choices.

EQUIPMENT TIP

The MSR-GK will burn just about any type of fuel.

The *MSR-GK* stove is quite different than both the Svea and the Coleman stoves. The MSR fuel tank is the Sigg fuel bottle itself. As a result, the lightweight burner is the only actual stove part. This makes for a very compact and lightweight unit. Sigg fuel bottles are readily available in most camping stores and have the advantages of being light, leak-proof and noncorrosive. The MSR-GK will burn white gas, blazo, aviation gas, car fuel, and even kerosene. It comes with a pump for priming and a built in flint that eliminates the need for matches. If kerosene is used, preheating will be necessary. Drawbacks to this dependable little

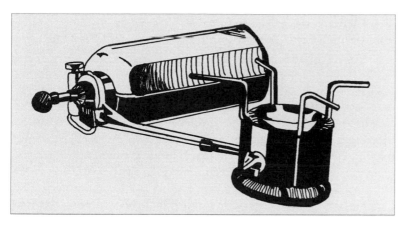

Figure 3-9
MSR-GK Stove attached to a
Sig fuel bottle

stove are high cost, noisy burning, and lack of simmering ability. However, owners tend to swear by this stove; they say it always works and burns very hot. (At least that's what this owner says.) MSR also has a model called the Whisperlite. It is smaller than the GK, quieter and has a simmer capability. MSR stoves are known for their dependability and high price.

Wind will affect any stove's effectiveness by blowing the heat away from the pot, cooling the surface of the pot, and drawing the heat out of the flame. Various stoves attempt to counteract this, usually with some sort of windscreen. On a final note, most manufacturers do not recommend filling stoves much beyond the three quarter mark since the expansion of gas during priming could cause an explosion if there is no available space in the fuel tank.

EQUIPMENT TIP

A simple windscreen can double the effectiveness of your stove.

COOKING KITS

Modern kitchens make use of numerous gadgets. In contrast, some campers seem to feel obligated to get by with little more than one pot and a spoon. I am a believer in having the necessary tools to make the job easy. If this means a pressure cooker, a Teflon spatula, and a dutch oven, so be it. I don't carry a kitchen sink, but I hate burning my fingers because nobody brought a pair of pliers.

The number of pots, pans, and other kitchen paraphernalia will vary according to the size of your group and the complexity of the meals. Nesting cooksets are those where the kettles (often called billies) fit into one another for ease of packing. The billies usually vary in size from one to four litres, and are generally made from aluminum. *Sigg* and *Mirro* are two manufacturers who are

EQUIPMENT TIP

Nesting cooksets require little space.

well known for quality products. A thick rather than thin aluminum pot will be resistant to scratches and dents, while ensuring more even heating. Pot handles should be sturdy enough to make it possible to hold the pot securely when full, and lids should always be used since they speed cooking time and prevent debris from being kicked into the meal. Often, a side handle or clamp handle is sold as part of the cookset; however, many campers find that a pair of ordinary pliers are the easiest tool to use when pots have to be moved around the campfire. Pliers will allow you to get a good grip on the pot from any angle or side, making their extra weight inconsequential. A coffee pot or percolator can usually be fitted into the billy kit and used for soups and other liquids as well as tea and coffee. Frypans usually form the base of the billy nest, and *Teflon* has proved to be great for camping. It requires little care other than the use of a plastic spatula. Sand or other hard agents such as steel wool should not be used to clean Teflon since the coating may end up in your food.

Inexpensive pie plates may be satisfactory as serving plates during good weather, but they chill too rapidly in bad weather. In the winter, plastic plates may have to be used, or even pouches in the case of one-pot meals or dehydrated foods. No matter what the season, it is a nice touch to heat the plates by putting them on top of a cooking pot for a few minutes prior to serving. Drinking cups can be tricky. The thin metal ones burn your lips and tongue on the first sip, then end up cold by the third or fourth taste. *Sierra cups* overcome this problem by using a combination of metals. But, they are quite expensive. Cutlery is an individual decision. Many campers find that a spoon and a belt knife suffice for just about everything.

Kitchen paraphernalia is a compromise between convenience, safety, weight, length of trip, weather conditions and menu. In order to guard against forgetting an important piece of cooking gear, I find it helpful to mentally walk through the entire meal preparation, item by item before I leave home.

EQUIPMENT TIP

Sierra cups are high tech. They won't burn your lips, but they may dent your pocketbook.

A Sample of Possible Cooking Gear

Frypan	Cups	Salt and Pepper shaker
Billies	Cutlery	Water bottle
Coffee pot	Can opener	Cooking grid
Plates	Pliers	Reflector oven
Egg carrier	Spatula	Matches and container
Fuel Funnel	Gas	Backpacker's stove
Stove	Fuel bottle	Backpacker's Mini-oven

STUFF BAGS

Stuff bags can be one of the most important pieces of equipment you have. They provide additional protection for much of your gear, keep you organized, make the handling of cooking paraphernalia much easier, and help keep everything dry. Stuff bags come in a variety of sizes ranging from 15–30 cm. (6–12 in.) in diameter, and 30–75 cm. (12–30 in.) in length. Check for strong materials, firm drawstrings, and good stitching. Coated material is best for protection against rain, but don't put your wet or damp clothes in a coated stuff bag or you will find the mildew sets in pretty fast. The better stuff bags have storm-flaps at the top so that the bags can be sealed more tightly.

Many sleeping bags do not come with a good stuff sack. This doesn't necessarily mean the sleeping bag isn't a good one, but you should get a good, strong stuff sack to protect it. For sleeping bags, especially if they are made with synthetic insulation, look for a stuff sack with compression straps that can be tightened in order to help reduce the overall size. I also recommend waterproof stuff sacks, particularly for sleeping bags. On backpacking trips, I find it handy to use several small stuff bags. All my underwear, socks, and toilet gear go in one, and my jeans and sweaters go in another. If the bags are different colours, it's easier to identify the correct sack, and all your clothing doesn't have to be dragged out each time you need something. Most canoe and backpacking specialty stores sell a variety of good quality, coated stuff sacks.

LIGHTS

A good light source is a small equipment item that it is easy to overlook. However, adequate lighting to visit the bushes at 3: 00 a.m., find your matches after dark, or illuminate the area in the event of an emergency, is necessary. Qualities to look for in a flashlight are durability, length of life if battery operated, brilliance, width of beam, waterproofness, and ease of operation. *Tekna* makes several very good flashlights.

Recently, I have been converted to the benefits of *candle lanterns*. Though they throw little light in an open area and are subject to wind and rain, candle lanterns have a very cheery soft light that is not dependent on the strength of your batteries. As long as you have an extra candle, the lamp can be easily rejuvenated. Several companies sell candle lanterns that can be hung inside a tent and I have found this practice to be very pleasant.

Figure 3-10
Wonder Lamp

However, it is important to be careful. If the flame comes into contact with the tent fabric, you may be sleeping outdoors for the rest of the trip, or worse.

Wonder Lamps (see Fig. 3-10) and *Petzl Headlamps* are combination headlamps/flashlights that many people find quite effective. They provide hands-free operation, and are good for cooking, reading, and even ski touring at night.

COMPASSES

Orienteering compasses, invented by Gunnar Tillander in 1933, are the best type of compass for wilderness travel. (For a discussion on the use of the orienteering compass, see Chapter Four.) The dial on the orienteering compass has the bearings or "ways to go" marked on the outside of the housing, and north/south parallel grid lines drawn on the inside. Equipped with a rectangular base and a direction of travel arrow, the orienteering compass can be used as a protractor. Silva is the foremost manufacturer of orienteering compasses, and their *3-NL* and *Type 3 Explorer III* are good basic compasses at reasonable prices. The *Silva Ranger* is an excellent compass for the more accomplished routefinder, combining luminous dials and a declination adjustment. All of these compasses are liquid dampened—a process of filling the housing with a liquid in order to slow the movement of the needle and prevent it from jumping about. This technique is superior to induction dampening.

WATER PURIFIERS

In North America it used to be common to drink water straight from most of the lakes and rivers that attracted canoeists and backpackers, but not any longer. Though there are many areas

Water bottles are invaluable when you have to camp or portage more than a short distance from fresh water.

where the water is still pristine, particularly in northern Canada, there are also a number of good camping areas where microorganisms like *giardia* lurk. Outside North America the problem is magnified with viruses such as hepatitis A, poliovirus, rotavirus, and cholera.

There are several inexpensive methods to purify water. These include adding tincture of iodine at the ratio of 5 drops per litre and letting the mixture stand for 30 minutes, and boiling water for a minimum of 10 minutes (longer at high altitudes).

CAMPING TIP

In some areas, a water purifier is a necessity.

Recently, filtration based water filters have become popular with campers travelling in areas where safe drinking water is not available. These filters are based on two approaches. The least expensive ones are simply resin filters that release iodine. The more expensive ones have microfilters to remove protozoan cysts like *giardia* and iodine matrices that eliminate the carriers of hepatitis A, cholera, typhoid, and polio. Although these water filters may sound like pretty esoteric pieces of equipment, if you are backpacking through countries or areas where the water is suspect, the investment could be one of the wisest travel decisions you make. If in doubt, purify your water. Remember, just because the local people drink the water doesn't mean you can.

BINOCULARS

Binoculars are worth their weight in gold to the camper who is interested in observing nature. However, binoculars can be quite expensive, and are often little understood.

Binoculars are generally distinguished by a set of figures such as 7 X 50, or 8 X 40. The first number, for instance the 7 in the 7 X 50, describes the magnification factor. Using these binoculars, objects will appear seven times closer than if viewed with the unaided eye. The second figure is the diameter of the objective lens. This is the glass at the front of the binoculars, the one that the image first enters. The larger the objective lens, the greater the amount of light entering the binoculars, hence the better they are for viewing at dusk or night. To compare binoculars in terms of light gathering ability, multiply the magnification factor by the objective lens diameter. The larger the resulting number, the greater the detail that will be seen in dim light.

Some manufacturers, Ashai Pentax for one, suggest using the *exit pupil measurement* to determine binoculars' capability to "see" in dim light conditions. This is calculated by dividing the objective lens diameter by the magnification factor. Therefore, a pair of 7 X 35 binoculars has an exit pupil measurement of 5 mm.; 8 x 40 binoculars will have the same measurement. This approach ignores the fact that a higher magnification factor increases performance in low light. Consequently, other manufacturers argue that the *twilight factor* is a better method for calculating and comparing binoculars' low light performance. This factor is calculated by multiplying the magnification by the objective lens diameter, then taking the square root. Thus a pair of 7 x 35 binoculars have a twilight factor of 15.7, while the 8 x 40 pair have a twilight factor of 17.9. The greater the number, the better the binoculars are for night viewing.

Binoculars differ in terms of their *field of view*. This refers to how much of the scene actually fits within the view of the binoculars. Some binoculars will describe the field of view as so many feet at a thousand yards, while others indicate an angle in degrees. Increasingly, binocular manufacturers are using metres per thousand metres to describe field of view. For comparison purposes, feet per thousand yards can be changed to metres per thousand metres by dividing the feet by 3.024. Thus, 372 feet at 1,000 yards becomes 372 divided by 3.024 or 123 metres at a thousand metres. To convert an angle such as 7.0, simply multiply it by 17.5. Thus a field of view of 7.0 becomes 7 X 17.5 or 123 metres at a thousand metres.

A wide angle pair of binoculars, with a large field of view, allow the user to see a much greater area without moving the binoculars. This is particularly important for bird-watchers, who are often trying to find a small object against a confusing background, then follow it as the bird moves quickly and unpredictably. Wide angle binoculars are those with a field of view of 165 metres at a thousand metres, or greater. A sailor, who is responsible for scanning the horizon, doesn't have a problem with field of view. Her priorities would be the magnification power and the ability of the binoculars to transmit light under low light conditions.

Binocular lenses are coated in order to reduce the reflection that normally occurs when light passes through glass. The quality of the coating varies greatly, often reducing or eliminating the effectiveness of twilight factor comparisons. To check the coating, hold the binoculars under a fluorescent light and angle them so you can see the light as it trips through the lenses. The light should have a violet-blue tinge. If white light is reflected, it may indicate an uncoated surface. Some manufacturers coat only the outside surfaces in order to cut costs; however, responsible companies have a reputation to maintain. Bausch & Lomb, Bushnell, Pentax, and Zeiss have excellent reputations. (I have a friend who has abused a pair of Carl Wetzlar binoculars for twenty years and they appear to be as good as the day they were bought.)

Binoculars will invariably be subjected to perspiration, rain, and snow. Given this, some campers believe in purchasing waterproof binoculars. These binoculars tend to be high quality, individually tested, and quite expensive. Don't confuse them with watertight binoculars, which won't survive much beyond a light sprinkle. I have never been convinced that the additional cost warrants the purchase of waterproof binoculars; when it rains I generally put up my tent and go to sleep.

Most binoculars come with focusing instructions. However, these are not always clear, concise and understandable. The first adjustment you should make corrects for the distance between your eyes. Some people have eyes close together, while others have eyes far apart. If, as you look through the binoculars, there are overlapping circles, black circles, half circles or quarter circles, squeeze the eyepieces closer together or pull them further apart until the circles disappear. Binocular manufacturers refer to this as "adjusting the interpupillary distance." The second adjustment is for focus. Check to see whether the right or left eyepiece has an individual adjustment, then close the eye that you would use to look through that eyepiece. Using the opposite eye, focus the binoculars on an object 10–15 metres (11–17 yards) distant, using the focusing ring in the centre of the binoculars. Then, close that eye and focus for the other eye using the eyepiece focusing adjustment. This technique allows you to adjust the binoculars

EQUIPMENT TIP

Birders need wide-angle binoculars.

EQUIPMENT TIP

Waterproof binoculars are not the same as watertight binoculars.

Protecting Your Binoculars

1. Avoid cleaning the lenses with anything but a clean cotton cloth or chamois. Fingerprints should never appear on the lens, since oil and perspiration can affect the coating.

2. Avoid dropping or jarring the binoculars.

3. Avoid unnecessary exposure to excessive heat, cold and moisture.

4. Unless you are a trained technician, don't attempt any major repairs.

5. Store your binoculars in a dry, dust-free area.

for any variation in your own eyes. If you have trouble closing one eye, or find that it causes undue squinting, cover the appropriate barrel with a lens cap while you make the adjustment.

Mini binoculars have become very popular among backpackers because of their compact size and light weight. Generally speaking, mini binoculars can provide equal magnification and field of view compared to most other binoculars, but they won't perform as well in dim light.

Binoculars can be a life-time investment. A good pair, with the aid of reasonable care, will see you through a lot of trips.

CAMERAS

Pictures, whether they are prints or slides, allow you to relive and share the best and the worst of the trip with friends and relatives, over and over again. But, selecting an appropriate camera is not always easy. Your decision should be influenced by the trip destination, mode of travel and your photographic interest and expertise.

Most photographers choose 35 mm cameras. They are small, relatively inexpensive, moderately lightweight and reliable. Single-lens reflex 35 mm cameras permit you to see precisely what you are about to photograph when you look through the view finder. This is accomplished by means of a mirror which permits the photographer to look directly through the lens. This advantage makes it much easier to take close-up photographs and other pictures where the subject position within the frame needs to be quite precise. Often, single-lens reflex cameras are able to accept a variety of lenses. Consequently with many of these cameras you can switch to a wide-angle lens for recording broad vistas or a telephoto lens for wildlife shots. These additional lenses, how-ever, add considerably to the weight of your gear. A few 35 mm single-lens reflex cameras have built in devices to allow for minor changes in the focal length of the lens without actually changing the lens. These cameras, though not inexpensive for the most part, will not take photos that are as sharp and clear as a 35 mm single-lens reflex camera with a variety of interchangeable lenses.

A long lens makes wildlife photography possible.

Most 35 mm range-finder cameras are less expensive than 35 mm single-lens reflex cameras. In part this is because the subject is not viewed through the lens, so a simpler mechanism can be employed. With most subjects close-up photos being the major exception, this is not a big problem. Typically, range-finder cameras don't have interchangeable lenses. There are a variety of range-finder cameras on the market that are marketed as water resistant or all weather cameras. For the novice or amateur photographer who simply wants a broad record of the trip, these are excellent cameras. In spite of the fact that with most of these cameras neither the focal length of the lens nor the lens itself can be changed, they do produce good photos. My family uses one because we don't have to worry about the kids leaving it in the sand, dropping it in the water, or even giving it a good thump. Ours is a Kodak Explorer and comes equipped with a motor drive, built-in flash and automatic re-wind—good features to have. For the most part, everyone in the family seems to be able to take a good picture with it, when we remember to aim!

EQUIPMENT TIP

All-weather range-finder cameras are a good choice for general purpose photography.

I also have a more sophisticated package of camera equipment that I take on long expeditions to remote areas. These are the trips where I want to spend time recording the wildlife and flora. My equipment includes two single-lens reflex camera bodies (the second one is carried in case the first one fails— something that happened to me at the five day point on a 30 day Nahanni River trip), a wide-angle (28 mm) lens, a standard lens (50 mm), a zoom lens (80 - 210 mm) and a telephoto (400 mm Novaflex). The 400 mm is difficult to carry, tough to waterproof and, in many situa-tions, I run the risk of severely damaging it. However, I finish most trips with pretty good photos.

Waterproofing cameras and other sensitive gear is important, but not something that I recommend becoming overly concerned with. After all, if the camera gear is always securely and safely packed away, great pictures are not going to be recorded. (I should confess that this has cost me some expensive gear ... but I do have floater insurance—no pun intended.) Some campers stick with water resistant cameras, an excellent choice. These

Taking a break on a lazy morning.

cameras don't need to be packed away and you can get some great pictures on wet, miserable days. Others use inexpensive, zip-lock poly bags or specialty, soft plastic container bags that have restrictive sealing systems to protect the camera. The latter are more secure, more expensive and tougher to get the camera out of in a hurry. Other approaches include war surplus ammunition cases that are equipped with rubber seals and specialty rubber or hard plastic cases also equipped with gasket seals. Whatever the technique, you need a secure place for your camera when the weather turns bad. But remember, the easier it is to get at your camera, the better the photographs are likely to be.

Cameras do enhance the after-trip experience, but they rarely make the trip itself a better event since it is very easy to get wrapped up in taking a picture while the pleasure of the moment slips by. I must admit, there have been times on long wilderness trips when I have noticed after the fact that I didn't actually experience the beauty of a scene because I was too busy recording it on film. Simple to operate and easily accessible cameras help avoid this pitfall. The water resistant 35 mm range-finder may be the best overall choice.

SUMMARY

The question to ask yourself when buying any type of camping equipment is "does it suit my needs?" Are you buying what you need, based on the type of canoeing, backpacking, or skiing you will be doing? There is no law that says you have to spend a lot of money on this sport. For the past twenty years the cost of camping equipment, particularly tents and sleeping bags, has been declining when measured in constant dollars. Camping has never been so cheap, unless you feel compelled to give way to the urge to buy all the high-tech, expedition style equipment. In that case, the sport will seem very expensive. Buy wisely, and build your store of equipment over time. Look for sales and don't be afraid to buy used gear. It's almost always very easy to tell what kind of shape used equipment is in, and the price savings can be substantial.

ADDITIONAL SOURCES

* Cunningham, G. & Hansson, M. (1976). *Lightweight Camping Equipment and How to Make It.* New York: Charles Scribner and Sons.

Simply having a map and compass
is not good enough. You also have
to know how to use it or

4

Map and Compass

No matter where you go, there you are!

If you want to know where you are going, if you want travel in relative safety, and if you plan to travel beyond highways and well established routes, then you must be able to read maps and use a compass.

Many years ago, while canoeing a whitewater river that flows into James Bay, I camped one night with two fellows who had recently finished their seasonal jobs as trip leaders for a summer camp. They had decided to take a "busman's" holiday, and paddle a northern river. When I asked them how they had come to choose this particular river, they said that they picked it when they saw the river marked on a restaurant placemat. This placemat turned out to be the only map they were carrying. These two, very experienced canoeists were taking a considerable risk. They had no notion of where the rapids and falls were, or even how long the trip might actually take. I would describe them as experienced but not too smart. Several years later, on the same river, I was four days downriver when I came across a bright red canoe. There were two people on shore, wringing out clothes, and another person paddling the canoe in circles while trying to snag items that had sunk to the bottom of the river. It turned out that the three canoeists had dumped at a very minor rapid, after having successfully negotiated some of the most difficult parts of the river. We brewed up some tea and were helping to dry out some of their gear when the senior member of the group asked me if I thought they would reach a "store" or some other place that day. I thought he was joking, but, as it turned out, the only map he had was one of eastern North America. On it, the river

MAP TIP

Carrying a map and compass is only the first step; equally important is your ability to use them.

was a vague blue line. I explained that if he and the two teenagers with him paddled very hard for four days, they might be able to reach the railroad line, from where they would be able to flag a train the following day. It was his turn to be shocked. They survived, but with one shoe apiece, wet gear, and little food—they wouldn't take any of ours—I am sure it wasn't a fun-filled four days. I would described them as inexperienced and not too smart.

Many backpackers and canoeists get into trouble on wilderness trips, and some die. I have always been somewhat surprised that more don't end up in the obituaries. Travelling without adequate maps and a compass is certainly one way of increasing the odds that you won't return. Experienced or inexperienced, it is always best to travel smart, and that means being knowledgable and prepared.

Adequate maps, a good compass, and the ability to use both are necessary for safe and successful wilderness camping trips. To travel without a map and compass is an act of foolishness. Those who are new to wilderness backpacking or canoeing usually start out knowing little or nothing about maps or how to use a compass. Their immediate concerns are focused on selecting the right equipment, being in shape for the trip, and finding suitable travelling companions. Trailing at the back of a group of hikers, or sitting in the bow of the third canoe, little route-finding skill is required. You simply follow the others. When or how do you get the knowledge and experience that effective route finding demands? Unfortunately, some people never do.

Everyone on the trip, or at least each canoe team or tent group, should be encouraged to not simply look at the maps, but to carry their own set of maps and track the progress of the trip, determine where the group "is," and predict daily travel distances and projected campsites. The time to learn route finding is before you lead a trip, and there is no teacher like experience. Route finding is an interesting component of any wilderness trip. If you leave the map reading to others, you are missing out. Used wisely, a good map is like a tour guide with a bit of preventative medicine thrown in. Maps identify points of interest that might otherwise be missed, dangerous areas to avoid or in which to exercise caution, and short-cuts. In the event of an emergency or other problem that requires a re-routing, the map identifies alternate paths.

Asking an Inuk to show us our location on a map proves to be a fruitless exercise. He knows precisely where he is simply by looking at the shape of the land, and rarely uses maps. The heavy clothing is for protection from bugs.

This chapter covers the basics of map and compass use, and examines the particulars necessary to understand the technicalities of contour maps and techniques of compass use.

MAP AND COMPASS

Maps and compasses should be inseparable companions for the serious outdoor traveller. There are, however, some wilderness travellers who haven't learned this. Canoeing is one mode of wilderness travel that encourages route finding indiscretions. Picture a group of four accomplished canoeists planning a ten day trip down a whitewater river. They have paddled the river before, so there is little concern for "finding" the way. They take their old maps, but see no need for a compass. After all, they figure that this trip is simply a matter of going downstream, and the maps identify problem areas such as falls and rapids. This group would argue that orienting the map and keeping track of their position are all that is required. On balance, the chances are that this group will have no cause to regret being without a compass. But, just suppose that on this trip the group experiences heavy rains, which change the nature of the rapids, and the canoes are seriously damaged or lost in an accident. Does the group try to walk out, relying solely on the old maps? Do they try to cut across country in order to reach a forest access road? If they get to the road will they find it overgrown and impossible to follow? Or, because they don't have a compass, are they forced to wait at the river until another group or a search party finds

Most portage routes are not marked on maps.

them? Travelling without a compass, and relying only on maps, can have severe consequences. Always carry up-to-date maps and a compass. And remember, you also have to know how to use them.

TYPES OF MAPS

There are a wide variety or types of maps in general use. Each has a specific purpose and special characteristics. For example, automobile road maps are designed, first and foremost, to fit into a typical glove compartment. They are also planimetric, from the Latin *planum* and *etria*, meaning flat ground and measurement. By definition, planimetric maps do not indicate elevation. These maps describe how to get from Toronto to Winnipeg, but they don't indicate whether you go uphill or downhill to get there.

Stick maps are commonly used by wilderness canoeists and backpackers. They are "straight line maps" that describe specific rivers or trails. Typically, these maps provide a great deal of detailed information within a limited area. They show little or no detail off the route, an obvious limitation. Stick maps are usually considered to be less reliable than a good topographic map.

Coastal charts are used by boaters. Generally, these maps emphasize depth of the water, natural and man-made aids to navigation, and natural and man-made hazards to navigation. Aeronautical charts are similar to coastal charts except that they are designed for the aviator. These maps concentrate on obstacles that impede aircraft traffic, particularly around airports.

Detailed trail maps are often available for well-used hiking or ski trails, particularly in provincial or national parks. Although these are often quite good, and are usually large scale, they should be used as supplements to current topographic maps.

For wilderness travel you need a map that will enable you to keep track of your precise position and plan your intended line of travel. For this reason, the best map for a wilderness traveller is a topographic map, often shortened to "top map." Topographic comes from the Greek word *topos*, meaning a drawing or picture of a place. Topographic maps are drawn to scale. The scale is the ratio between a distance on the map and that same distance in the field. For example, a scale of 1 to 1,000 means that every unit of 1 on the map translates into 1,000 units in the real world. Thus, a distance of 1 centimetre or 1 inch on the map represents 1,000 centimetres or 1,000 inches in the field. Three of the more common scales used on Canadian topographic maps are one unit to two hundred and fifty thousand units, one unit to fifty thousand units, and one unit to twenty-five thousand units. These scales are generally printed on maps in the following manner:

> 1: 250,000, 1: 50,000 and 1: 25,000

In addition, conversion to metric is making more 1: 100,000 maps available.

When considering scales, it is important to remember that the smaller the second number, the larger and clearer the details will be on the map. At the same time though, highly detailed top maps cover a smaller area. Therefore, relying on detailed maps may result in the need to carry many maps on a long trip. Most areas in Canada are covered by 1: 250,000 topographic maps. As well, many areas are covered by larger scale maps. In order to purchase Canadian topographic maps, write to:

> Map Distribution Office
> Energy, Mines and Resources Canada
> Ottawa, Ontario
> K1A 0E9

This office will send you a map of Canada showing all the top maps available for the various regions. On the reverse side, there is an excellent summary of maps and canoe tripping written by Eric Morse. If you live in a large city it is likely that there will be a local supplier of the most sought after maps.

If you require maps for the United States, write to:

> Map Distribution
> United States Geological Survey
> 1200 South Eads Street
> Arlington, Virginia
> U.S.A. 22202

GENERAL DETAILS ON TOPOGRAPHIC MAPS

At the bottom centre of the map, in the margin, you will find the name of that particular topographic map. The name of the map is generally derived from a principal feature located in the mapped area. This might be a town, lake, mountain, or geographic area. The map also has a distinct number. For example, in the case of the Ontario map named "Minden," the map number is 31D/15. The number is usually located in the lower right-hand corner of the map. Maps are ordered by name and number.

In the corners of each map are small numerals noting the latitude and longitude. These numbers identify the specific place

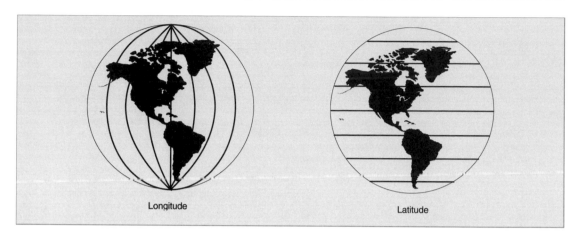

Longitude

Latitude

Figure 4-1
Lines of longitude and latitude

MAP TIP

Out-of-date maps can be quite misleading, sometimes with serious consequences.

on the earth represented by that particular topographic map. The lines and numbers that run north and south from pole to pole are the lines of longitude. The lines that run from side to side or east to west, are parallel lines that indicate latitude.

If you check the lower left-hand corner of your topographic map you should find dates that indicate when and how the information for that specific map was gathered. For instance, the map may be based on or updated from aerial photographs. In fact, these days, most topographic maps are based primarily on aerial photos. Culture checks are sometimes done for updated editions that are issued between aerial photograph observations. Culture checks are usually based on ground observations and, as the term implies, are meant to note any changes of a cultural nature, such as new roads, buildings either built or torn down, and dams. Any changes, natural or man-made, to an area after the last date noted on a map will not be shown. Thus, if you are using a 1949 version of the Finger Lakes map in upper New York State, you will find both the natural and the cultural changes to be considerable. Up-to-date maps are quite helpful, while out-of-date maps are often quite misleading.

MAP SYMBOLS AND FEATURES

It is important to be fully conversant with common map symbols in order to be able to visualize the "big picture." In addition, you should check your map for unusual physical features, such as string bogs or foreshore flats, before you leave home, then read up on these features at your local library.

Sometimes it's difficult to know whether to portage or paddle.

Map Features and Their Symbols

Symbols are used to convey details of the landscape to the map reader.

Cultural Features (Black)

Road—hard surface	dual highway	2 lanes	
Cart Track	– – – –	Cemetery	C
Trail or Portage	·········	Church	✝
Railway (single track)	+++++	Post Office	P
Railway (multiple track)	⊬⊬⊬⊬	Buildings	▄ ▌ ◼
Railway (abandoned)	+ + + +	Telephone Line	⊥⊥⊥⊥⊥
Horizontal Control Point	△594	Power Line	– – – · – – –
Bench Mark	↑255	Windmill	⚲
Sort Elevation	.410	Lighthouse	✪
Boundary Marker	▣	Historical Site	⊕
Mine or Quarry	⚒	Tower	⊙
Well	◯	School	⚑

Water Features (Blue)

Lake or Pond		Intermittent Lake	
River		Spring	○
Stream		Marsh	⚶ ··· ⚶
Rapids	⊬~~⊬	Inundated Land	
Dam or Falls	⊢E	Icefield	
Mud			

Vegetation Features (Green)

Woods		Vineyards	⊡

Elevation Features (Brown)

Contour		Index Contour	~500~
Depression Contour		Sand Dunes	

Cultural Features

Cultural features include roads, trails, houses, public buildings, power lines, bridges, historical sites, cemeteries, towers, and elevation markers. These are generally shown in black, although heavy duty and medium duty highways may be shown in red or orange. Symbols for cultural features are larger than they would be if they were drawn to scale.

Water Features

Water features such as rivers, canals, lakes, and oceans are noted in blue. Narrow rivers are usually indicated by a narrow blue line, while large rivers may be a blue band. On some maps, rapids and falls are marked by "R" and "F" respectively. In the case of a falls, the points on the end of the bar point downstream.

Vegetation Features

Vegetation features such as wooded areas, vineyards, scrub bush, and orchards are displayed in green.

Elevation Features

Elevation features such as hills and valleys are represented on topographic maps by thin brown lines called contour lines.

Contours

Contour lines are the essence of topographic maps. They encourage the reader to calculate and even visualize the slope of the land. Recall the situation where a group is stranded on a river bank after losing their canoes. Should they stay put and wait for help, or try to travel cross-country? Many factors come into play, one of which is the slope of the land.

A contour line is an imaginary line drawn on the map, along which every point touched by the line is at the same height above sea level. It is imaginary in the sense that it doesn't exist in the real world, just on the topographic map. If you examine a top map, you will see that some contour lines are heavier than others. These are *index contour lines*, and if you follow one on the map, you will find that somewhere it has a number on it. This number indicates the height above sea level of all the land touched by that contour line. The difference in height between one contour line and the next contour line is called the *contour interval*. The contour interval varies from map to map, and is usually noted at the bottom of the top map. The contour interval of some maps is

Figure 4-2
Contour lines represent
elevation.

as little as five feet. A small contour interval is used when there is very little difference in height over the entire map. On other maps, the contour interval may be fifty feet, a hundred feet, or more. In mountainous areas a large contour interval is required, otherwise the entire map would be a mess of brown lines. When contour lines are close together they indicate steep areas. Contour lines crossing a river take on a "V" shape. The point of the "V" aims upstream.

When interpreting contour lines, you will notice that a hill appears as a series of round circles. If the hill is steep at the beginning with a relatively flat top, then the circles will be close together at the outside, and further apart near the centre of the circle. If the hill starts as a gentle slope then becomes steep at the top, the reverse would be true.

Contour lines represent elevation. Contour lines allow the traveller to anticipate rapids, falls or gorges that may not be marked on a map. Contour lines can also be used to help anticipate good camping spots, and determine whether they are exposed or sheltered. Judgements regarding lookout points, ridges to follow for easier travel, and likely places to spot wildlife or seek out freshwater springs can all be predicted using contour lines. Reading contour lines takes practice. Use your topographic map and try to discover which lakes are highest, where the lowest elevation on the map is, then find and mark all the contour lines of a specific height—practice, practice, practice.

Topographic Map Features

1. **Contour lines, drawn in brown, show elevation and enable you to visualize the shape and slope of the land.**

2. **Water features, such as lakes and rivers, are drawn in blue.**

3. **Vegetation is marked in green.**

4. **Cultural features, such as towers and buildings, are marked in black.**

5. **The name and scale of the map are printed near the bottom centre, as is the contour interval.**

6. **The map date is noted in the bottom left corner.**

7. **Latitude and longitude are marked in the corners of the map.**

8. **Index contour lines note height above sea level.**

Other Indicators

There are other height indicators on a top map. For instance road intersections, mountain summits, lake surfaces, bench marks, and triangulation points are often accompanied by numbers that indicate the height above sea level. These features are usually marked in black.

Topographic maps are divided into squares using *grid reference lines*. On the right-hand side, Canadian topographic maps have a brief explanation of military grid reference lines, as well as a short description of how to use them. Basically, this involves taking an east reading and a north reading, commonly referred to as an *easting* and a *northing*. With respect to Fig. 4–3, locate Moore's Falls. Reading along the bottom of the map, the easting, notice that the dam at Moore's Falls is between line 73 and line 74. Use the reference number 73 as the first two numbers for a grid reference point. Next, determine how far the dam is from line 73. If you break the square into tenths, this particular dam falls about eight-tenths of the way across the square; therefore, the first three digits of a six digit military grid reference point for Moore's Falls would be 738. Then read up, or take a northing. In this case, the northing would be 63 and six-tenths, or 636. These figures are then combined to make one, six digit figure which gives the precise reference point. By precise, we mean it will be

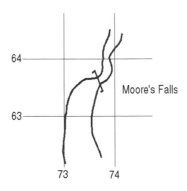

Figure 4-3

Time-Keeping

When travelling it's wise to keep a record of your time so you can "guesstimate" the time required to travel over a variety of terrains. The advantage of having previously documented your travel time becomes apparent when trying to make decisions, such as whether to make camp or continue travelling. Determining the best route in an emergency situation is made easier if you can guesstimate your travelling time over a variety of terrains. However, don't forget that travelling time will vary considerably from trip to trip as well as over different types of terrains.

within 100 metres of the exact point. This is because each of the grid lines is separated by a distance of one kilometre. The six digit military grid reference point for the dam at Moore's Falls is 738636. The nearest point that would have the same grid reference is about 63 miles away. When using the grid designation, you must make it clear which map you are referring to. Remember that the easting comes first.

Choose a half dozen prominent features on a map of your own, and then determine their grid references. Rescue work, locating campsites or interest spots, and determining meeting points are examples of situations when this technique can come in handy. If you forget how to do it, remember that there are directions on the map.

Every topographic map has a scale, generally found at the bottom centre of the map. This scale can be a helpful means of measuring distances on the map. First, measure your proposed route of travel with a compass, ruler, or a piece of string. Then convert, using the scale, to units of your choice. A string is particularly handy for measuring distances on maps because it can be used to trace the routes of wriggly streams or looping trails. For practice, get an old top map, perhaps the one you used for determining military grid reference points, and try calculating the distance between major features. Use a small piece of string and the scale at the bottom of the map.

Map Drawing Exercise

It follows that if you understand what maps are, and can visualize map features, then you should be able to draw one. Test yourself by taking an ordinary sheet of paper and drawing a map based on the following instructions.

Place the paper so that the long sides are at the top and bottom. The scale is one kilometre to one centimetre or one inch to one mile—your choice. Clear Lake is a large lake, covering about 1/5 of the paper, located in the centre of the map. It is roughly oval in shape and runs on a S.W. to N.E. axis. At its uppermost point, there is a small river that runs two kilometres (1.2 miles) to the north. This river is fairly straight, with three sets of rapids near its middle part. A small lake running east to west joins the other end of the river. The river exits from the west end of this lake, called Finger Lake. Finger Lake, shaped like its name, is 5 and 1/2 kilometres (3.3 miles) long and 1/2 kilometre (0.3 miles) wide. A river enters Finger Lake from the east. This river, called Dog River, runs due east off the map. A railroad comes onto the map from the south, due south of the southernmost point of Clear Lake. The railroad line runs north, meeting Clear Lake at a fishing and hunting camp. The camp is comprised of one large building back from shore, and five smaller buildings near the shore. There is a small orchard behind the large building. Two small springs are located just west of the orchard. The railroad skirts around the north-west side of Clear Lake, crossing the river at the rapids, then running north to Finger Lake. At that point, it turns east running off the map. A four lane divided highway runs east-west immediately north of Finger Lake. The height of Clear Lake averages 782 feet, depending on the season. There are three small islands in a cluster on Clear Lake immediately south of the river that joins it with Finger Lake. A hydro line runs north to south immediately west of Clear Lake. The southeast shore of Clear Lake is swampy.

Check your map with Appendix D, but not until you draw all the features!

There is a simple technique used by many campers for route planning and on-trip navigation. Simply recopy your intended route, be it a river, lake or trail, from the top map onto a blank piece of paper. This will reduce the many distracting and initially irrelevant details found on the map, and help to familiarize you with the route. Add the most important features along a 7–10

Figure 4-4
Orienteering Compass

An orienteering compass has three arrows: a—orienteering arrow; b—magnetic needle; c—direction of travel arrow.

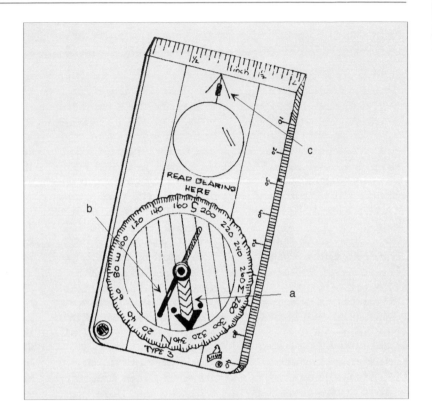

kilometre (4–6 mile) corridor. These include navigational aids, possible campsites, hazards, and points of interest. Then note all the contour lines that cross your route and calculate the elevation differences between these points. With experience, these figures will greatly assist you in predicting the class of white water or the difficulty of the hike. This type of planning is in addition to a top map, not instead of one.

THE COMPASS

Around 2,500 B.C., the Chinese discovered that if a particular type of ore was put on a small piece of wood, then floated in water, it would turn until one end pointed in the general direction from which the sun shone when it was at its peak. This was the first compass, and today's compass is not a whole lot different. The compass is simply a strip of magnetized steel, balanced on a pivot. The needle is free to swing in any direction, and will eventually come to rest with one end pointing north.

As discussed in the last chapter, the compass most suitable for campers is the standard orienteering design. Just as with the top

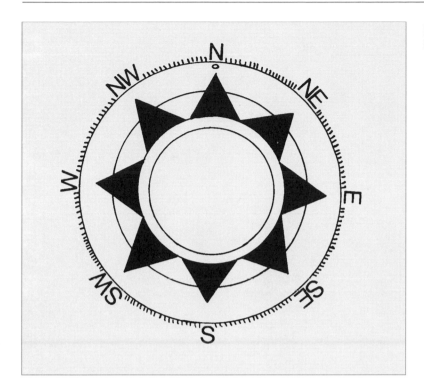

Figure 4-5
Compass Rose

map, it is important for any serious outdoors person to become thoroughly familiar with the compass. Most compasses come with a set of instructions. Save the instructions. They are usually very well written, and provide a lightweight and handy summary of how to use the compass.

If you bought the correct compass, it is mounted on a plastic or glass base with one or more scales on the sides. These scales can be used to measure distances on the map. Most compasses have a small hole in the base plate. Run a string or thong through the hole, and you will not only have a handy method for carrying the compass, but you can also use the string or thong for measuring roundabout distances on the map.

There are three different arrows on your compass. Each has a specific purpose. Understanding the differences between the arrows is critical to knowing how to use a compass.

The *Direction of Travel Arrow* (see Fig. 4–4) is the one that points in the direction of intended travel. The *Magnetic Needle* points towards the north magnetic pole. Unfortunately, when travellers get confused, they often follow the Magnetic Needle instead of the Direction of Travel Arrow. The *Orienteering Arrow* is used to orient the map and/or compass towards north. The

MAP TIP

Save the instructions that come with your compass. They will be a handy reference guide and are easily stored in your first aid kit.

Figure 4-6
Calculating a bearing.

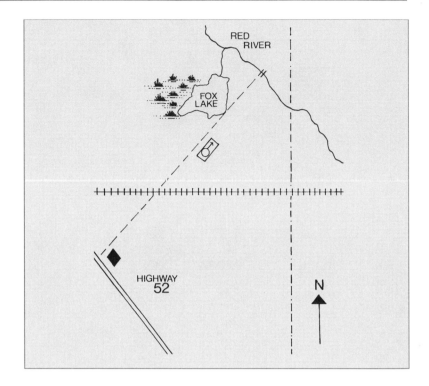

compass housing is what makes an orienteering compass unique. It can be rotated while the base plate and the Direction of Travel Arrow remain stationary. The compass housing is usually filled with a liquid, a process known as *dampening*, to prevent the magnetic needle from bouncing around and continually overcorrecting. Orienteering compasses used to be electrically dampened, but liquid dampening is more effective.

BEARINGS

On the outside ring of the compass housing are the *directions*. The four cardinal directions are north, south, east and west. These are sub-divided by the inter-cardinal directions of northeast, northwest, southeast, and southwest. Eight additional compass points sub-divide the eight cardinal and inter-cardinal points. More precisely, the intended path of travel, or direction, is described as a *bearing*, with *degrees* being the unit of measurement. There are 360°—or ways to go—in a full circle. Thus, a bearing or travel line could be 175°, 245°, 009°, 349°, or any other number of degrees not exceeding 360. East is represented by 90°, west by 270°, and south by 180°. North is 360°.

Reciprocal bearings are opposite ways to go. The reciprocal of north is south; the reciprocal of east is west. Written in degrees the reciprocal of 90° (east) would be 270° (west). It is important to be able to calculate reciprocal bearings quickly since they are required whenever you decide to reverse direction, triangulate or determine your position in the field. If your first bearing falls between one degree and one hundred and eighty degrees, simply add one hundred and eighty degrees to come up with the reciprocal. If the original bearing falls between one hundred and eight-one degrees, and three hundred and sixty degrees, simply subtract one hundred and eighty degrees to determine the reciprocal.

Calculating the Reciprocal Bearing

5°	**+ 180°**	**= 185°**
19°	**+ 180°**	**= 199°**
265°	**- 180°**	**= 85°**
81°	**+ 180°**	**= 261°**
240°	**- 180°**	**= 60°**

MAP AND COMPASS

Armed with a map and a compass, it isn't difficult to calculate the bearing or "way to go" for a proposed trip. With reference to the sketch map in Fig. 4–6, we will use the place where the highway and building meet as a proposed departure point, then calculate a bearing in order to travel directly to the quarry. If you were to actually attempt to travel this route without an orienteering compass or protractor, you would likely examine the map, think "northeast," and go. However, given the distance to be covered, it is unlikely that your travel would be straight and true. Calculating and following compass bearings is simple, and far more accurate than travelling by pure instinct. To determine the bearing in this example, follow the steps described in the following box.

Calculating A True Bearing

1. Draw a line on the map from the departure point along the intended path of travel.

2. Lay your compass along the line so that the Direction of Travel Arrow points in the direction you wish to travel.

3. Turn the compass housing, not the body of the compass, until the Orienteering Arrow points towards north on the map. This is easiest to accomplish by lining up the grid lines in the compass housing with the grid lines on the map.

4. Your direction of travel, or bearing, is now indicated at the Direction of Travel Arrow where it says *Read Bearing Here*. How convenient!

Compensating for Declination

Area	Intended Direction of Travel	Declination	Therefore You	Revised Bearing
Vancouver, B.C.	150°T	25°E	subtract	125°M
Churchill, Manitova	340°T	0°	—	340°M
Minden, Ontario	15°T	11°W	add	26°M
Devon Is., N.W.T.	270°T	90°W	add	360°M
Whitehorse, Y.T.	170°T	31°E	subtract	139°M
Fort George, P.Q.	219°T	16°W	add	235°M
T = True	M = Magnetic			

Now you know how to draw a travel line, lay the compass on that travel line, and calculate the bearing. Are you all set to head off? Almost, but not quite. The problem you have yet to overcome, is that of *declination*. Things would be much simpler if the compass needle pointed to *true north*; however, it doesn't. The magnetized needle on the compass points to the *magnetic north pole*, whereas top maps have their grid reference lines oriented to true north, or the north pole. This hasn't been a problem in your calculations so far because up to now you haven't made use of the magnetic needle. But, after you determine your bearing from the map, it will be necessary to use the magnetic needle in the field. It is easiest to compensate for declination, the difference between the magnetic north and the true north, at this stage. If you are using a compass in eastern Ontario or New York State, for example, you will find that your compass points to the left of true north. This is because the magnetic north pole is located to the north and west of Hudson Bay. Logically, it is apparent that if you *add* the correct number of degrees to any magnetic compass reading, this would make up for the difference between magnetic north and true north. If we are working from a bearing on the west coast, the problem would be reversed. Our compass would be pointing in a direction which would be on the right-hand side or to the east of true north. Therefore, in order to compensate, we would *subtract* the correct number of degrees.

The top map will tell you how many degrees you must add or subtract in order to compensate for declination. One version of the Minden Map shows the difference between magnetic north and true north as 10° and 45 minutes. (There are 60 minutes in a degree just as there are 60 minutes in an hour.) When you take into consideration the fact that the declination in this area is increasing slightly, year by year, you will want to correct for an 11° difference, on this particular map. It is always important to check the annual change and take it into account. As well, you will find some maps show a substantial difference in declination for different areas on the same map. This is particularly true in areas near the magnetic pole. Always use the declination figure closest to your line of travel.

Routefinding in the fog.

When calculating any bearing on this version of the Minden Map, it is necessary to add 11° to make up for the difference between magnetic north and true north. If magnetic north is west of true north, you add. If magnetic north is east of true north, you subtract. *This is true when you are working from map to field. If you are working from field to map, the process is reversed.* That is, you would subtract a westerly declination and add an easterly declination. Some people use the rhyme "east is least and west is best," adding to east and subtracting from west. If, however, you can picture the two poles, it should be a process of logical deduction in order to determine whether to add or subtract, depending on whether you are working from the map to field, or from the field to map.

Some people prefer to compensate for magnetic declination before determining the bearing. This can be accomplished by drawing magnetic north lines on the map and orienting the compass to them, rather than to the true north grid lines. The first method is actually easier, providing you understand the logic behind the calculation. The second technique leaves your map with lots of pencil lines.

So far you have completed three steps: (1) calculated the bearing; (2) corrected for declination; and (3) determined the distance you need to travel. Now it's necessary to determine the actual direction in the field. Assume your calculated bearing is 68°, and follow the steps in the chart on the following page to determine direction in the field.

Determining Direction in the Field

1. Given a bearing of 68°, rotate the compass housing until 68° is opposite the direction of travel arrow.

2. Hold the compass in the palm of your hand at waist level, making sure the Direction of Travel Arrow is pointing away from you.

3. Ensure that the compass is not being affected by a belt buckle or other piece of metal.

4. Slowly turn your body by moving your feet. Do not turn the compass independently. Turn your body only, until the Orienteering Arrow and the Magnetic Needle are in line with one another. The Magnetic Needle should cover the Orienteering Arrow. Make sure the red end of the Magnetic Needle is the end that is pointing towards the north designation on the compass housing. When you have done this, you should be looking the same way the Direction of Travel Arrow is pointing.

5. You are now facing 68° or the way to go.

6. Holding the compass steady, look up and sight an object along the line of the Direction of Travel Arrow. This might be a tree, a bush, or a corner of a building.

7. Walk to the object you have sighted and you will be travelling on a bearing of 68° magnetic.

When following a bearing to a destination, do not walk while looking at the compass; instead, after you have sighted an object, put the compass down and then walk to the object. Sighting an object allows you to walk around trees, ditches, or other obstructions. When you reach the sighted object, stand with your back to it and sight another object. This technique is the best method for travelling in a straight line.

THE IMPORTANCE OF KNOWING YOUR LOCATION

Maps are often tucked away out of sight until trouble occurs. Trouble may take the form of being lost or suffering an accident. Instead of keeping the map packed away, a better idea is to continually use the map in order to keep track of where you are, at all times. Although it may sound silly, if you always know where you are, you will never be lost. And, you will never have to try and find your position from scratch, a difficult task.

Keeping track of your exact position while you hike or canoe will make you proficient in map reading. Soon you will anticipate side trails, small tributaries and other points of interest.

TRIANGULATION

If you are comfortable with the map and compass work discussed to this point, triangulation should pose no problem. Triangulation is a technique for determining your position, either as confirmation when you may not be entirely sure where you are, or in a situation where you know you are lost. Work through the following example, step by step, and you will probably conclude that the technique is logical and fairly simple.

Picture yourself standing on a hill from where you can see, off in the distance, a lake to your left, a fire tower straight ahead, and a hill to your right. (The picture in your mind should be similar to the layout in Fig. 4-7.) To determine your precise position in the field, you calculate the bearing to each landmark by pointing the compass' Direction of Travel Arrow at the object and rotating the housing until the Magnetic Needle covers the Orienteering Arrow. Once you have this bearing, adjust for declination, determine the reciprocal, and dial this reciprocal bearing on your compass. This is the bearing from the object to you. Then, by laying the compass on your map and drawing a pencil line through the object along the reciprocal bearing you have calculated, you will have a line that runs from the object through your current location. Repeat this process for two more identifiable objects, and the point where the three lines meet is your location. Using the example in Fig. 4-7, assume you have determined the tower to be on a bearing of 305°, the hill at 84°, and the lake at 216°. Calculate the reciprocal bearings by completing the chart on page 87, then draw the intersect on Fig. 4-7. After you complete the exercise, compare your calculations with the answers at the end of the chapter.

MAP TIP

Should you find an error on a current official map and be able to provide detailed information about it, write to:

IN THE UNITED STATES:

Map Distribution United States Geological Survey 1200 South Eads Street Arlington, Virginia U.S.A. 22202

IN CANADA:

Topographical Survey Office Government of Canada 615 Booth Street Ottawa, Ontario K1A 0E9

Figure 4-7
Triangulation exercise

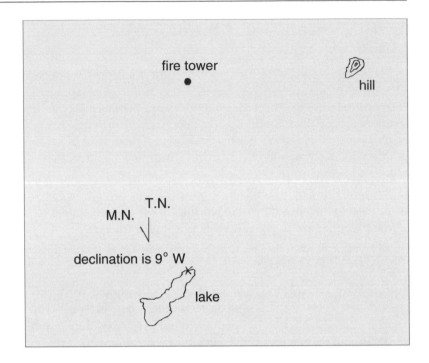

Steps for Triangulation

1. **Point the Direction of Travel Arrow at the landmark.**

2. **Rotate the dial until the Magnetic Needle covers the Orienteering Arrow (Direction of Travel Arrow remains pointing at the landmark).**

3. **Read the bearing at the Direction of Travel Arrow. This is the bearing you would follow to go to that landmark.**

4. **Correct for declination, remembering that you are now working from field to map, then take the reciprocal of the corrected bearing because it is necessary to find the bearing from the landmark to your position.**

5. **Dial the reciprocal bearing on the compass, place the side of the compass base on the landmark on the map, then rotate the entire compass until the Orienteering Arrow points towards north.**

6. **Draw a line from the object in the direction of the Direction of Travel Arrow.**

7. **Repeat this for at least two other prominent landmarks. Where these lines meet is your position.**

Triangulation Problem

	BEARING	Declination	Corrected Bearing	Reciprocals
Tower	305°			
Hill	84°			
Lake	216°			

USING A COMPASS IN A CANOE

Wilderness canoeing brings special challenges to route finding. Consider the situation where you reach a large lake, intending to paddle to a portage on the other side. In some cases you may not be able to see the portage on the other side. In order to prevent unnecessary paddling, although this can often be the best part of the trip, you prefer to use your map and compass to calculate a bearing from your present position to the portage. After correcting for declination, use the compass to sight where the portage should be. It is often possible to make note of a particular tree or rock and paddle to it. If that is not feasible, lay the compass down on a pack in front of you so that the Direction of Travel Arrow runs along the keel of the canoe. Dial the corrected bearing and turn the canoe so the Magnetic Needle covers the Orienteering Arrow. At this point you have oriented the compass and the canoe. While paddling to the portage it will be necessary to correct for waves, winds, and currents, and whether or not the pack with the compass on it contains the billy kit!

Triangulation may be employed from within a canoe for a variety of reasons. You may wish to determine your exact position along the shore of a large lake, or where you are on a long wide river. Taking bearings off islands and high, visible points of land will help you with this task.

OFF-BEARINGS

The following is a typical example used to illustrate the importance of off-bearings. Consider someone who parks on an east-west concession road, then walks due south to do some bird watching. After an hour, he walks due north to his car. It would

How to Avoid Getting Lost

1. Carry an up-to-date topographical map, and know how to read it. Don't allow yourslf to get separated from your map.

2. Carry an orienteering compas, on your person, and know how to use it.

3. On long trips, carry an extra set of maps.

4. While travelling, be sure to pinpoint your exact position every ten to fifteen minutes. Always anticipate and watch for the next landmark.

be a long-shot to bet that he would hit the road exactly at his car. In fact, he could be anywhere from 100 metres to two kilometres (110 yards to 1.2 miles) from the car. This isn't a problem if the road is perfectly flat and straight. He would be able to see for several some distance. But it is more likely that the road curves or is hilly. Therefore, on reaching the road he wouldn't know in which direction to walk. He might try two kilometres (1.2 miles) one way, then give up and walk the other way, when in fact he was within 100 metres (110 yards) of his car when he decided to change direction. This would be frustrating if you had a chocolate bar, good weather, and lots of time and patience. Under deteriorating weather conditions, it can be downright dangerous. The solution is to return to the car by walking not due north, but at an off-bearing which will definitely put you to one side of the vehicle or the other. You then know for certain which way to walk on the road. This same technique should be used when following a bearing in your canoe while looking for a portage.

EXPERIENCE IN NAVIGATION

There isn't anything that will make up for practical experience in wilderness navigation. Knowing how to interpret contour lines, keeping track of your position at all times, and being able to calculate and follow compass bearings are necessary skills that need to be refined through practice.

Wilderness travellers who get caught in difficult situations, such as bad weather or an accident, have a curious habit of distrusting their equipment. More specifically, they often believe that their compass is malfunctioning and is no longer reliable. At that point, the urge to trust their own internal sense of direction takes over. Many studies have demonstrated that it is not possible to travel in a straight line using only your "sense" of what appears to be a straight route. Sooner or later, you will start to go in circles. The compass is almost never wrong, and, since most of us travel in groups of two or more, it is a simple matter to check one compass against another. Everyone should carry a compass.

ADDITIONAL SOURCES

- Kjellstrom, B. (1976). *Be Expert with Map and Compass.* New York: Charles Scribner and Sons.

- Randall, G. (1989). *The Outward Bound Map and Compass Handbook.* Toronto: Douglas & McIntyre.

- Rutstrum, C. (1973). *The Wilderness Route Finder.* New York: Collier Books.

Answers to the Triangulation Problem

	BEARING	Declination	Corrected Bearing	Reciprocals
Tower	305°	9°	296°	116°
Hill	84°	9°	75°	255°
Lake	216°	9°	197°	17°

Preparing a big meal after a hard day of paddling in the Kipawa area of Quebec.

5
Diet and Nutrition

Recipe for Loon soup: Do not make Loon soup.
The Eskimo Cookbook

Not long ago I watched a slide show documenting a 30 day canoe trip down the Horton River. The Horton is a stunningly beautiful river located about 400 kilometres east of the Mackenzie. It has moderate rapids, striking scenery, and great wildlife. The river ends at the Arctic Ocean, where it empties into the west side of Franklin Bay. I have seen hundreds of slide shows illustrating canoe and backpacking trips around the world, but at the end of this show I realized that I had just missed something—I had not seen a single photograph of food, cooking or people eating. There were lots of pictures of canoeing, white water, wildlife, mountains, and hiking, but not a single meal. I was amazed. My experience on long trips, both backpacking and canoeing, has been that food is dwelt upon, in the resulting slide show, with the same intensity and preoccupation that a food writer in the Sunday *New York Times* might give it.

With the exception of this one slide show, which I should add was an excellent presentation, the issue of what food to pack has been an important, highly visible, and often talked about element of every wilderness trip I have heard about or been a party to. This is not surprising. Food is critical, both for biological and psychological reasons. If you don't have enough, people get very, very ornery. If you don't have the right type, they still get ornery. Even those responsible for selecting the food, and deciding how much to take, get ornery. The bottom line is that good food, and lots of it, is a critical aspect of every wilderness trip. At least three times a day, and for some of us it may be as often as five or six times a day, food is evaluated in terms of quantity and quality. To make matters more difficult, preferences regarding amount and type vary considerably. Some folks are very picky, while others will eat almost anything. I have camped with freeze dried food specialists, nutrition gurus, vegetarians, and even some environmentalists who claim a preference for "fireless food," all of whom had very different views regarding what constitutes appropriate fare. Such differing views can make meal planning a challenge.

This chapter examines some of the basic issues that are important when it comes to selecting and packing food for a wilderness trip. These include such factors as weight, tastiness, variety, bulk, resistance to spoilage, ease of preparation, length of the trip, and nutritional value. Also presented in this chapter are a potpourri of meal ideas. The meal suggestions will have special appeal for those who like to sample different recipes, and also for those who are too busy or too indifferent to get very excited about creating their own menus.

WEIGHT

The single-mindedness that drives some campers to pursue the goal of minimal food weight in their menu planning and packing has fostered and supported the many freeze-dried food companies that presently exist. To be fair, this devotion to weight reduction does not apply only to food, but is also aimed at equipment. Sleeping bags, tents, clothing and even toothbrushes have become lighter and more compact at the insistence of campers who are only too willing to pay more for less!

For many campers, particularly those who travel long distances through regions that are difficult to get into, the issue of weight drives many menu decisions. If you are doing a fourteen day backpacking trip in Auyuittuq National Park (see Chapter 10), you are only going to be willing and able to carry so much food. If you are a two person canoe group flying from Fort Simpson to the headwaters of the Nahanni in a Cessna 185, you are only going to carry about 135 kilograms (300 lbs.) of food and equipment if you expect to clear the mountain peaks. Gone are the days when Arctic explorer David Hanbury travelled north from Edmonton at the turn of the century to spend a year and a half living off the land.

If weight is going to be a critical factor, then the obvious question to ask is "what is a reasonable amount of food to carry, by weight, per person per day?" Unfortunately, the answer is not as simple as the question. While it would be convenient to say one kilogram (2.2 pounds) per person per day fits all occasions, and let it go at that, a "one weight does em all" answer would be neither realistic nor correct. If, however, we think in terms of a range, it can be said that many people pack and carry food at between 900 and 1400 grams (2-3 pounds) per person per day for up to ten days of backpacking or 25 days of canoeing. The shorter the trip, the higher the food weight per day. However, please note that this is not expedition style camping, where special restrictions come into play. The 900 to 1400 grams (2-3 pounds) per person per day range is simply a starting point for planning purposes. I have seen it used by groups paddling to James Bay and others hiking in the Yukon. When combined with the gear carried, this planning figure allows a goal for total weight per person, an important planning factor for backpacking trips where there are upper limits to the amount of weight you want to sling onto your back every day. Variations on this figure will be affected by how much of the food is dry, versus how much is whole. In some cases I have encountered people carrying less than 900 grams (2 pounds) per person per day on extended backpacking trips. In fact, it is possible, with dried and pre-packaged items to get down to a 650 gram (.7 pounds) average.

One-cup meals are a good idea when you want to get a fast start on the day.

Serious trip planning should involve budgeting for food weights. But try to remain flexible. If you keep track of the food weight you carry on several different types of trips, you will soon build a food/weight repertoire that makes your menu and trip planning easier and more efficient.

TASTINESS

For most of us, taste preferences are an important menu consideration. We like to buy, think about, and eat food that pleases the palate. I will admit that I have met some campers who buy and eat food based on what they think is nutritionally good for them, with little regard to how it tastes; however, most of us put taste high on the list of what is important when menu planning.

On shorter trips of one to three days, where the weight factor is not so important, menus are often based largely on taste preferences. Large meat dinners, fancy lunches, and bacon and egg breakfasts are the order of the day. Here, the major consid-erations are whether the food needs any special protection, such as refrigeration, and if can it be effectively prepared outdoors— the answer to the latter question almost invariably being yes, providing the cook is willing to be inventive.

Reflector ovens can be used to prepare cakes, pies, cookies and muffins.

On longer trips, tastiness can be approached in several ways. For example, you may choose to incorporate two "special" dinners for every week of menu planning. Then, although every meal may not be the ultimate taste treat, there is always a special meal to look forward to. Or, you can pack special treats, such as somebody's favourite chocolate bar or the makings for a lemon pie (pizza or bread pie crust with lemon Jello for the filling). Keep these items separate and secret, then bring them out as the need for a special treat arises. I have heard of trips where each person was required to bring one very special treat; then, every few days, a treat was prepared and shared.

CAMPING TIP

Tasty meals can make or break some trips.

The importance of including foods that are pleasing to the palate cannot be overestimated. They can easily make the difference between "good" and "great" when things go well, and they can save the day when everything else goes wrong. People are generally versatile and forgiving until they are fed meals that, to their way of tasting, are inedible.

I remember a trip in the Kipawa area of western Quebec when, after a hot, buggy day of portaging along a small river, we paddled to our campsite on an island near the northern end of an open lake. The kicker was that the wind was strong enough to require an all-out-every-muscle paddle for about 45 minutes in order to reach the island. We had worked for a good ten hours that day and on reaching the island the group was exhausted. While waiting for dinner, I was starting to feel a bit down in the dumps. This was day twelve and it had rained every day. I was cold and I could see we were going to eat the old starchy standby ... plain spaghetti! The others appeared to share my sentiments. No one talked, and the camp chores were done in the silent mechanical fashion that comes to a group twelve days and several hundred miles into bug country. I was sitting on a rock watching the sun drop when someone handed me a hot plate. Then the smell struck me. The cook for that meal had used a variety of herbs, a fresh onion, and other goodies that turned an old standby dinner into what seemed, in that time and place, to be a culinary extravaganza. The group finished dinner with a few good jokes and shared laughter. The mood was altogether different, and it was a simple but tasty dinner that did the trick. A terrific sunset appeared and the rain disappeared!

VARIETY

There are two schools of thought with respect to variety—those who find it necessary and those who don't. Some menu planners select a breakfast menu, and then simply multiply it by the number of days on the trail. Those who are even less committed to variety will do the same for lunch and dinner. I think this is pretty boring, and even a good recipe can become dismal after you have eaten it for three or four days in a row.

Many people, however, find that a menu must include variety to get campers interested and stimulate their taste-buds. Psychologically, change is important for most of us. At the absolute minimum, I recommend at least three different breakfast, lunch, and dinner menus for trips lasting a week or more. Since fresh food can be used for the first few days, this is not difficult to achieve. And, to put some surprise in the menu, have an occasional meal that is never repeated. This could be a major production that requires a rest/cooking day, such as fresh baked beans, prepared from scratch and done in a sand pit.

CAMPING TIP

A minimum of three different breakfast, lunch and dinner menus helps satisfy our need for variety.

BULK/AMOUNT

Some people, particularly young people, eat a certain "bulk" or amount of food. My experience has taught me that it is a waste of time and energy trying to convince these types that they have had enough to eat, from a nutritional perspective, when their stomachs keep growling "give me more." Many teenagers, particularly boys, eat by the teenager bulk rule: *eat til you can't eat any more without throwing up.* Those with such unrestrained appetites have become accustomed to eating a certain amount of food, usually an incredibly large amount, and no measure of logic is going to change their eating habits.

Making bannock.

Unless you are prepared to be plagued by constant pleas for more food, I strongly recommend ensuring that your menu has some bulk items in it. While it's true that if you are travelling for six weeks in the Canadian arctic the participants will have to come to grips with the fact that resupply costs restrict the amount of peanut butter you can carry, shorter trips will benefit from extra allotments of macaroni, rice, and instant mashed potatoes. My response to those who are always hungry is to encourage them to cook up half a kilo (1 pound) of rice and have a feast. I also encourage fishing and gathering of edible plants. Not all the food has to come from the wannigan.

RESISTANCE TO SPOILAGE

The length of time different foods keep without spoiling varies considerably. Select, pack, and prepare food with this in mind. Spoilage can be caused not only by the passage of time, but also by crushing, exposure to water or air, and heat. Fresh meat at the bottom of the wannigan will last far longer than if it is left in the top of a darkly coloured canoe pack sitting in the sun.

CAMPING TIP

Many fresh foods will last for several weeks if stored properly.

Many items, such as fresh eggs, salami, bacon and cheese, keep for long periods of time when stored and carried properly. I have carried and eaten ordinary pre-sliced, vacuum packaged 500 gram (1 pound) packages of side bacon for as long as three weeks during the summer. I have one rule: when I open the vacuum sealed package, I eat the entire package. Whole pieces of back bacon or peameal bacon can be carried for extraordinarily long periods of time. Cheddar cheese, in five or even ten kilo (11 or 22 pounds) blocks, can be stored in a wannigan for two months with few problems. If, after the first month, the edges look a little too green, simply slice them off. I generally carry eggs for a week, eating them for my first few breakfasts on long trips. On shorter trips, I like to have eggs for breakfast at least every other day. Smoked meats, such as salamis, are excellent to carry on extended trips. They are a valuable protein source and will, if properly cared for, last indefinitely.

In all cases, be sure to use good judgement. All foods should be stored properly to ensure minimum spoilage. If you think food has been spoiled, then don't take a chance. The hospital is too far away and certain types of food poisoning are not worth any risk (see Food Poisoning in Chapter Seven—Emergency Care).

EASE OF PREPARATION

If you are not particularly turned on by cooking over a camp stove or open fire, if you are camping with young children or others who are inept at cooking, or if you are on an expedition where special constraints exist, ease of preparation may be one of your chief concerns when planning menus. Freeze-dried foods, one-pot meals, and premixed foods lend themselves to these situations. In fact, almost every trip should have some simple meals for days when weather makes preparing a two or three course meal an onerous task. Having several one-pot meals available, and a selection of soups and cold food such as gorp for eating inside the tent, makes sense. Build these into a particularly extended trip in the ratio of about one for every five days. If you are going into an inhospitable region, increase this ratio.

LENGTH OF TRIP

As implied earlier, the length of the trip will have an important influence on the menu. Weight, variety, spoilage issues, and nutrition are different for a three day trip compared to a six week trip. For three days, the amount of food, its nutritional quality, and variety are minor issues. However, for a six week trip, these issues are very important. For trips of seven days or more, even consumable items such as soup, scouring pads, flashlight batteries, and toothpaste have to be considered in terms of their weight.

For very long trips, it is obvious that it is next to impossible to carry enough "typical" camping food. Consider a forty day backpack trip. At one kilogram (2.2 pounds) per person per day, it would be necessary to start the trip with 40 kilograms (100 pounds) of food per person. Carrying this weight of food, plus equipment, does not sound like an enjoyable outdoor experience. For a trip of this sort it would be necessary to cache food, have food drops, stop at re-supply stores along the way, hunt, or gather edible plants.

Few of us do menu planning for forty day trips. Instead, we wrestle with the problem of 1.5 kilograms (3.3 pounds) per person per day for five or ten day trips. However, even on short trips, food weights may seem excessive. In these cases the most common solution is to reduce the per day weight of the food by including more dried food and leaving heavier items at home. Another trick is to eat as many of the heavy meals as early in the trip as possible. The drawback to this approach is that the heavier meals are often the most appetizing and nourishing.

Gnawing on a piece of rockbread. (See recipe on page 111.)

DIET AND NUTRITION

Many authors have become rich writing about diet and nutrition. Experts bombard us with claims and counterclaims, making it difficult for the lay person to understand or believe much of what is said. In order to make some sense of diet and nutrition issues, as they relate to camping and menu planning, I think it's necessary to understand some of the terminology and basic concepts.

The total of all the foods you eat is your diet. What happens to the food after it has been ingested, digested and absorbed by the body is known as nutrition. Nutrients are the different substances found in food. They are necessary for the body to fulfil a variety of tasks

There are about 40 elements required for healthy human nutrition. Water and air are the two most immediate. Scientists classify the others into five groups. These are protein, carbohydrates, fats, minerals, and vitamins. Strategically combining these five elements in your diet is the puzzle that alternately intrigues and befuddles the camper who takes menu planning seriously.

One approach for creating a healthy diet is to select food items according to their percentages of carbohydrates, fat, and protein. A healthy diet is composed of approximately 55% carbohydrates, 30% fat, and 15% protein. With this approach, the only other factor to consider is calories. Calories are an indicator of the potential energy which may be released from foods. Knowing caloric requirements helps determine quantities.

Let's take a closer look at the five groups of elements. *Protein* is used and required by all living things. Humans are about 18% to 20% protein by weight. Protein forms the basic structural components for the body, acting as its building blocks. Protein is necessary for the creation of hair, nails, muscles and cartilage. As well, the body requires protein for growth, repairs, and maintenance. Protein is a catalyst agent for many of the metabolic reactions that take place in the body. Nutritionists differ as to what they believe are the best foods to eat in order to ingest usable protein. Many, including the traditionalists, are usually in this group, and they argue that proteins of animal origin, such as eggs, milk, meat, fish and poultry, are generally superior foods.

Carbohydrates, such as starches and sugar, are energy foods. During and after digestion they get broken down and yield glucose. Glucose is used by the body's cells to provide energy. The carbohydrates that don't get used for energy production are converted into fat and stored in various parts of the body. These

Nutrient Tasks

1. **Energy production.**

2. **Maintenance and repair of such items as bones, blood cells, and muscle.**

3. **Growth.**

4. **Reproduction and lactation.**

5. **Regulation and coordination of body processes including the many internal chemical reactions required for everyday living.**

are the foods that are responsible for the layers of fat that accumulate around the stomach, arms and thighs. Foods that are high in starch content include potatoes, macaroni, spaghetti, oats, corn, rice, noodles, bread, pies, cakes, and many breakfast cereals. Sugary goods (my specialty!) include most candy, jam, pie filling, cake, icing, honey, molasses and syrup.

Fats are excellent sources of energy, stimulate caloric intake, and act as an insulator for many of the vital organs within the body cavity. By weight, fats can provide energy in the form of calories at more than twice the rate of either carbohydrates or protein. Fatty foods are easy to recognize both visually and texturally. They include heavily marbled meats, bacon, butter, cooking oils, margarine, peanuts, salad oils, cheese and eggs.

Minerals are necessary for a balanced diet. They act as strength-giving constituents for bones and teeth, and as structural parts of soft tissues. Minerals are also important regulators of a variety of body functions.

Vitamins are organic catalysts. They are essential to muscle and nerve functions, and are necessary for full utilization of other nutrients by the body.

Nutritionists divide foods into groups according to their nutrients. Associating foods in this way provides the basis for menu planning by category or food group, in the home or on a wilderness trip. Menu planning according to food groups focuses attention on the need to have a balanced diet, one that is based on variety.

The most common food guide divides food into four major groups; however, there are food guides with seven, ten and twelve groups. The four group food guide includes: (1) eggs, meat, legumes, and nuts; (2) milk, cheese, and other milk products; (3) bread and cereals; and (4) vegetables and fruits.

MEAL TIP

Fats are an excellent source of energy.

Daily Suggested Servings

Group	Item	Serving Size
1. (2 servings daily)	Eggs meat legumes	2 medium 250 gm lean cooked 250 ml
2. (2 servings daily)	milk cheese	250 ml (adults)* 250 gm
3. (4 servings daily)	bread cereal rice spaghetti noodles	1 slice 80 gm 125 ml 125 ml 125 ml
4. (4 servings daily)	broccoli pumpkin grapefruit potatoes banana apple	125 ml 125 ml 1/2 medium 125 ml 1 1

* Double this figure for children since they require larger amounts of calcium.

Calories are used as a measure of the expenditure of energy or work by the body. Energy comes from the foods we eat. Some comes from foods that have been recently consumed, while other energy comes from foods that have been stored in the body for a period time. Typically, the body burns calories from recently consumed food before it resorts to burning stored fats.

In theory, it is possible to balance caloric input and output—you eat only as much as the body can currently use. If you eat more than the body can use, the excess is stored as fat. A state of equilibrium, where intake matches output, is preferable to a situation where body stores of fat fluctuate.

In order to determine how many calories are required to "operate" the body, you first calculate how many are required to maintain a body at rest. *Basal Metabolic Rate* (BMR) is the minimum energy expenditure required to keep the body alive when at rest. BMR works out to about one calorie per hour for every kilogram (2.2 pounds) of body weight. Thus, a person, at rest, weighing 75 kilograms (165 pounds), has a BMR of 75 x 24

During the winter you have to eat fast if you want a warm meal.

hours. Such a person would need approximately 1800 calories every day in order to maintain basic body functions without drawing on reserves. Some nutritionists and fitness experts subtract ten percent from this figure for women since their caloric needs are generally less than those of men. Energy expenditures in excess of BMR, such as walking, hiking, biking, are converted to calories and added to the resting figure in order to calculate a total daily figure. Activities can be graded accorded to how strenuous they are.

Sedentary or very light physical activities include reading, writing, playing cards, and watching television. Activities of this sort burn approximately 80 to 100 calories per hour. Activities requiring medium physical effort, such as light housework, gardening, walking, delivering mail, and city driving, burn approximately 160 to 250 calories per hour. Very strenuous activities, such as difficult backpacking, squash, tennis, rock climbing, cross-country skiing and running, are at the upper end of the scale, requiring 350 calories or more per hour.

Remember that it would be quite unusual to play tennis for more than a few hours each day. This is true of most of the strenuous activities, so even if a person is heavily outdoors-oriented, vigorous activities are typically interspersed with periods of rest or moderate activity. Wilderness travellers are likely to burn anywhere from 2800 to 4800 calories per day depending on the season, degree of travel difficulty, and individual body size and fitness level.

Calorie Table

Food Description	Serving Size	Approximate Calories
BEVERAGES		
beer	375 ml	171
carbonated soft drink	375 ml	156
whiskey	45 ml	120
wine	125 ml	114
milk	30 ml	102
milk—evaporated	125 ml	165
milk—whole	250 ml	153
milk—buttermilk	250 ml	85
grapefruit juice (can)	250 ml	90
orange juice (can)	250 ml	128
FRUITS AND TOMATOES		
grapefruit	1/2 medium	44
lime	1 medium	14
orange	1 medium	44
tomato	1 medium	21
apple	1 large	76
banana	1 medium	89
blueberries	125 ml	43
peach	1 medium	46
raisins	125 ml	162
raspberries	125 ml	35
watermelon	1/2 slice	22
VEGETABLES		
celery	125 ml	12
corn	1 ear	89
lettuce	2 large leaves	6
peas	125 ml	71
peppers, green	1 medium	17
potatoes, white	1 medium	105
potatoes, sweet	1 medium	158
radish	3 medium	6
turnip, yellow	125 ml cubed	40
BREADS AND CEREALS		
oats, rolled	65 ml	98
rice, brown	30 ml	103
rice, white	30 ml	102
wheat, whole	125 ml	153
cornflakes	125 ml	80
flour, enriched white	65 ml	99
macaroni or spaghetti	65 ml/cup	108
white enriched, bread	1 slice	83
whole wheat bread	1 slice	72
rye bread	1 slice	73

Calorie Table (continued)

Food Description	Serving Size	Approximate Calories
MEAT AND FISH		
beef, hamburger	110 gm	364
beef, corned (can)	110 gm	244
lamb chop	110 gm	307
pork, back bacon	110 gm	264
pork, side bacon	110 gm	756
pork, chop	110 gm	264
bologna	110 gm	266
liver, beef	110 gm	153
sausage, pork	110 gm	480
wiener	2 medium	206
cod	110 gm	86
halibut	110 gm	162
oysters	5 medium	102
salmon	110 gm	257
MISCELLANEOUS		
cheese, cheddar	30 gm	107
cheese, cream	30 ml	106
eggs	1 medium	72
peanut butter	15 ml	81
butter	15 ml	108
lard	15 ml	128
mayonnaise	15 ml	106
candy bar, average	60 gm	271
honey, strained	15 ml	62
sugar, brown	15 ml	48
sugar, white	15 ml	42
syrup, corn	15 ml	57

DRIED FOODS

Dried foods have been a boon to camping. They are light-weight, require little space and, often, are easy to prepare. However, the cost and nutritional value varies considerably, depending in part on the method used to dry the food.

Thirty years ago, almost all dried foods used by campers were freeze-dried. Still popular, freeze-dried foods are very expensive. In the freeze-drying process, meats, vegetables and fruits are quick frozen, after which they are put in a vacuum chamber, and a small amount of heat is applied. This changes the ice crystals to water vapour. The vaporization process removes about 98% of the water. As with most dried products, freeze-dried foods are best kept sealed and stored in a dark, cool place.

A pancake breakfast on the shore of James Bay.

Along with freeze-dried foods, there are a variety of dried fruits available in grocery stores. Apricots and prunes are the most common. Sold in sealed bags, the moisture content of these fruits is usually between 20 and 30%, by weight. Sulphur is used to help keep the fruit chewable and fresh tasting.

Heat dried foods are also used by campers. Heat-dried foods can be processed at home, using a variety of techniques, or they can be purchased commercially. Recently, heat-dried fruit has become a specialty item in grocery stores and mall outlets. If the drying is done at home, it is a relatively low cost method for preserving foods. If bought retail, heat-dried food can be very expensive. The heat drying process involves circulating warm, dry air around the food in order to carry off the moisture. For most food items, the air should be between 32° and 46° Celsius (90°—115° Fahrenheit). If the air is too hot, the food is slow cooked, not dried. Heat dried foods often use no more than 20% of the storage space required by the same wet foods and heat dried foods are, of course, much lighter than whole foods. Heat drying can reduce food spoilage since items that are ripening too fast, or produce from the garden that can't be consumed immediately, can be heat-dried. Once food has been dried, no additional energy is required. By contrast, frozen foods continue to require energy until they are consumed.

There are two ways to start drying your own food. One is with a commercially made dehydrator, the other is to rig a simple homemade device. The principle is simple. Air is moved at 38° Celsius (100° Fahrenheit) across and around food. The smaller the food pieces, the easier and faster the drying process. Placing small food scraps on screens laid over a radiator or hot air register may do the trick. Placing the food on racks inside a slightly open oven turned to low is another technique. Flack's (1977) book, titled *Dry and Save*, has a good section on building your own dehydrator. Commercial dehydrators cost anywhere from $200 to $500 and while this may seem like a lot of money there are benefits. For example, you don't have to constantly turn or rotate the food, or dry food only on sunny days. A commercial dehydrator means simple, easy drying with bulk capability. When looking at commercial dehydrators, be sure to check and compare drying capacity, energy required for operation, ease of shelf rotation, ease of cleaning, sturdiness, temperature control, and airflow. Information on commercial dehydrators can be obtained from many specialty camping stores.

MEAL TIP

If you do a lot of camping, a commercial dehydrator can save you money.

Sample Menu

	BREAKFAST	LUNCH	DINNER	SNACK
DAY 1	granola cereal, milk, coffee, & juice	hot dogs, buns, mustard, relish, onion, & lemonade	tomato soup, corned beef hash, potatoes, corn, coffee, & tea	popcorn, marg., salt, & hot chocolate
DAY 2	bacon, eggs, ryebread, marg., juice, coffee	ryebread, peanut butter, jam, juice & cheese	mushroom soup, spaghetti & sauce, coffee & tea	Snackin Cake, flour, marg., dried egg, & tea
DAY 3	familia, bacon, juice, coffee,	rockbread, jam, peanut butter, cheese, & juice	vegetable soup, spanish rice, tea & coffee	bannock & hot chocolate
DAY 4	oatmeal pancakes, syrup, juice, coffee	tuna casserole, Baker's semi-sweet, & juice	rye crisps, baked bean soup, tea & coffee	oatmeal cookies (cooked in reflector oven) & tea
DAY 5	granola cereal, milk, juice, & coffee	mount logan bread, cheese, & juice	onion soup, meat & macaroni with cheese, coffee & tea	cornbread, marg., jam, juice
DAY 6	familia, bacon, Tang, & coffee	gorp, date & nut loaf, & juice	tomato soup, freeze-dried stew, coffee & tea	home-dried fruit, & hot chocolate
DAY 7	cornmeal pancakes, milk, juice, & coffee	rockbread, margarine, jam, cheese, & juice	macaroni, cheese, milk, coffee, tea & granola bar	bannock & tea

WINTER MENU PLANNING

Winter camping presents special menu planning problems. Unless conditions are very unusual, it isn't realistic to incorporate the elaborate menus that may be *de rigueur* at other times of the year. During the winter, it is very difficult to keep a wood fire burning with enough heat to keep pots and frypans working well. Even lightweight stoves can be tricky to use in winter. On a cold day, heat dissipates so quickly that it often requires tremendous effort to warm a single pot. By the time you transfer the food to a plate or bowl and eat half of it, the rest is cold. I recall sitting in the snow outside a snow house one fine winter afternoon, pumping a Svea stove as fast as I could in order to try and thaw out the dinner. When the stew looked about as warm as it was going to get, I took it off the stove and began to eat. The first mouthful was warm, the second was tepid, the third was cold, and by the fourth the meal was starting to freeze. The air temperature was minus 30° Celsius (– 23° Fahrenheit) and dropping fast. I wanted a warm meal before retiring for the night—at about 5 pm.—but couldn't get enough heat from the stove to do the trick.

The easiest way to deal with winter cooking problems is to stick with prepackaged, dried, one pot meals that can be eaten right out of a cup or bag. Lasagna, hash and stews can be purchased in this form. Avoid foods that are frozen. Having to thaw and then cook the meal requires too much energy (fuel and effort). What you might be able to accomplish on a good winter day will be impossible on a bad one, and it is on the bad day that a hot, nutritious meal is most important.

MEAL TIP

During winter, stick with one-pot meals.

MENU SUGGESTIONS

The following menu suggestions include a variety of breakfast, lunch, and dinner ideas. Most of these meals are based on ingredients that are easy to find, and simple to pack and prepare. Not all these recipes are gourmet delights, but they are tried and true, almost-fool-safe recipes that lend themselves to variation and experimentation. As always, I strongly recommend taking simple spices and herbs to stimulate your taste buds and satisfy your creativity.

Breakfasts tend to be pretty straightforward. Fast and easy to prepare, these are the meals that need to be high in nutrient value since they provide the fuel to get you started and keep you going through the day. Most trips benefit from at least three different breakfast menus.

I have always found lunches to be the most difficult meals to plan. You can't be sure if time and resources will permit a quick fire or if you will have to eat in the canoe or high on the trail. Sometimes you can be stuck in the middle of a portage with no access to water. As a result, lunches are often bland and unimaginative. I recommend at least four different lunch ideas. These will add considerable variety to your overall menu. At least one lunch should be a hot meal, and I always carry extra soups which, in the event of bad weather, can be incorporated into any lunch.

Dinner is usually the most relaxed and extensive meal because there is time to prepare it. Except for hiking around the campsite,

CONVERSIONS
240 ml. = 1 cup
1 kg. = 2.2 lbs.
110 gm. = 3.5 oz.
15 ml. = 1 tbsp.

you aren't likely to be packing up and travelling after dinner. Try your hand at baking, either before or after dinner. It is not difficult to come up with five good dinner ideas.

Most of the following menu ideas are not compatible with winter camping since most require more than one pot, and are not eaten out of a cup. Familia, halvah, and gorp are exceptions. They are good winter menu items.

ADDITIONAL SOURCES

- Assiniwi, B. (1972). *Indian Recipes.* Toronto: Copp Clark.
- Edwald, E. (1973). *Recipes for a Small Planet.* New York: Ballantine Books.
- Flack, D. (1976). *Dry and Save.* Santa Barbara, California: Woodbridge Press.
- Gunn, D. (1988). *The Expedition Cookbook.* Denver: Chockstone Press.
- Hodgins, C. (1983). *Wanapetei Canoe Tripper's Cookbook.* Cobalt, Ontario: Highway Book Shop.
- Kinmont, K. & Axcell, C. (1976). *Simple Foods for the Pack.* San Francisco: Sierra Club.
- Lappe, F. (1971). *Diet for a Small Planet.* New York: Ballantine Books.

Breakfast Ideas

1. FAST FAMILIA

Familia is a basic homemade breakfast that can provide 40% of daily required protein. Make a batch at home and give it a try before heading out. Vary the ratios in order to suit your taste. I like mine with lots of raisins and brown sugar.

- 350 ml. rolled oats
- 125 ml. sunflower seeds
- 350 ml. rolled wheat
- 125 ml. raisins
- 400 ml. milk powder
- 125 ml. dried fruit
- 100 ml. ground nuts
- 125 ml. soy grits
- 100 ml. chopped nuts

Mix the ingredients thoroughly. This recipe will yield six to eight 200 ml. servings. To serve, simply fill a cup three quarters full of familia, add boiling water to cover, stir thoroughly and let sit for two or three minutes.

2. OATMEAL PANCAKES

These take time to prepare. Save them for lazy mornings when a quick start is not important. After trying these pancakes, you may never wish to use a premixed package again.

- 375 ml. rolled oats
- 2 eggs (rehydrated powdered eggs)
- 125 ml. whole wheat
- 15 gm. oil
- 15 gm. baking powder
- 15 gm. honey
- 5 gm. salt
- 375 ml. milk (rehydrated powdered milk)

Mix to make a batter, then fry like ordinary pancakes. This recipe serves three. If you don't want to carry syrup, try making some by mixing 250 ml. of brown sugar with 5 gm. of margarine and 2 gm. of vanilla, then add 250 ml. of boiling water. If you prefer, try substituting berries for the vanilla. If you have extra berries, add them to your batter.

3. CORN MEAL PANCAKES

These take time to prepare, but are a nice change of pace.

- 375 ml. flour
- 20 gm. milk powder
- 160 ml. cornmeal
- 10 gm. sugar
- 5 gm. baking powder
- 2 gm. salt
- 2 eggs (rehydrated, powdered eggs)
- 90 gm. shortening

Mix all the ingredients, then add water until you have a nice pancake batter. Let the batter stand for 10 minutes and the consistency will improve. These pancakes burn more easily than others, so don't use a fire that is too hot. This quantity serves three.

4. INSTANT CEREALS

There are a host of instant pre-packaged cereals on the market that make for good tasting, fast breakfasts. Cream of Wheat and Quaker Oats are two well known names. Many of these cereals come in several flavours, allowing you to mix and match, and giving people a chance to try something different if they didn't like the last flavour. These cereals are inexpensive, easy to prepare, and they can be purchased just about anywhere. Combine these cereals with long lasting German style packaged pumpernickel, or other whole grain bread, and you have a veritable feast.

1. BANNOCK

There are a zillion recipes for bannock. I have come to rely on bannock as a lunch item, baking it the night before. Bannock is a simple bread made from flour, baking soda, salt, shortening and water. Fill a cup three-quarters full of flour, then blend in a spoonful of baking soda, two spoonfuls of shortening and a pinch of salt. The secret is to mix the dry ingredients thoroughly. Use a small billy if necessary. When the dry ingredients are mixed, add water until you have a smooth dough. The bannock can be fried, baked or roasted on a stick. Brown it on all sides until the dough is cooked through. I prefer my bannock done over a low heat in a covered frying pan. It's even better if you add raisins, diced onions, berries, vanilla, or honey. For a real taste treat, use milk instead of water. When you can poke the bannock with a thin twig, and the twig comes out dry, it's ready. Hot or cold, spread some jam or peanut butter on the bannock and enjoy. Whole wheat flour can be substituted.

If all this mixing business sounds like too much fuss, then I have a well kept secret to share with you. There is a product called *Brodies XXX Self Raising Cake and Pastry Flour*. It is a pre-mixed, baking soda and salt already added, virtually no-fail bannock bread substitute. Right from the package, with a little water, you can make bannock that will be the envy of lightweight campers from miles around. If you want to be really sneaky, re-package the mix before you head out, and tell everyone that it is your very own secret recipe. The stuff is fantastic. I have done blind taste tests with old-time, ultra conservative bannock makers who would turn their noses up at a pre-mixed recipe. To a person, they gave it a two thumbs-up rating.

2. GORP

Like bannock, Gorp comes in a thousand varieties. It is an easy to prepare, quick energy lunch meal or snack. There is no hard and fast recipe, so feel free to mix and match according to your own inclinations.

- 50 ml. Smarties
- 50 ml. chopped licorice
- 100 ml. raisins
- 200 ml. shredded coconut
- 50 ml. cashews
- 150 ml. chopped dried fruit
- 100 ml. peanuts

Mix and store in a large bag. As a snack, just dig in. For lunch, combine a half cup of gorp with a hunk of cheese and a drink. Gorp also goes extremely well with a tin or two of Cross & Blackwell's tinned cakes.

3. TUNA CASSEROLE

Simply cook a batch of macaroni and some peas the night before and keep them sealed in a bag or pot with a tight lid. Leave them in the coldest place you can find until lunch. This might be in the bottom of a wannigan or under a canoe seat. At lunch time, add tuna (tinned) and a small jar of mayonnaise. The mayonnaise stays fresh until you open it, then it must be consumed that day. If you wish, add edible greens such as chopped cattail, bulrush, plantain or young dandelion leaves for flavour and eye appeal. This lunch is a terrific change of pace.

4. CORNBREAD

Combine the following ingredients, adding only enough milk to make thin dough.

- 750 ml. flour
- 3 eggs (rehydrated powder)
- 700 ml. cornmeal
- 250 ml. sugar
- 5 gm. salt
- 250 gm. shortening
- 50 gm. baking powder
- 500—750 ml. mile

Bake until golden brown.

5. ROCKBREAD

Rockbread is a very dense, high-nutrient bread. Rockbread is prepared *before* the trip, and is particularly suitable for canoe trips where the heavy weight will not be problematic. The bread usually lasts three to five weeks provided that it is kept dry.

- 450 ml. strong coffee
- 250 ml. powdered milk
- 1 kg. whole wheat flour
- 250 ml. chopped nuts
- 200 ml. liquid honey
- 10 ml. salt
- 200 ml. blackstrap molasses
- 250 ml. raisins or dried fruit

Mix the dry ingredients together. Then use water to make a paste with the powdered milk, and mix the paste with the coffee, honey, and molasses. Combine the wet and dry ingredients, kneading until you achieve a consistent dough-like texture. If necessary, add additional whole milk or whole wheat flour in order to achieve this consistency. Cut the dough into 1 kg. (2.2 pounds) pieces and shape like loaves. Bake at 110˚ Celsius (230˚ Fahrenheit) for approximately five hours. Be sure the bread is cooked on all surfaces by putting an edge of the loaf on an overturned plate. After baking, the crust will turn hard, and the inside will firm up considerably. After they cool off, put the loafs in plastic bags and refrigerate them until trip time.

6. HALVAH

This is a quick meal which is tasty and high in nutrient value.

- 250 ml. shredded coconut
- 50 ml. sesame seeds
- 200 ml. honey (liquid)
- 100 ml. milk powder

Put the shredded coconut and milk powder into a bag or pot. Add the sesame seeds and mix thoroughly. Add honey while stirring until a thick consistency is reached or, better still, toss the ingredients into a poly bag and knead it until the halvah is thoroughly mixed. It's a sticky meal to prepare and eat, but tastes great.

7. MOUNT LOGAN BREAD

This is light enough to be quite tasty, while heavy enough to be quite filling. Mount Logan bread is prepared *before* the trip.

- 240 ml. whole wheat flour
- 2 eggs (rehydrated)
- 240 ml. white flour
- 100 ml. raisins
- 240 ml. rolled oats
- 100 ml. nuts
- 100 ml. soy flour
- 10 ml. baking powder
- 100 ml. brown sugar
- 5 ml. baking soda
- 200 ml. margarine
- 100 ml. honey
- 100 ml. molasses
- 400—500 ml. water
- 100 ml. oil

Mix all the dry ingredients, then work in the margarine and oil. Add raisins, honey and dried fruit, along with the honey and molasses. Add enough water to a make nice firm dough. Bake in a greased pan at 190˚ Celsius (375˚ Fahrenheit) for approximately two hours.

Dinner Ideas

1. HASH PIE

- 1 tin corned beef
- 4 medium potatoes (or equivalent in flakes)
- 1 onion
- corn (3 servings freeze-dried or heat-dried)

Fry the hash and chopped onion in one pan, while boiling the potatoes and cooking the corn in separate pots. When ready, spread the corn on the hash, then cover with mashed or sliced potatoes. Cut into slices like a pie, and serve immediately. Spices really help this meal.

2. BAKED BEAN SOUP

- 15 gm. margarine
- 2 gm. salt
- 15 gm. flour
- dash pepper
- 375 ml. milk
- dash baking soda
- diced onion
- 600 ml. baked beans in tomato sauce

Using a low fire, melt the butter in a frypan. Add the flour after removing the pan from the heat. Blend well as you add the flour. Add the onion, milk, salt, pepper and continue stirring. Combine the baking soda and beans, then add them to the thickened soup mixture. Be sure to stir constantly or it will burn. Continue heating until the beans are hot.

3. SPAGHETTI

This is a favourite standby, and doesn't require any explanation. Onions, garlic, dried ground beef and tomato paste or soup will really help this meal.

4. SPANISH RICE

Cook your rice while frying an onion and three or four strips of side bacon. When the bacon has become quite crisp, pour the grease into your storage container, crush the bacon and add a small can of tomato paste. Allow this mixture to simmer, then add it to your drained rice. Use salt and pepper to taste.

5. MEAT AND MACARONI

Cut canned meat (Kam) into strips and line them across the bottom of a greased frypan. Cover the meat with cooked macaroni and add strips of cheddar cheese on top of the macaroni. Using a low fire and frypan lid, cook slowly until the cheese has melted through the macaroni. Add spices such as bay leaves or oregano, then salt and pepper to taste.

6. LENTILS & RICE

This meal is just the ticket for vegetarians.

- 240 ml. brown rice
- pinch of garlic powder
- 240 ml. lentils
- pinch of oregano
- 100 ml. soy grits
- pinch of bay leaves
- 80 ml. bulgar
- 15 ml. of oil or margarine
- 200 ml. dried vegetables

Cook the rice in two litres of water, while sautéeing the onion. After the rice is cooked, add the other ingredients and let everything simmer until all the grains are cooked. The garlic, oregano, and bay leaves are optional. Add salt and pepper to taste.

Snack Ideas

1. SPICE COOKIES

- 250 ml. flour
- 2 eggs (rehydrated powdered eggs)
- pinch of baking soda
- 200 ml. oatmeal
- 2 pinches of cinnamon
- 200 ml. raisins
- 125 ml. brown sugar
- 20 ml. powdered milk
- 125 ml. shortening

Mix all the ingredients to a doughy consistency, roll out flat, then cut the cookies out (1/2 cm. thick) and bake in a reflector oven. Let the cookies cool before eating.

2. JERKY

- 2.5 kg. lean beef
- 240 ml. vinegar
- 1 litre of water
- 250 ml. salt

Cut the meat into very thin strips. All excess fat should be removed. Boil the meat in the water, vinegar and salt for about 10 minutes, then squeeze as much moisture out of the meat as possible. Put the beef on oven racks or on a cookie sheet and "cook" for about 3 hours at 98 Celsius (200° Fahrenheit) *with the oven door slightly ajar.*

3. HONEY FRUIT

- 480 ml. dried fruit
- pinch of cinnamon
- 20 ml. honey
- pinch of brown sugar
- 700 ml. water

Slice and dice the fruit and mix with the honey, sugar, cinnamon and water. Bring to a slow boil and let simmer for 20 minutes. Drain off the excess water and let cool.

4. GINGERBREAD COOKIES

These are a camp favourite for young and old.

- 360 ml. white flour
- 5 ml. cinnamon
- 120 ml. whole wheat flour
- 10 ml. egg powder
- 120 ml. soy flour
- 120 ml. brown sugar
- pinch of salt
- 120 ml. molasses
- pinch of baking soda
- 120 ml. milk powder
- 2 pinches of baking powder
- 200 ml. margarine
- 240 ml. boiling water

Mix the dry ingredients, then work in the margarine. Add the molasses and boiling water, then cut into shapes and bake in a greased frying pan.

In many wilderness areas fish are abundant and easy to catch.

6
Survival

The most tiresome thing about the dead is having to
keep up both sides of the conversation.

Jane Rule

Camping is quite different from surviving. Camping implies
a planned outdoors excursion, where things are known,
expected and prepared for. These days, the use of technological innovation plays a big part in camping. ABS canoes,
laminated paddles, lightweight pack frames, and specialized
clothing are part and parcel of "going camping." Survival, by
comparison, is most often an unplanned activity, where response
to physical and environmental conditions is largely improvised.
In survival situations the high tech component is either less
important or altogether absent—if you haven't got any water or
food, a water purifier and a shiny cookset with state-of-the-art
no-stick coating isn't going to be of much help.

This does not mean that planning cannot be undertaken for
survival situations. But planning for survival is speculative, since
the specific nature of a survival situation is difficult to anticipate.
The airplane falls out of the sky, the canoe and supplies are lost
in the rapids, or the rock gives way and you find yourself in the
wrong place at the wrong time. Many things can go wrong, and
they can go wrong in many ways. We can't anticipate everything.
Survival in the bush is different from survival in the city because
in the bush we rely on the skills and equipment we have brought
with us, along with whatever we can scrounge from nature. In
the city we entrust our lives to those who are paid to provide
help—medics, police, fire personnel, and so on.

Survival situations can be divided into two broad categories—
those that could have been avoided through the practice of
reasonable care and caution, and those that were brought on by
unusual and unpredictable weather, technological failure, or just
plain bad luck. In some circumstances, it is difficult to differentiate

IN THIS CHAPTER

- **Water**
- **Food**
- **Heat**
- **Shelter**
- **Signals**
- **Pain, Fatigue,
  Boredom and
  Loneliness**

between these cases. Should the rapids have been run or portaged? Was the mountain well beyond our level of ability? Should we have made camp when the weather first turned ugly?

Accountability for a life-threatening situation that has resulted from incorrect route information could rest with the person who supplied the information or the person who accepted and believed the information. Its difficult to be certain who is at fault, and, without considerable detail about the specific situation, impossible to fully attribute blame. Determining who is "at fault" is not simply undertaken to criticize the source or prepare for a lawsuit, but to find out if the problem is linked to the faulty judgement of the trip leader or participants. This is a very important consideration since one error often leads to others. If a survival situation is a result of bad judgement by the trip participants, serious thought should be given to what steps should be taken to avoid compounding errors.

Faulty judgement tends to lead to more faulty judgement. Consider a case where two people go out for afternoon hikes. One carries no map or compass. The second person carries not only a map and compass, but also a daypack with food items, matches, and a raincoat. They both get disoriented, dusk comes, rain starts to fall, and temperatures drop. Which hiker would be most likely to make a rude camp and prepare to spend the night? The answer is obvious; it would be the one who went out prepared. The hiker without the map and compass will be sorely tempted to compound the error by making another mistake; he will try to walk out. Look closely at the details surrounding accidents where judgement errors are involved, and you will often find that there is a chain of events, with one error in judgement leading to the next error in judgement. Often, the errors increase in severity.

The importance of being prepared—being adequately knowledgeable, skilled and equipped—is obvious. Prepared campers are least likely to find themselves in a survival situation, but if such a situation does occur, prepared campers will be best able to deal with the ensuing problems. In the previous illustration, the hiker with the food, raincoat and matches is not experiencing a survival situation. Preparation has resulted in an unexpected, but hardly life threatening, night in the woods.

Beyond knowledge, skills, and equipment, the question of who will survive and the survival mentality itself have been the subject of much discussion and research. Certain qualities or characteristics are associated with survival. These include such wide ranging variables as a positive feeling of self-worth, a well defined set of values, the ability to reason logically, flexibility, creativity, decisiveness, patience, and a great deal of optimism. The survivor may or may not be a leader. In fact, some people who are leaders under normal conditions may become disoriented and unable to lead under adverse conditions. A survival situation may be the catalyst that brings out leadership qualities in people who don't typically act as leaders.

A common fallacy is that an emergency brings people together. More often, an emergency tends to sharply divide a group, making common action and rational decision making very difficult. People isolate themselves from the group, blaming the elements at first, then muttering about the leadership that put them in the situation. These types are easy to recognize—they put their efforts into attributing blame and complaining about their condition, rather than working to solve the problem. Groups that react well to adverse conditions are those that have a high degree of cohesiveness, where trust prevails, and where members recognize and accept the dependency they have on each other. In this type of group, individuals feel stronger for being a part of the group. Reflect on and evaluate the group you camp with. How would your camping buddies behave under survival conditions? Would they come together and set aside individual differences and opinions in order to work as a team and minimize the dangers of the situation? Or would the personalities clash, degenerating into divisiveness and conflict.

Ptarmigan and grouse are easy to catch, if you can spot them.

Knowing our limits is a good way to avoid life threatening conditions. The camper who maintains a physical, mental and skill reserve can deal reasonably well with unexpected conditions. Campers who push themselves to the limit have nothing to spare when the unexpected occurs.

There is no question that preparation, including survival training, can help to both forestall and, if necessary, cope with a survival situation. Preparation may take many forms, and include activities such as reading survival books, practical skill development, simulation exercises, learning to identify edible plants, and participating in strategy games.

One of the key decisions to be made in many survival situations, particularly if the predicament has resulted from an accident, is whether to move or stay put. Depending on the circumstances, either action could turn out to be the right or wrong one. It is important to consider the fact that experience shows us that search parties have great difficulty and little success

Sticks, bark and leaves can be used to make effective survival shelters in the late spring, summer, and early fall.

finding people who move from a crash site or who continually wander when they become lost. Many stories have been told about how the crash site or old campsite has been located, but the survivors have left the area and cannot be found. Many people who have tried to walk out of the bush from an accident site have died regretting their decision.

That having been said, there are, broadly speaking, three reasons that justify trying to walk out of a survival situation. These include: (1) you are sure you can walk out, probably long before you are even identified as missing; (2) you are certain that you won't be located in your present position, perhaps because you aren't where you are supposed to be or you didn't tell anyone you were going; or (3) the present location is dangerous and you must move for reasons of physical safety. If you are not certain that you can walk out, and physical safety is not an issue, stay put. People, particularly those who are downed in aircraft, do not realize that most of Canada is not designed with easy hiking in mind. In summer, forests are tangled jungles full of insects. Rivers, lakes and streams are numerous, requiring continual dunking and long detours. In the barrens, compasses are unreliable. In the mountains, storms come swiftly and strike with incredible ferocity. And, in winter, travel without snowshoes is next to impossible.

Survival needs can be examined in the context of four categories: water, food, shelter, and heat. These are physical requirements, but don't forget that the psychological issues of survival are just as important. Only those with cool, calm heads will be able to use the skills required to satisfy physical needs. This is demonstrated every year by the number of experienced people, particularly hunters, who die in relatively mild conditions.

The following survival hints and techniques are based on generalizations. A textbook cannot mirror real-life survival situations. So, once again, the reader is cautioned to learn and practice skills in the field. Don't wait until an accident occurs. Learn and practice now.

WATER

Without water, no one will survive for more than a few days, even if all other circumstances are ideal. It isn't possible to say precisely how long a person can survive without water, since temperature, humidity, physical effort, exposure, and foods will affect survival time. In Canada it is usually not very difficult to find water.

Running water is generally good and quite drinkable. By comparison, still, brackish water is not desirable unless there is no other option. Since water flows downhill, the best place to look for fresh water is at the bottom of a hill, or in gullies and gorges. (Unfortunately, this is not the place where you would most likely be seen by a search party.)

If you are in doubt about the quality of your water supply, boiling the water will usually purify it. If you do end up boiling your drinking water, you will notice that it has a flat taste. This flat taste can be removed by shaking the water up, by blowing bubbles in it through a plant stem, or by adding a little bit of charcoal from your campfire. Why bother doing this in a survival situation? Well, one of the keys to successful survival is aiming beyond "just getting by." You should try to make yourself as comfortable as possible, and the best place to start is with clean, plentiful, good-tasting, drinking water. The psychological benefits of good water and good food cannot be underestimated.

In the winter, try to find open water. If this is not possible, you may have to melt snow or ice. Remember, however, that it is not good practice to eat snow directly, since this will tend to dehydrate the body, particularly if the weather is very cold. Melting ice is preferable to melting snow because it requires less fuel for the amount of water produced. Ice and snow can be melted in a fairly crude container, such as one shaped from birchbark or other natural fibre. The trick is to try and prevent the flame from coming into direct contact with the container, particularly the part of the container above the water line.

SURVIVAL TIP

If you are uncertain about the quality of your water, boil it for 5-10 minutes.

SURVIVAL TIP

During the winter, you should drink about twice as much water as in summer—about 4 litres per day.

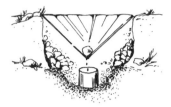

Figure 6-1
A solar still can be made by digging a hole, one metre by one metre (one yard by one yard), lining it with plant material, then covering it with a clear piece of plastic weighted in the middle with a stone. With a good seal around the outside edge, condensation will drip into a container placed at the bottom of the hole.

Under no circumstances should you drink salt water. In the north, look for snow, frozen ice away from the sea, or icebergs trapped in frozen sea ice. If you are lucky enough to find an iceberg, or just a small part of one, chip off the outer coating of salt spray, and melt a chunk of underlying ice. When faced with sea or ocean water in warmer climates, dig down several feet, a hundred metres (110 yards) or so from the ocean on a sand beach. Once below the water table, your chances of finding pure water are very good. This is a simple and almost guaranteed way to find drinkable water in a tropical climate. Yet, there are many recorded cases of death from dehydration because people trapped after a plane crash or shipwreck had no idea that, as they looked out on the ocean, drinkable water was just a few feet under the sand on which they stood.

If you are trapped at sea without a supply of drinking water, try to collect rainwater or dew. In the desert, collecting water is a critical task. Desert temperatures and low humidity will dehydrate your body in a very short period of time. Finding an oasis, digging into an old river bed, or building a solar still (see Fig. 6–1) are possibilities to keep in mind.

Finally, remember that eating requires lots of water for digestion and removal of wastes. Proteins in particular require a great deal of water. If you are short on water, watch what you eat. Stay away from very dry foods, and others that require a long time to digest.

FOOD

Although you can survive for some time without food, it is psychologically important to have something to eat. Getting and preparing food also helps satisfy another need—having something to do and occupying your time.

Having a rudimentary knowledge of, along with the ability to identify, edible plants is valuable for all campers. However, it is important to remember that to reach the stage where you can walk through the woods pointing out edible plant after edible plant requires years of study. Instead of spending years trying to acquire "expert" status, work on becoming familiar with half a dozen, common, edible wild plants. Learn to recognize them in all seasons, and try your hand at preparing them. (Don't forget that many common plants are extremely poisonous. See Chapter 7 for a discussion of common, poisonous plants.)

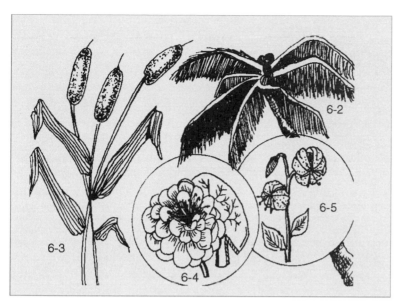

The cattail *(Typha latifolia)* and the coconut *(Cocus nucifera)* are considered to be universal survival foods since either one or the other is found in most regions of the world. Mountain peaks and polar ice caps are the exceptions. The coconut contains a white, pulpy fruit and a milky liquid. Locating a cache of coconuts will almost guarantee that your nutritional requirements can be met in style. The cattail is common to wet, marshy areas. It is an excellent survival food. If you learn to recognize and prepare only one survival food, make it this one. The flowering head of the cattail can be eaten like a vegetable in the spring when it is young. During the summer and fall, when the head is brown, it can be dried and pounded into cattail flour. The inner stem is quite delicious and makes a celery-like snack. The root, once it has been cleaned and the outer layer peeled away, is similar to a potato and can be eaten raw or boiled. If the taste is too woody, swallow the starchy material that separates out when you chew a cattail, then spit out the rest.

Pond Lilies *(Nuphar advena)* are easy to identify and collect. The roots should be peeled and boiled, after which they make a tasty treat. The roots of the Tiger Lily *(Lillium tigrinum)* are prepared in the same way, although they can also be eaten raw like the cattail.

Fiddleheads are my favourite. They are the uncurled fronds of ostrich ferns *(Matteucia struthiopteris)* and are sold both fresh (while in season) and frozen in many grocery stores. Fiddleheads

SURVIVAL TIP

Every camper should be able to recognize and prepare cattails as a survival food.

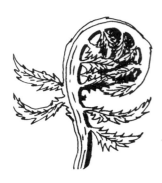

Figure 6-6
Fiddlehead

are collectable for only a short period of time each year, but their taste appeal makes them worth hunting. Wash the fiddleheads and then boil them for two or three minutes. If you are preparing them at home, try one of the more exotic methods of preparation, such as sautéeing in butter and wine.

A wide variety of teas can be made from the leaves and needles of different plants. Birch leaf tea is an aromatic beverage made by steeping the young leaves of a birch tree in hot water. Be sure to cut or tear the leaves before adding them to the water or it will take forever to make the tea. Spruce tea is made by boiling young spruce needles in water. Cedar bark tea is made the same way. Use small pieces of bark, collected by holding a pot against the side of cedar tree and brushing a stick against the bark in a rapid up and down motion above the pot. Labrador tea (Ledum groeniandicum) is a well known survival drink available in summer and winter. Collect the leaves and prepare them in the same way as you would young birch leaves. The labrador tea plant is quite common to northern forested areas. One of the chief means of identification is the characteristic hairy underside of the plant's leaves.

Traps and snares can be employed to catch small game. Pick up a coil of thin wire from your hardware store, and stick it in your first aid kit. Then you will always be prepared with the necessary tool to make simple but effective snares. Rabbits are one of the easiest small animals to snare. They are abundant and often use easily discernable trails. Simply set up a slip loop and dangle it over the rabbit run (see Fig. 6–8). The bottom of the loop should be about 7 centimetres (3 inches) off the ground, with a diameter of approximately 10 centimetres (4 inches). If the loop is hung from a horizontal branch, the branch should be least 22–25 centimetres (nine or ten inches) off the ground. Use sticks to block the area of the run not directly in line with the snare. This will force the rabbit into the path. Always check snares on a regular basis or other predators will dine on your catch.

Squirrels are another common and easy to catch source of food. The balance pole snare is based on the principle that squirrels like to use shortcuts (see Fig. 6–9). Use three or four snares on each pole, with rotten apples or any other smelly food as bait. If you don't have any food to spare, bait the snares with a shiny object such as a belt buckle or aluminum foil.

The porcupine is known as the hunter's survival food. This is because it is slow moving and very easy to catch and kill. Once you find and corner the animal, often up a tree, it only requires

Figure 6-7
Labrador Tree

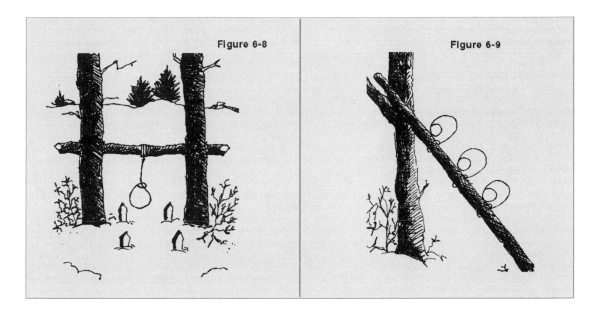

Figure 6-8

Figure 6-9

a stout stick to finish it off. Preparing porcupines for eating is not as difficult as you might think. Roll the animal over on its back and make a longitudinal incision beginning at the stomach. You start with the stomach because there are few quills in this area. (The animal rolls into a ball when cornered.) As with skinning any animal, make your cut deep enough to get inside the skin without actually breaking through into the body sac. Once you have started to roll the skin off, it generally falls away quite easily. Killing porcupines outside the context of an actual survival crisis is unacceptable. The animal has no defense against man and isn't particularly tasty.

Fish are a good source of protein. String can be used as line, and, if necessary, safety pins can be used as hooks. Bones such as ribs from small rodents can make effective fish hooks, and braided inner bark from trees such as elm or basswood makes good line. I always keep ten metres of monofilament line and a half dozen hooks in my first aid kit. This way I can set several lines with relative ease and increase my chances for success. If you run out of food on a long trip, fish are likely going to be one of the easiest food sources to locate and catch. Do yourself a favour and stick some fishing line, hooks, and a lure or two in your first aid kit today.

Grouse and ptarmigan have two main defense mechanisms; they stay still and their colour blends effectively with the environment. Consequently, it is hard to spot these birds. But, once

Figure 6-8
Rabbit Snare

Figure 6-9
Squirrel Snare

SURVIVAL TIP

Keep a supply of fishing line and assorted hooks in your first aid kit as "survival insurance".

spotted, it is often possible to kill them with a stone, or snare them using a long pole with a loop on the end. Other small animals and birds should not be overlooked, though they tend to be more difficult to catch.

Once you have found or caught your food, cooking it is the next concern. Boiling, drying and roasting are three common options. Boiling is the least complicated. Cut the meat or other food into small equal size pieces, place these in your cooking container, cover with water and bring to a boil. Add water as it boils off, so that the meat is always covered. Boiling results in very little food value being lost since you finish with a nice broth. Almost any type of container can be used for boiling. Although the result won't quite be like the home cooking you grew up with—or if it is, please accept my condolences—boiling is the easiest food preparation technique under survival conditions.

Roasting or barbecuing produces very tasty meat. However, considerable nutrition is lost as shrinkage occurs. This loss can be somewhat diminished by charring the outside of the meat and then placing a pan underneath to catch the drippings. Charring is accomplished by placing the meat very close to the fire for a few minutes. Be sure to rotate the meat regularly and use green sticks to hold it in place. This method of food preparation requires that the meat be kept a considerable distance from the fire. Hence, a greater quantity of fuel is required.

Frying requires a pan, some grease, and much more fuel than does boiling. For these reasons, frying is not recommended.

HEAT

Human survival is possible only within a narrow temperature range. If it's too hot, the body dehydrates and dies. If it's too cold, the body loses heat faster than it can be generated, blood stops flowing and the heart fibrillates. In the north, many people die because they get too cold. To combat this, body heat can be generated in a number of ways. These include internal generation through the burning of energy, and the use of external sources such as fires. This chapter focuses on fires as a source for heat and as a means of cooking food.

Different kinds of fires burning under different conditions produce varying degrees of heat. Building a campfire seems a simple activity, and in good weather with lots of material at hand this is true. But when you have to make a fire quickly from nearby materials after three days of rain, or when your hands are so cold you can't hold the matches, then fire building is more challenging.

SURVIVAL TIP

Boiling is the easiest way to prepare a meal, and little of the nutritional value is lost.

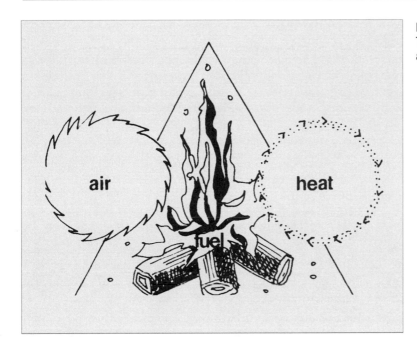

Figure 6-10
The three essential elements of a campfire—fuel, heat, and air.

Understanding how fires work, and the specific elements and conditions under which fires work best, will make you a much better fire maker under all conditions.

To make a fire, you need three things: fuel, heat, and oxygen (see Fig. 6–10). Fuel is the basic ingredient. Heat is required to raise the temperature of the fuel to the point where it will burn. Once the fuel is "burning," the heat produced through combustion creates more combustion. In other words, the process regenerates itself. Oxygen is the third and final element that is a must for campfires. Even though you may have fuel and heat, if oxygen cannot get to the fire, it will die.

Think of the campfire as a living thing. It must eat (fuel), breath (air), and keep warm (heat). Fires are extinguished by dousing with water (cooling them off), spraying with carbon dioxide or other chemical (strangling them), or by not providing food/fuel (starving them). If you are having trouble getting a fire started, reconsider the three basic elements. Is it getting enough oxygen? Is there too much or too little of the right kind of fuel? Is there enough heat to get the fuel to the point of combustion?

Simple fires, such as campfires, are built by using fuel with a relatively low ignition temperature. The ignition temperature is the point at which the fuel, whatever it happens to be, starts to burn. From experience, you will likely know that small pieces of wood such as chips and shavings initially burn easier than whole logs. Leaves will burn even more easily. Dead wood burns better than live wood, for the same reason that wet wood is harder to burn than dry wood. Green wood has sap in it, which acts to cool the fire off. Green wood and wet wood will burn, but only at higher combustion temperatures. The higher temperature is needed in order to offset the cooling effect of the water or sap in the wood.

Why not make campfires from leaves since they have one of the lowest ignition temperatures and are readily available? The explanation is simple. Leaves and other fuels with low ignition points won't provide nearly as much heat as other types of fuel and they burn too quickly. In fact, the combustion point of leaves is so low that it is very difficult to start other fuel, such as logs, burning, unless you have a very large pile of leaves. Better to start with a fuel that has a higher ignition temperature, then it will be easier to move up to larger sticks and logs.

Hardwoods are the best heat producers since they have high ignition temperatures. The downside is that hardwoods are more difficult to start burning. Softwoods have lower ignition temperatures; therefore, it is easier to start a fire with softwood, but unless you move up to hardwood as the fire develops, you won't get as much heat as you might need. Tinder is another name for small bits and pieces of tiny branches, bark, and the like. Generally, the smaller the tinder, the lower the ignition temperature. Birchbark is an excellent fire starting material because it contains oils that make it flammable even when fairly wet, and it burns much hotter than leaves or very tiny tinder.

With campfire fuel, the rule is simple: start small and work your way up. Small, dry tinder, dead twigs, or birchbark will do wonders as the initial fire starter. Under exceptional conditions, creativity may have to govern the finding and use of appropriate tinder. Fuzz sticks are twigs that have been sliced on all sides, similar to fancy carrot sticks. Assuming the wood is dry, fuzz sticks are very good for fire starting.

SURVIVAL TIP

Dead, dry twigs from the bottom of coniferous trees are one of the best fire starters.

If it has been raining for some time, dry wood may be hard to locate. Try finding a stand of coniferous trees, then go into the middle of the stand and pull off the dead branches at the bottom of the trees. These twigs are one of the best fire starters available. Unless someone else has beaten you to the spot, you should be able to gather several good size handfuls in just a few minutes. Plan to start your fire with the smallest of the small twigs. The best of the lot will be the ones that crack if bent even slightly. The cracking noise tells you the twig has no moisture in it. Even during heavy downpours, when the rest of the bush is soaking wet, these twigs are almost always dry. Use these tiny twigs to build a series of cross-hatched layers. The result looks like a log cabin with plenty of holes and a centre that is filled with wood. The holes are necessary, otherwise the fire won't get enough oxygen. Before you start the fire, be sure to have plenty of additional fuel handy, up to and including the size you wish to use as the final or equilibrium fuel. There are few things more aggravating than watching your fire go out because you have run out of fuel.

When you are ready, light your match and insert it through one of the holes. Make sure the match is placed in the lower middle of the pile of twigs. Remember, fire burns up. Putting the match on top of the twigs, or in some other spot where fuel is not above the heat, will likely mean failure. As the twigs burn, add larger and larger fuel until you have a fire that suits your needs.

If the fire fails, reconsider the three basic elements: fuel, heat, air. If you used a match, heat is not the issue. If you have plenty of holes in your design, allowing the fire to breathe, air is not the issue. More likely, the fuel used has too high an ignition point, perhaps because it was wet or too large, Or, you may have tried to move up your wood size too fast. On a bright, sunny, dry day, fires burn almost automatically. Failure is difficult to achieve. On such a day, building the fire up from twigs to logs may be a one or two step process. However, on a wet, cold, dull day, fire starting requires better fuel, more heat, and a slower development strategy.

In some circumstances, it may not be possible to find dry wood, even in a stand of mature coniferous trees. I recall a case in point while on a canoe trip in northern Quebec. It rained for 22 out of 28 days on this trip. We were at the three week mark, and it had been raining for almost a week straight. By that stage, there was nothing dry. The worst thing to do at the end of a hard day of paddling and portaging would have been to give up and go to the tents with a cold meal. The group needed something hot, just to cheer the spirit. We cut down a large, standing piece of deadwood, dragged it under a tarp, and began to literally take the tree apart. By sawing it into pieces, carving out the core, and then slicing small slices off, we ended with a sizeable pile of dry shavings. This was enough to start a small fire, which we then used to dry more wood. It took almost an hour, but the result was a great campfire that produced a hot meal and cheered everyone's spirits immeasurably.

SAFETY TIP

If you plan to gather rocks to encircle your campfire—an environmentally questionable practice—avoid those which are near a river or lake. These may contain moisture and could explode.

Check your campsite for animal tracks before you decide to stay the night.

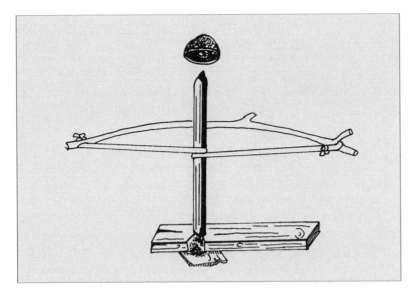

Figure 6-11
Using a firebow requires skill and practice. The tinder goes in a notch cut into the baseboard. The stick is then twisted back and forth very quickly. The resulting friction should create enough heat to produce a smouldering coal.

On other occasions, when travelling in areas where burnable wood of any kind is difficult to find, I have often carried wood. In these cases, I pick up pieces of wood that I know will start a good hot fire. Once I have a strong fire going, I know that I will be able to burn virtually whatever type of wood can be found.

Although relatively unlikely, it is possible under survival conditions to find yourself without matches. Many survival courses teach the use of flints. I argue that flint, though it's a handy tool, is usually carried only by people who make sure they have plenty of matches stored in different locations. Cigarette lighters, magnifying glasses, sparks from battery terminals, flares, and gasoline can be used to get your fire started. Except for gasoline, these are methods of generating the necessary heat to achieve ignition. Gasoline alters the fuel to make it more combustible, and is itself a fuel that burns at a high temperature with a fairly low ignition point.

Using a firebow is an interesting, though somewhat esoteric, approach to fire starting (see Fig. 6–11). Being able to use a firebow requires considerable practice. It is not a skill you will learn when trapped in a survival setting. Most folks who are adept with this technique carry the bow and tinder materials with them. To create a workable firebow requires time, patience and skill gleaned from practice. Old bird nests often make good fire bow tinder. The firebow stick is rotated at high speed by means of the bow. This creates the friction necessary to ignite the tinder which is located in a notch beneath the stick. Don't expect great flaming tinder. Be satisfied with a small glowing coal. Blowing gentle puffs of air will raise the temperature slightly and create the flame. This tinder is then transferred to a pile of low ignition temperature fuel, such as the remains of the bird's nest. Nests of small birds that use small twigs and dead plant material are best. Suffice to say that it will take you a long time to get a mud nest to burn.

SHELTER

A good hot fire in the middle of an open field during a winter storm is of little practical value. Although it may look pretty, the heat dissipates before it produces any real benefit. Whether heat is generated by your body or comes from an external source, some sort of shelter must be used in order to trap the heat and gain maximum benefit. The rule is simple: under extreme weather conditions, find shelter or die. This section emphasizes shelters for cold weather protection.

Tents are reasonably good insulators. Shelters that are based on tent-like features secure some of the same benefits. Enclosed, stable structures that incorporate breathability are the most desirable. The typical lean-to shelter lacks most of these qualities. With a large front opening, the lean-to shelter allows heat to immediately rise and exit. Survival shelters should be small, with few openings, and close to the ground. Alternatively, the sleeping platform should be raised so that it is close to the roof.

Barring the discovery of a natural shelter, such as a cave, one of the easiest survival shelters to construct is made out of logs, branches, and leaves shaped in a low tunnel form. Use two parallel logs covered with sticks as an emergency shelter. Cover the sticks with leaves, then add tree bark for shingles. Avoid low areas and gullies since rain will collect there. And, as much as possible, make use of naturally occurring formations in order to minimize your energy output. It is not advisable to build a fire in this type of shelter. Such a shelter works well in the summer and early fall when the weather is not too cold. Even if the weather dips slightly below freezing, leaves can be used as body cover in order to make a crude, but livable, overnight environment.

Rock shelters combine protection and heat. For this reason, they are better than simple wood shelters when colder conditions prevail. There are many variations of rock shelters, and creative thinking will produce even more. Start by locating a vertical rock at least 1 metre (3 feet) high and 2 metres (6 feet) in length. It is best if the rock wall is adjoined by a rock base or has a parallel rock beside it (see Fig. 6–12). If possible, add several small rocks

SURVIVAL TIP

Under extreme weather conditions, finding shelter should be your first priority.

Figure 6-12
After the stones have been heated, cover the shelter with any materials at hand in order to trap the heat.

to form a wall on one end. Lay a fire along the length of the rocks and keep it burning using dead dry wood that will produce lots of heat. The heat from your fire will be stored in the rocks and, as you sleep beside or on the rocks, the same heat is radiated off throughout the night, keeping you warm and toasty. Be sure to finish the shelter by leaning sticks at an angle against the rock, with leaves, branches or bark on top of the sticks, keeping the roof as low as possible. Lay down a bed of leaves in order to protect yourself from any rocks that are too hot, then remove the leaves as the night wears on.

Shelters such as lean-tos that are designed to be maintained with an ongoing fire are, by comparison with rock shelters, very uncomfortable. The body is warmed on one side only, and the fire is a glutton that must be constantly fed. You wake up cold and miserable every half hour. A rock shelter will radiate heat for about twice as long as it is heated. If necessary, you can get four hours of sleep, heat the rock for two more and get a second four hours of sleep. Be sure though, to keep plenty of fuel on hand as it will be next to impossible to gather wood in the dark. If you can find two parallel rock walls a few feet apart, the rock shelter can be extremely comfortable. Often these shelters are too warm in the early stages and you may find that it is necessary to remove clothing in order to be comfortable. Avoid sweating. It's not central heating, but it does work.

SURVIVAL TIP

Survival shelters should, if possible, be built facing east. This means they will get early morning sun and be blocked from approaching weather systems which usually travel west to east.

Figure 6-13
Vertical cross-section of a snow shelter

Although the rock shelter is good even on the coldest winter nights, many people prefer snow shelters. If you have a sleeping bag or other bedding material, snow shelters are easy to build and offer excellent protection from storms. Snow houses are similar to igloos in purpose; however, the design does not require the same degree of skill for construction.

A multi-person snow shelter can be constructed by piling up a large mound of snow and then digging it out (see Figs. 6–13 and 6–14). A mound of snow two metres (six and a half feet) high and three metres (10 feet) in diameter will make a comfortable shelter for three or four people. The initial mound of snow can be made with a shovel, snowshoes or even skis. Once the snow is piled high, pack or tramp it down. This encourages the snow to "set" and helps ensure a sturdy house. Digging the shelter out is time consuming but the finished product is worth the effort.

While digging the shelter out, throw the snow you remove from the inside onto the top. This will increase the wall thickness and make the shelter more secure. Walls should be a minimum of 30 cm. (1 foot) thick. As well, the door opening should be at the lowest part of the shelter, 90 degrees to the prevailing wind. Sleeping platforms are always raised. If you like, a small fire can be used to warm up the inside of the shelter to the stage where the walls begin to drip. Then, when the fire is extinguished, the walls will glaze over and become even more secure. If you add a smoke hole on the lee side, cooking and living in the shelter becomes quite comfortable. If you are fully equipped, candles can be used to light the interior.

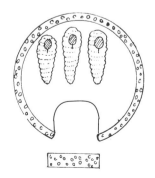

Figure 6-14
Overhead view of a snow shelter

Many campers prefer this type of shelter to a tent when winter camping since snow shelters are warmer and provide far more living space. For waiting out a winter storm, a snow shelter is ideal. It would not be unusual to have -30° weather outside while the temperature inside the snow shelter hovers near the freezing

Survival Tips

1. Plan for things to go wrong.

2. Pack extra food, clothing, and survival gear, even on very short trips.

3. Practice survival skills (ie, lighting fires under windy conditions, cooking).

4. Learn to identify edible plants.

5. Mark your location to make it easy for a search party to find you.

mark. This will not happen with even the best expedition tents. In fact, the only type of tenting arrangement that is more comfortable than a large snow shelter is a wall tent with a wood stove—not something you are likely to have in a survival setting.

Snow shelters take time to construct (4–6 hours) but they will last for days with few repairs because of the strength inherent in the shape. One word of caution though: people who suffer from claustrophobia may have difficulty living in a snow shelter. Once the sun goes down, and the candle or flashlight is turned out, snow shelters are pitch black and dead quiet. Those of us who are accustomed to city living rarely experience the pure darkness and utter silence that such a shelter creates. I recall one night in a snow shelter when, once the candle was out, a very panicky voice convinced me that unless I could get the candle going again in a matter of seconds, someone was going to go berserk! All I could picture was the body beside me making a diving leap through the wall. The weather outside was a crisp forty below and the shelter represented the difference between comfort and disaster. Claustrophobia in a snow shelter will only be alleviated by maintaining a light source, at least until the person who suffers from the problem goes to sleep. Then you hope like heck he doesn't wake up until the light of day.

A one person snow shelter can be made by carving snow blocks out of packed snow in a coffin or trench pattern (see Fig. 6–15). These are then used to make a lean-to type of roof over the trench. This type of shelter may be good for one night, but is very confining for long periods of time. In areas of heavy snowfall, a one person shelter can be dug into the side of a snow bank (see Fig. 6–16).

Figure 6-15
The coffin shelter is made from carved blocks of firm snow. If necessary, tramp the snow down and let it set before you attempt to carve the blocks. Carving vertical blocks is the fast method, but if the snow is shallow, they may have to be carved horizontally. Two triangular pieces must be cut for the ends.

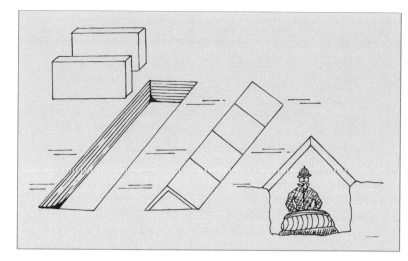

Figure 6-16
A different type of one person snow shelter can be constructed by digging into the lip of a large snow bank. Lots of snow is required but, because the sleeping area is raised, this shelter is warmer than the coffin shelter shown in Fig. 6–15.

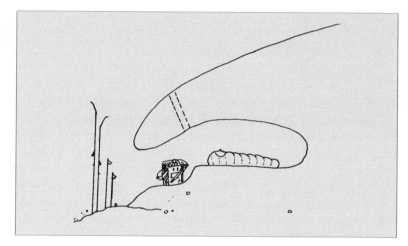

In contrast with cold weather, protection during the warm summer months usually means seeking relief from mosquitoes and blackflies. The characteristics that make for a warm survival shelter will create a haven for mosquitoes. In warm summer months get to an open location, such as a small island, point of land, or hilltop where the wind will help minimize bug problems. Although it doesn't sound appealing, dirt and mud spread over your face and hands may be one of the few techniques you can use to reduce the effects of bugs. Definitely try to stay covered, but at the same time remember that mosquitoes and black flies are attracted to body heat and carbon dioxide. A hot body is like a runway for bugs, equipped with landing lights!

Under extremely hot conditions, such as you might find in the southwest region of the United States, shelter from the sun is critical. In such situations, exposing yourself to the sun, let alone travelling during the day, is a questionable practice at best. Try to locate a place to hole-up, using whatever shade you can find.

SIGNALS

Anyone caught in a survival situation should make plans to signal search parties. Don't wait until you see an airplane before you try and figure out how to signal it. The bigger the signal, the better. Often, a downed aircraft or wrecked canoe is highly visible from the air and is generally the first thing spotted by search parties. This is another reason that supports staying at the accident site. (It also is a reason for purchasing a red or yellow canoe.)

Ground-to-air Communications

The following are signal codes for ground to air communication.

1. Require a doctor, serious injury	—
2. Require medical supplies	=
3. Unable to proceed	X
4. Require food and water	F
5. Am proceeding in this direction	→
6. Probably safe to land here	△
7. All well	LL
8. Yes, affirmative	Y
9. No, negative	N

Note: Signals should be at least 10 metres (11 yards) high in order to be visible from the air.

Anything in a group of three is considered to be a distress signal. Three fires, three large rock cairns, or even three piles of sod or snow blocks may be used. If you choose to leave the area, build the markers and leave an indication of your intentions and travel route. Know how to use flares, an E.L.T., or any other emergency signalling devices that may be carried.

PAIN, FATIGUE, BOREDOM AND LONELINESS

Pain obstructs rational decision making. Fatigue is also a factor that impairs mental faculties. Both of these are common to survival situations, so dealing with them must be given top priority. When people are hurt or tired, they don't make good decisions. Attend to your wounds and get some rest. Then start making decisions.

Boredom and loneliness are after effects that set in while waiting for the rescue. Boredom and loneliness encourage many people to try and walk out of a survival situation. Unfortunately, there are many cases of people who, though they were surviving quite nicely, simply got bored and died while trying to walk out. After medical attention and rest, develop a routine, get busy, and don't let yourself get bored. There are many things to do. These include setting traps, scrounging equipment, mapping the local area, and preparing wood for signal fires. Don't let your success be the first step toward failure. Take nothing for granted and your chances for survival will increase.

ADDITIONAL SOURCES

- Angier, B. (1974). *Field Guide to Edible Wild Plants.* Harrisburg, Pennsylvania: Stackpole Books.

- *Down But Not Out.* (1973). (C.F.P. 217), Ottawa: Information Canada.

- Fear, E. H. (1979). *Surviving the Unexpected Wilderness Emergency.* Tacoma, Washington: Survival Education Association.

- Ferri, G. (1989). *The Psychology of Wilderness Survival.* Hanover, Ontario: Skyway Publishing.

- Medsger, 0. P. (1972). *Edible Wild Plants.* New York: Collier Books.

- Olson, L. D. (1990). *Outdoor Survival Skills* (5th Ed.). Chicago: Chicago Review Press.

An anonymous grave in the barrens

7

Emergency Care

For advice about money, ask a banker. For doctors, try nurses.

W. Gifford-Jones

This chapter focuses on issues and problems related to the provision of wilderness first aid or emergency care during the course of a backcountry trip. It is important to emphasize that reading this brief chapter will not provide the reader with the level of knowledge and skill required by those who travel in wilderness areas, and certainly not those who act as leaders. This chapter does not take the place of a first aid course, particularly one geared to dealing with the special problems that occur when trying to respond to medical problems in wilderness settings. There is no substitute for practice, feedback, and opportunity for simulations that you will get from a qualified instructor during a hands-on course.

This chapter is valuable for several reasons. It may, for example, demonstrate to those who have not taken a first aid course the wide variety of issues and complexity of material that necessitate taking a course. Hence this book will act, for some people, as a catalyst for applied training, as well as useful preparation for such training. This chapter may also serve as a refresher for those who have studied and practised wilderness emergency care. Finally, this chapter may be useful as a reference document.

If you are looking for an applied first aid course, consider one of the courses offered by the Red Cross or St. John Ambulance Society. As well, if there is a community college in your town or city, contact the registrar and ask if the college offers a course specifically for wilderness travel enthusiasts. Local canoeing, climbing, backpacking, or cross-country ski clubs are also good places to inquire about courses geared to the out-of-doors.

IN THIS CHAPTER

- **Prevention, Preparation, and First Response**
- **Priorities**
- **The Body**
- **Respiratory Failure**
- **Bleeding**
- **Shock**
- **Fractures, Strains, Sprains, and Dislocations**
- **Heat and Cold Injuries**
- **Hypothermia**
- **Poisoning**
- **Foreign Bodies**
- **Dressings and Bandages**
- **Transportation**

PREVENTION, PREPARATION, AND FIRST RESPONSE

By anticipating difficult and dangerous situations, taking steps to minimize hazards, and being prepared to respond to accidents, wilderness travellers minimize the inherent risks involved in being out-of-doors and at a distance from medical treatment facilities. Prevention is based on planning, adequate clothing, dependable equipment, and ensuring that the skill level of the participants and leaders corresponds to the type of trip being undertaken. When, in spite of all planning and precaution, an accident occurs, and physical or psychological well-being is at stake, emergency care skills are needed.

Anyone travelling into a remote area should have a comprehensive medical examination prior to the trip. And, for personal medical histories to be of any value, they must be shared. If there is a trip leader, he or she should assume responsibility for ensuring that medical histories are complete and detailed, and that copies of the medical histories, or summaries, are taken on the trip. In this way, should treatment or evacuation be necessary, medical information will be readily available. As well, a copy of the medical histories should be available in a central location in the event that the information taken on the trip is lost or destroyed. (See Appendix C for a sample medical history form.)

If you are ever called upon to provide emergency care for someone who is not part of your group, check for a medic-alert bracelet, neck tag, or any other cards or information that may provide you with any details regarding medical history, current medication being taken, or treatment required. If the person is part of a group, be sure to ask the group members if there is any medical information available, or if the person has been taking medication for which there may be instructions. Remember, people with special problems, such as allergies to penicillin or other common drugs, are likely to be carrying information describing the problem and necessary treatment. If you are subject to unique and special medical problems, do yourself and your camping friends a favour, get a medic-alert bracelet and let your friends know about your condition.

While performing any type of emergency care assistance, it is important to keep an accurate record of signs, symptoms, treatment given, and reactions to treatment. Times, dosages, and all other relevant information should be noted in order to assist medical authorities with later evaluation and treatment.

When providing emergency care, the benefits of giving continual reassurance to the victim and maintaining a positive attitude cannot be overestimated. Being calm, cool, and at least appearing to be competent, can be helpful in relaxing the victim and reducing—or at least not exacerbating—some of the effects of shock. Be honest, but optimistic. If the victim does not know you, be sure to identify yourself, indicating you are trained in first aid, and ask if you can help. Continue to talk to the victim, even if he or she appears to be unconscious or non-responsive. In many cases, the victim may be able to hear, even though unable to respond, and the confidence you provide by talking in a supportive and caring manner will be very beneficial. At the minimum, talking will help you sort things out and calm others.

Overloaded canoes are a prescription for disaster.

People react very differently in the face of accidents or emergencies. Some are calm, others are not. People who a few moments earlier appeared to be pillars of strength can fall to pieces, and some of the less obviously strong types will become heroes. For the emergency care worker, the trick is to use people according to their strengths. Trying to shore up bystanders who are in shock will be a waste of time. Instead, concentrate on giving everyone a job. Getting blankets, starting mouth to mouth resuscitation, looking for lost equipment, applying direct pressure to a wound, going for help, reading from the first aid book, retrieving the medical histories, or, in some circumstances, crowd control, are just some of the important activities that will keep people busy, involved, and focused on the positive.

PRIORITIES

Wilderness emergency care consists of four major areas:

1. Prevention
2. Diagnosis
3. Treatment and Stabilization
4. Transportation/Evacuation

Prevention techniques are critical. If proper planning and preparation doesn't take place, there is a greater likelihood that problems will occur, and it is more likely that emergency care skills will be insufficient to deal with difficulties. Without proper planning and preparation, the group will have to depend completely on luck. Most of the time, luck will be sufficient. But when your luck runs out, minor accidents become serious problems, and there is a far greater likelihood that serious, life-threatening mishaps will result in tragedy.

If the weather is pleasant, this situation is a minor annoyance. In bad weather, it can be life-threatening.

Diagnosis is the first step after an accident has occurred. Here, it is important to find out as much as possible about the person's medical history, and what medicines or treatments are appropriate and available.

For most wilderness injuries, treatment and stabilization are necessary before evacuation takes place. Exceptions would be those cases where additional injury is imminent if the victim is not moved quickly. Treatment priorities are: (1) breathing; (2) bleeding; (3) broken bones, (4) burns and shock.

Breathing is the most important issue. If the brain is deprived of oxygen, even for a very short period of time, death or severe brain injury will result. Therefore, the first step in diagnosis is to check for airway patency, and then breathing. While checking for a clean and unobstructed airway, be sure to look for false teeth or other oral obstructions. If breathing is absent, then artificial respiration should be started immediately. Seconds count.

If the victim is breathing, but unconscious, take steps to ensure that vomitus will not be aspirated (sucked into the lungs) if the patient becomes sick to his stomach. This is typically accomplished by placing the victim on his side with the head down, assuming that other injuries don't prevent this.

Once you are certain the victim is not in further danger from the elements, and breathing has been established, check for bleeding. Serious bleeding, such as that which occurs if an artery has been opened, requires immediate attention. Direct pressure to the wound may be necessary in order to control bleeding. Open wounds should be covered.

SAFETY TIP

Treatment priorities should be second nature:
 – breathing,
 – bleeding,
 – broken bones,
 – burns and
 – shock.

SAFETY TIP

Direct pressure may be required to control arterial bleeding.

After bleeding, fractures are the next priority. All fractures need to be immobilized prior to evacuation. Fractures of the neck and spine are particularly critical since they can result in paralysis. If a fracture of the spine or neck is suspected, it will likely be best to try and bring medical assistance to the victim, rather than attempt evacuation without the proper equipment.

Treatment for shock, prior to transport, is important since this will help reduce additional complications. As soon as possible, make the victim warm and comfortable, but avoid overheating. Never give a severely traumatized victim anything to drink.

The following sections of this chapter provide an overview of wilderness emergency care by first describing the body and its major systems, and then discussing specific emergency care problems and issues. However, before proceeding, four points deserve further emphasis.

1. Books are not a satisfactory substitute for an emergency care or wilderness first aid course taught by an experienced and competent teacher. Such courses provide practical, hands-on experience.

2. Unless the victim is in immediate physical danger or is not breathing, avoid moving him until you are certain there is no spinal or neck injury.

3. First aid and emergency care techniques change with the times. Different approaches to treatment, as well as new techniques and drugs, make re-training a must. In order to be up-to-date, take a refresher course every couple of years. You will never regret being "over-trained" in emergency care.

4. Even doctors can find it difficult to determine if death has occurred. The earliest signal is the absence of movement, but that in itself proves nothing. Even if you can detect no breathing and no heartbeat, you will never be sorry for continuing to provide rescue breathing too long as compared with not long enough. Quit only if there are multiple victims and it becomes necessary to rank them. If at all possible, continue treatment until a doctor is available to make the final determination.

THE BODY

Basic understanding of body structure and how the body works is as important to a first aider as knowledge of a car is to a mechanic.

SAFETY TIP

Fractures need to be immobilized before transporting the victim.

The head is comprised of the skull and jaws. There are twenty-two bones in the head, eight of which comprise the skull. It is the skull that surrounds, supports, and protects the brain. Damage to the skull will almost certainly affect the brain.

The spine or vertebral column is composed of a long series of bones, 26 to be exact, that surround and protect the spinal cord. The spine begins with the neck and concludes with the tailbone or coccyx. The vertebra are held together by strong ligaments. The spinal cord acts as a distribution line, and is responsible for sending signals to the rest of the body. Damage to any part of the spine risks interrupting the body's main communications conduit, often resulting in paralysis. One major focus of first aid training concentrates on recognizing and dealing with spinal injuries. If spinal injury victims are not diagnosed, then immobilized and transported with great care, the "treatment" may simply exacerbate the original injury.

The chest area is surrounded and protected by twelve pairs of ribs attached to the spinal column. Each pair of ribs is attached to a single vertebra, and the top ten pairs are attached at the front to the breastbone. The lower pair are floating ribs. The chest structure provides protection for many of the body's vital organs, including the heart, lungs, and liver.

The pelvis is located under the abdomen and includes the hipbones, sacrum, and pubic bone. It provides protection for a number of the lower abdominal organs including the bladder.

Each arm, including the hand, is comprised of 29 bones. The upper arm fits into the socket located at the junction of the shoulder blade and collar bone. The humerus is the upper arm bone. It is connected to the main body via the shoulder girdle. The lower arm is comprised of two major bones, the radius and the ulna. Each leg contains thirty bones, the largest being the thighbone or femur. A fracture of the thighbone is very serious, in part because of the associated likelihood of damaging a major artery. Like the arm, the lower leg is comprised of two bones, the fibula and the tibia.

The metacarpal bones are found in the palm of the hand. The metatarsals are the corresponding bones in the feet. The size of these bones, and their location, often make them subject to injury. Though injuries to these bones are unlikely to be life-threatening, they can be very painful and may result in the inability to use a hand or put weight on a foot.

The human skeleton is flexible because it incorporates joints. Movement results when the brain sends signals down the spinal cord, through a system of nerves, to muscles linked to the nerve endings. These muscles respond to the brain's commands by contracting or relaxing, and the arms, legs, hands, feet, chest, and head respond accordingly.

Cartilage covers the portions of the bone that come into contact with each other at the joints. Cartilage is very, very smooth. Its function is to reduce friction when the bones rub against each other. People who suffer from damaged cartilage, particularly in their knees, often complain of extreme pain. Think of the loud grinding noises a car engine running with no motor oil would make and you should be able to sympathize with people who have damaged cartilage.

Grizzlies are easily recognized by a hump over the shoulders.

The bones are held together by ligaments. Without ligaments, the bones would "wander" from each other, and the result would be regular and massive dislocations. As mentioned earlier, muscles control the movement of the bones, but muscles and bones are not directly connected. Instead, the muscles are attached to tendons, which in turn are attached to the bones.

Damage to muscles, tendons, cartilage, ligaments, or bones is a serious problem for wilderness travellers—even if the injury itself is relatively mild. In the upper body, this type of injury can result in the inability to carry the basics for survival: food, sleeping bag, or tent. Damage to the lower body is even worse since it may leave the victim unable to walk.

The operation of the body is based on four systems: the nervous system, the respiratory system, the cardiovascular system, and the digestive system.

The *nervous system* is responsible for initiating and controlling movement. In humans, this system is very highly developed. The voluntary component of the nervous system includes the brain, spinal cord, and the complex of nerves that run from the spinal cord throughout the body. This is the system that controls planned physical movement. As mentioned earlier, any injury to either of the two major components of this system—the brain and spinal cord—may result in full or partial paralysis. The involuntary component of the nervous system is so named because it is normally outside direct conscious control. Also originating in the brain and spinal cord, the involuntary nervous system controls all involuntary muscles, glands, and blood vessels.

The *respiratory system* controls the supply of oxygen to the body and the removal of waste products such as carbon dioxide. It is perhaps the easiest of the systems to understand and visualize. When you breathe in, air enters the body through either the nose or mouth. This air then travels down the windpipe and into the bronchial tubes found in the lungs. These bronchial tubes subdivide into smaller and smaller sections, the smallest are called bronchioles. Oxygen from the air you breathe in is transferred from the bronchioles to blood vessels, via alveoli. The alveoli are tiny air spaces composed of tissue that is thin enough for diffusion to take place between the bronchioles and very small blood vessels. As oxygen goes from the bronchioles into the blood vessels, carbon dioxide travels in the opposite direction. Exhaling brings the carbon dioxide up through the bronchial tubes, into the windpipe, and out the nose or mouth.

FIRST AID TIP

If the sac encasing the lungs is punctured, the victim may be unable to breathe without direct assistance.

The lungs are encased in a sac called the pleura. Normally, there is no air in the pleura. When the diaphragm and ribs pull in such a way as to extend the pleura, an imbalance is created since the air pressure outside the body is suddenly higher than the air pressure in the lungs. This causes air to be pulled through the mouth or nose down into the lungs. Then, when the diaphragm and ribs force the pleura to contract, air is expelled. If the pleural sac is ever punctured, for example by means of a chest wound resulting from a misdirected ski pole, no pressure imbalance will be available to pull air into the lungs. When this happens, the victim will be unable to breathe without direct assistance.

The *cardiovascular system* controls circulation of the blood. Given that the blood carries oxygen and carbon dioxide within the body, taking oxygen from the respiratory system and giving back carbon dioxide, the cardiovascular and respiratory systems are closely intertwined. The heart is the pump that pushes blood on its trip through the body. From the right hand side of the heart, the blood travels first to the lungs, where it hands over carbon dioxide to the bronchioles and takes on a load of oxygen. The blood then returns to the left side of the heart, from where it is pumped throughout the body. On this trip, the blood travels through arteries, transferring oxygen to cells as required. Like the bronchial tubes, the arteries get progressively smaller. At their smallest size, the arteries transfer the blood to veins. It is the veins that carry the blood back to the right side of the heart, picking up carbon dioxide and other wastes along the way.

The smallest of the arteries and veins are called capillaries. Many of them, particularly those in the hands, feet and head, are quite close to the surface of the body. When the weather is hot, the body will automatically dilate these capillaries in order to help radiate heat and keep the central body temperature down. When it is very cold, the capillaries will be constricted in order to minimize heat loss. In hot or cold weather, it is important to help—or at least not hinder—the body by ensuring that these areas are properly exposed or covered according to the prevailing conditions.

The *digestive system* includes the mouth, esophagus, stomach, intestines, gall bladder, pancreas, liver, and spleen. Most of these organs are found in the lower abdominal cavity and are protected by a layer of fat. However, even with this protection, it is not difficult to damage these organs. For example, a blow to the left side of the abdomen, near the ribs, can rupture the spleen.

The digestive system is responsible for controlling the flow, breakdown, and absorption of food and drink within the body. After food enters the mouth and is sufficiently chewed, it travels down the esophagus to the stomach. The esophagus is a muscular tube, lined with tough membrane. The stomach is simply an expanded section of the esophagus that further aids in the digestion of the food. After the food has been liquified in the stomach, it is ready to travel through the intestines. In the small intestines, digestion is completed and absorption of the usable elements in the food takes place. Anything not usable continues on into the large intestine where it is dried out and then expelled.

Any animal behaving out of character, no matter how small or friendly, should be suspected of carrying rabies and therefore avoided.

RESPIRATORY FAILURE

Respiratory failure is the most critical concern for a first aid worker. If the victim isn't breathing, then problems such as bleeding, broken bones, burns, and shock are secondary issues. Most cases of respiratory failure in the wilderness are the result of accidents in the water. However, heart attacks, electrical shocks, and drug use may also cause respiratory failure.

Given the severity of respiratory failure, coupled with the amount of wilderness activity taking place on and near water, it is reasonable and prudent to expect all members of a wilderness trip to be proficient in *artificial respiration*. I certainly wouldn't be keen on joining a wilderness trip where I was the only person able to provide artificial respiration.

There are many different techniques for giving artificial respiration. The most widely taught and accepted technique goes by a variety of names, including "mouth to mouth," "rescue breathing," and "direct." Using this technique (see Fig. 7–1), air is expelled from the rescuer's lungs directly into the victim's mouth. Assuming a tight seal, the air is literally forced into the victim's lungs, and the rescuer watches to see the victim's chest rise with each breath. This technique is direct, and the effectiveness can

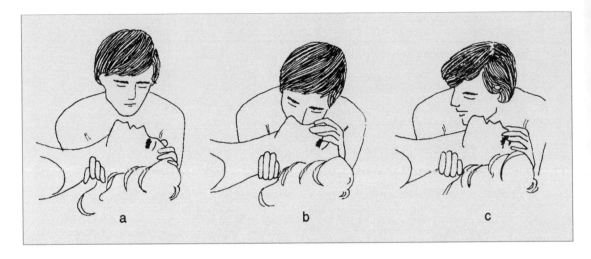

a   b   c

Figure 7-1
Rescue Breathing: (a) check the mouth for obstructions, lift the neck and tilt the head back; (b) pinch the nostrils, seal the mouth, and exhale directly into the victim's mouth; (c) release the nostrils and the seal around the mouth. The best way to test for airway patency is to watch for the victim's chest to rise and fall.

be visually measured by the rescuer. If the chest of the victim does not rise, then the mouth and throat are checked for obstructions before rescue breathing is continued.

If you encounter an accident victim who is not breathing, your first response should be to start artificial respiration as soon as possible. The heart may continue beating for several minutes following the cessation of breathing, but if the lungs are not getting fresh air, the brain will soon suffer damage. Therefore, get the victim into a position from which you can start rescue breathing, quickly check the mouth for obstructions such as false teeth or vomit, clean the mouth out if necessary, then begin rescue breathing. In order to ensure that the air is going into the lungs, rather than the stomach, tilt the neck as far back as you can. This position effectively closes off the route to the stomach, and leaves the passage to the lungs wide open. (Tilt your own head back as far as you can, then try and swallow. Most people will find it very difficult or impossible to swallow in this position.) Once the neck is extended, pinch the nostrils and breath air into the victim's mouth, making sure your lips form a tight seal around the lips of the victim. As you breath in, watch to see if the victim's chest is rising. If it shows no signs of expanding, and you find that you are unable to blow much air into the victim, re-check the mouth and throat area. If necessary, use your finger to reach as far as possible down the victim's throat in order to check for anything that shouldn't be there. Occasionally, a victim's tongue may be in the way, and will have to be pulled back into place. Rescue breathing should continue at a normal breathing pace, about twelve times per minute, until the victim is fully able to breath on

Falling in the wilderness has entirely different implications than does falling in the city.

Figure 7-2
The correct application of cardiopulmonary resuscitation requires considerable practice under the supervision of a qualified instructor.

his own or until a doctor pronounces him dead. Even if the victim appears able to breath on his own, be sure to keep a close watch since relapses are common. Vomiting on the part of a recovering victim is also common and can interfere with breathing. Be prepared to clean the vomit away.

Two other artificial respiration techniques, the modified Sylvester and the Holger Nielson, are sometimes used if there are additional injuries, such as a neck injury or broken jaw, that make the direct method ineffective.

Cardiopulmonary resuscitation, or C.P.R., is a form of external cardiac massage. Properly applied, C.P.R. forces the heart to keep pumping. Along with artificial respiration, C.P.R. is commonly used in emergencies such as electrocution, heart attack, and suffocation.

C.P.R. is a simple technique, but it requires considerable precision. The degree of pressure, the pressure points, and the frequency are all very important. Heart Associations normally

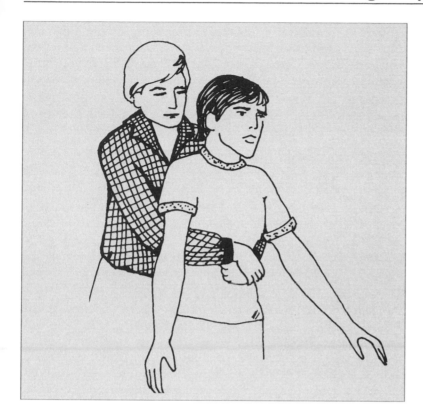

Figure 7-3
Heimlich Manoeuvre

organize and supervise short courses designed to teach C.P.R. and qualify practitioners. The following is a short description of C.P.R. technique, but is important to stress that this is not a rescue technique that can be adequately learned from a book. It requires instruction and practice under the guidance of a trained C.P.R. instructor.

If one person is attempting to provide both artificial respiration and C.P.R., the rescuer would normally start with the former and after four breaths check the carotid artery (located in the neck) for a pulse. If no pulse is evident, it can be assumed the heart is not beating, or at least not beating in a manner sufficient to get blood to the brain. At this stage, C.P.R. would be applied by pressing the heel of the hand on the lower part of the sternum. (More specifically, four or five centimetres—one and a half to two inches—above the xyphoid process.) This pressure compresses the heart, between the sternum and vertebral column. It is important that the hand be placed slightly above the tip of the sternum, otherwise it may fracture and puncture the liver.

C.P.R. is applied with fingers off the chest, straight arms, one hand on top of the other, and with pressure applied at a rate of sixty times per minute (see Fig. 7–2). The technique is quite tiring and, since it is normally combined with artificial respiration, two rescuers work together. If only one rescuer is present, fifteen compressions of the heart are followed by two quick breaths of rescue breathing, then fifteen compressions, and so on.

Respiratory failure can also occur if a victim's throat is obstructed with food or other object. Sometimes known as *cafe coronary*, this condition can be caused by swallowing a large piece of meat or other food that has not been sufficiently chewed. Peanut butter is another food that may cause this problem. People with missing teeth, or dental problems that make it difficult to properly chew food, are particularly prone to this problem. When it occurs, the victim is usually silent and may actually pass out before anyone notices. Then the problem may be mistaken for a heart attack. If the accident is treated quickly, breathing will begin automatically. To clear the airway, the rescuer grasps the victim from behind, locking his fists just below the sternum (see Fig. 7–3). A sharp tug will force air out of the victim's lungs and, hopefully, dislodge the obstruction. This treatment, known as the *Heimlich manoeuvre* or *abdominal thrust*, has saved many lives. Many more could have been saved, if people had been trained to recognize and treat this problem. Trying to dislodge food caught in the throat by reaching down with fingers will usually cause the food to be pushed further down the larynx.

Increasingly, or so it seems, people who are highly sensitized to insect bites or stings are taking to camping. For most people, an insect bite produces a somewhat painful swelling, with associated redness and swelling to mark the spot. However, for those who are highly sensitized to bites or stings, allergic reactions can result in death. Most people who suffer extreme reactions to insect bites or stings are aware of their condition and carry appropriate medication. In these cases, the victim should be able to help with the diagnosis and treatment. There are, however, those cases where a severe reaction to a bee or wasp sting is occurring for the first time. If a person suffering from an insect bite develops swelling around the eyes or mouth, hives, nausea, vomiting, or has difficulty breathing, it is reasonable to conclude that a severe reaction is in the offing. In these circumstances, getting medical aid is imperative. The victim should be put in a restful position and action taken to reduce shock. If breathing stops, initiate artificial respiration.

SAFETY TIP

Severe reactions to insect bites should be diagnosed and treated by medical authorities as quickly as possible.

Sucking chest wounds occur when a puncture or tear in the chest pokes a hole in the area between the chest wall and lung. They can be caused by ski poles, sharp sticks, or large splinters breaking off broken paddles. The lung on the injured side will deflate, and the victim will be unable to breathe. Air will be sucked in and out through the hole in the chest, resulting in a sucking noise. A sterile dressing, preferably coated with petroleum jelly, should be placed over the wound after the victim exhales, and then held tightly in place. In this situation, speed is imperative. If the first aid kit is not immediately available, use any clean piece of cloth, plastic, or cellophane to cover the wound. Treatment for shock should be instituted immediately, and evacuation given top priority.

SAFETY TIP

Use a sterile dressing to seal a sucking chest wound. Speed is critical. If the victim is unable to breathe after the application of a dressing and pressure on the wound, rescue breathing may be required.

BLEEDING

Bleeding wounds differ considerably in terms of severity. They are classified as follows:

1. **Abrasions** These result from skidding or sliding contact with a rough surface. Sliding down a rock face on your knees while wearing shorts will cause this type of wound.

2. **Laceration** These are rough, uneven, jagged wounds caused by slicing contact with an uneven object. Knives, hatchets, and swipes from a bear's paws are great sources for this type of injury.

3. **Punctures** These wounds result from the penetration of a thin object through the skin. The proverbial ski pole is a common basis for this wound. (I have heard that hummingbirds flying under the influence of too much nectar can cause this injury, but I have yet to see it.

4. **Contusions.** These are crushing type wounds and are often accompanied by severe bruising. Dumping your canoe and then getting slammed between the overturned boat and a rock will almost certainly produce severe contusions.

Although wounds come in a variety of shapes and sizes, and originate from many different sources, treatment can be focused on two concerns: *stopping the bleeding* and *controlling infection.*

If possible, the wounded area should be elevated. This helps reduce blood pressure in the area of the wound, thereby assisting the clotting process. Direct pressure is a technique used to stop or reduce bleeding when it is apparent that clotting is not going to take place without intervention on the first aider's part. Large,

Figure 7-4
Direct pressure is sometimes
required to stop the flow of
blood.

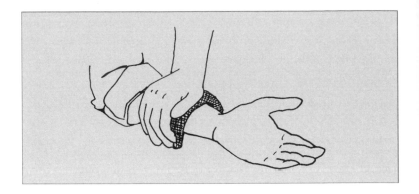

deep gashes or slices, such as might be caused by a misdirected axe, are examples of wounds that will likely require direct pressure. When applying direct pressure, it is best to lay a sterile cloth or bandage across the wound, then apply pressure with your fingers or hand (see Fig. 7–4.) If a sterile bandage is not immediately available, and the wound is particularly severe with large quantities of blood being lost, apply pressure immediately and look for a bandage later. Concerns about infection take a back seat if blood loss is substantial.

The use of direct pressure is not always appropriate if the wound is contaminated with foreign bodies, such as glass fragments, or if there are exposed bones. In these cases, causing further complications to the injury must be measured against blood loss. Where blood loss is not life threatening, it may be best to let the blood continue to flow rather than applying direct pressure, which will almost certainly jam debris deeper into the wound or further damage broken bones. In these cases, where broken bones or foreign bodies complicate the wound, a soft sterile dressing can be used to cover the wound, a ring bandage (see Fig. 7–5) is then applied to surround the wound, followed by a final covering bandage wrapped over the entire wound. The advantage to this approach is that the wound is protected, but direct pressure is avoided.

SAFETY TIP

***Tourniquets are a
treatment of last
resort.***

Tourniquets are used only in extreme circumstances. They should be viewed as a technique of last resort. The possibility of severe tissue damage restricts the use of tourniquets to extreme situations. One situation where a tourniquet may be required is following amputation of a finger, toe, hand, foot or entire limb. In essence, a tourniquet is used in situations where the alternative is bleeding to death. Once applied, a tourniquet should not be loosened until medical authorities assume responsibility for treatment.

Even on short hikes, like this one to the top of Sunblood Mountain near Virginia Falls, a first aid kit should be included with your gear.

Internal bleeding is not as obvious as many other wounds, and is therefore more difficult to diagnose. Symptoms of internal bleeding include thirst, dizziness, fainting, shallow irregular breathing, and a weak pulse. Often, symptoms of internal bleeding are similar to the symptoms of shock, and shock will typically accompany internal bleeding. Keep the victim warm and comfortable, and do not give any fluids. Treat internal bleeding as you would treat shock.

Bleeding from the ear is uncommon. The most likely cause is a skull fracture. Lay the victim in a prone position with the head slightly raised. Do not plug the ear. Tilt the head in order to allow the blood to drain from the ear. Treatment is similar to treatment for shock, with the exception of keeping the head slightly raised.

Ear injuries often result from attempts to clear the ear channel of foreign material such as bugs, dirt, or small stone chips. Children in particular will try to clear things from their ears by pushing other objects in, causing damage to the skin or ear drum. Adults should know better, but sometimes they can't resist sticking a probe down the ear channel. The best method for clearing a foreign object from an ear is to rinse the ear in lukewarm water, thereby softening the object and encouraging it to come out of its own accord. The standard rule is *never put an object smaller than your finger into an ear.*

Nosebleeds are not unusual. In fact, some people suffer nosebleeds quite regularly. Nosebleeds can be caused by relatively minor blows to the nose, untrimmed finger nails, or even a good sneeze. Victims should be encouraged to sit up with the head

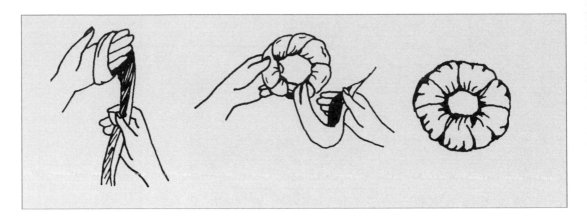

Figure 7-5
Ring bandages are useful for burns or cases where foreign objects are imbedded in the skin. These bandages prevent pressure from bearing down directly on the wound.

tilted slightly back, pinch the nostrils tight just below the bone, and breathe through the mouth. Most nosebleeds treated in this fashion will stop within five minutes. The nose should not be plugged.

Stopping the flow of blood is only the first part of the treatment for victims suffering from bleeding. The rescuer must also be concerned with preventing or minimizing the risks of infection during both the evaluation and treatment of the condition. Cleaning your hands and the area surrounding the wound with a mild antiseptic soap should be a matter of course, unless the loss of blood is so dramatic as to make gaining seconds imperative. Cleanliness at the beginning of the treatment process can go a long way to reducing the recuperative period.

SHOCK

Shock automatically accompanies many injuries. It is caused by circulatory insufficiency, a condition where not enough blood is being pumped through the body. The biggest single cause of shock is loss of blood.

Symptoms of shock include rapid pulse, shallow breathing, cold and clammy skin, dizziness, or unconsciousness. Basic treatment includes having the victim lie down, face up, with head and shoulders slightly lower than the rest of the body. Precise placement will be dependent on other injuries. The victim should be kept warm by putting blankets, sleeping bags, or other insulating material both under and over him. The goal is to prevent heat loss. However, be wary of overheating the victim since that will increase the problems associated with shock. Victims of shock should not be administered anything by mouth.

Shock may result from an acute heart attack, in which case treatment is different. Heart attacks are usually diagnosed from symptoms that include tight, vice-like, severe pain in the chest area. This may be followed by collapse and loss of consciousness. The victim's face will be ashen. In these cases, the victim should be kept in a sitting or half-sitting position. If available, nitroglycerine or amyl nitrate should be administered. Loosen the victim's clothing and provide continuous verbal reassurance. If vomiting occurs, try to help the victim minimize the amount of physical effort involved. If a heart attack is suspected, immediate evacuation, once the victim appears stabilized, is critical. The rescuer should be prepared to begin C.P.R. and artificial respiration if the heart fails and breathing stops.

Serious cases of shock can result in death, even where the original injury normally are not life threatening. It is for this reason that early treatment for shock is imperative, and removal to a medical facility, where intravenous equipment and a blood supply is available, should take place as soon as possible.

SAFETY TIP

Shock can be life threatening. Fast and effective treatment for shock is imperative.

FRACTURES, STRAINS, SPRAINS, AND DISLOCATIONS

A fracture is a bone separation. Fractures come in many types, shapes, and sizes, but are normally differentiated as either simple or compound. *Simple fractures* are those where the break is still within the skin, and the bone is not visible. *Compound fractures* are those where the bone has broken through the skin and is therefore exposed.

With simple fractures, because the bone is not visible, it is sometimes difficult to tell if in fact a fracture has occurred. In these cases, the presence of secondary symptoms or signs is used to diagnose the fracture. These include deformities in the suspected area of the fracture, acute soreness, situations where the victim heard a snap or pop, inability to move the suspected limb naturally or at all, and grating of the bone when the limb is moved. Shock should always be a consideration when treating a known or suspected fracture.

SAFETY TIP

Shock will almost certainly accompany a fracture.

Fractures should be immobilized as soon as possible in order to prevent further damage and discomfort. Immobilization must be completed before transportation takes place, otherwise additional damage to the affected area is almost certain. Splinting is the most common immobilization technique, and can be accomplished with paddle shafts, ski poles, or trimmed branches. The victim's own body can be used as part of the immobilization technique by tying or wrapping a broken arm to the chest, or bandaging one leg to another. Whatever the specific technique, fractures are generally immobilized by tightly securing the area above and below the fracture to ensure that free movement of the fracture area is minimized. The more secure the injured area, the more comfortable the victim will feel. If possible, stuff padding in the hollows formed between the body and the splint.

Compound fractures require additional attention since they are usually more serious fractures and the fact that they are open to the air makes them far more susceptible to infection. A compound fracture should be gently covered with a sterile dressing to combat the risk of infection.

Fractures of the back or neck are extremely serious. As noted earlier in this chapter, damage to the spinal cord may cause serious and irreversible paralysis. Consequently, the first rescuer on the scene of an accident location that may involve a back or neck injury must be extremely careful. Spinal injuries may be suspected in cases where there has been impact to the head or back, whiplash, or a fall. The victim may suffer partial paralysis to the hands and fingers in the event of a neck fracture, or partial paralysis to the toes or feet in the event of a fracture of the back.

Back or neck injuries must be completely immobilized, and in some circumstances it may be best to wait for special immobilization equipment—neck braces and the like—before attempting to transport the victim. Putting a victim with a spinal injury on a backboard requires at least three rescuers, one of whom must be specifically trained in casualty transportation. The neck must be kept in perfect alignment with the spine.

Strains are the product of torn muscle. Strains can result from a variety of circumstances, but are most common to situations where a victim tries to lift weights beyond the ability of the muscles involved. In effect, the mind wishes to accomplish more than the body can. *Sprains* are similar to strains, but result from torn or severely stretched ligaments at a joint. It is not always easy to differentiate between a fracture and a strain or sprain. If in doubt, assume the worst and treat the injury as a fracture.

Applying a cold compress and a firm bandage to strains and sprains can significantly reduce the haemorrhaging and swelling, thereby decreasing the recuperative period. Speed is important. The sooner a cold compress is applied, the less severe the injury is likely to become. Sprained ankles are very common out-of-doors, particularly in rugged areas where the terrain is uneven. In some cases, it will be necessary for a victim suffering from a

SAFETY TIP

Compound fractures are highly susceptible to infection. Keep the area clean and be sure to cover it with a sterile dressing.

SAFETY TIP

Cold compresses should be applied for strains and sprains as soon as possible.

strain or sprain to hike out. In these cases, use a firm bandage, wrapped tightly around the ankle and foot, to provide as much support as possible. By using a walking stick, the victim can minimize pressure on the affected area.

Dislocations occur when bones are displaced, and sometimes away, from a socket. Finger, shoulder, and jaw bones are most susceptible to dislocation. Symptoms include extreme pain in the area, discolouration, tenderness to touch, and deformity. If medical help is nearby, dislocation should be treated as a fracture. Relocating a dislocated bone normally requires considerable technical skill. If done improperly, further injuries to nerves, blood vessels, and muscles are likely. In remote areas, where medical assistance is not available, and will not be available for some time, attempted relocation may be the only recourse if the absence of a pulse or other symptom suggests that a more serious condition, such as gangrene, may result. The difficulty in relocating a bone increases with time. Therefore, the decision to attempt relocation should be considered fairly soon after the accident. Normally, force applied outward from the dislocation will result in correction, or at least a reduction in the pressure on nerves, blood vessels, and muscles.

Extended wilderness trips are not the place to try out edible wild plants for the first time.

HEAT AND COLD INJURIES

Burns are common, heat related injuries. They are classified as major or minor, and result from contact with a heat source such as fire, electrical outlet or wires, chemicals, or friction.

Dry heat, such as campfires, hot cooking utensils or food, and friction, are the most common sources of burn injuries for outdoor enthusiasts. As usual, prevention is far preferable to the cure, and simple caution exercised around the campfire will go a long way to preventing burn injuries. Tipped pots and hot cooking plates left unattended are very common burn sources. A scald is similar to a burn, but is caused by moist heat such as steam. Lifting the lid off a pot of boiling water, without ensuring your hand is off to the side, may cause scalding as the steam escapes.

Burns are considered to be minor if only the outside layers of skin are damaged. In these cases, treatment involves immersion in cold water for at least three minutes, as soon as possible following the accident. This treatment will not only help reduce the actual burn damage but will also reduce the associated pain, in many cases bringing some immediate relief. Many victims, and children in particular, will prefer to leave the affected area in water until the pain has dissipated.

Hats are mandatory, even on short trips. They help prevent sunburn, sun stroke and heat stroke.

Major burns penetrate below the surface of the skin, damaging the muscles or fat tissue. They are serious. Burns that cover more than one third of the body surface are also categorized as major. Major burns, burns covering more than 15% of the body, and burns to the face, neck, hands, or genitals will likely result in shock and accompanying trauma. Although breathing and bleeding take precedence in terms of diagnosis and treatment, major burns are clearly life threatening and incredibly painful. Without immediate attention, major burns, and the accompanying shock, will kill. Major burns are characterized by whole blood loss, accompanying shock, infection, extreme pain, and an extended healing process. Procedures for evacuation should be implemented immediately. In the meantime, treat the victim for shock, clean the burn area as much as possible without actually going into the wounded area to remove clothing or other debris, and cover the burn area with a ring bandage (see Fig. 7–5), sterile dressing, and another bandage. Creams and lotions are not usually recommended since they tend to increase the possibility of infection and make later examination by medical specialists more difficult.

Sunburn is also much easier to prevent than to cure. Recently, considerable evidence has linked exposure to the sun with cancer. Societal attitudes are changing, and much of the glamour that has in the past been associated with a rich, dark tan has faded. Covering up and using protective creams is the norm. However, having said this, sunburn continues to be a common ailment among outdoor enthusiasts, particularly those with fair hair and light skin. In part, this is because sunburn is often difficult to detect while it is actually occurring. Later in the evening, or even the next day, is when many victims realize that the damage has been done. Most cases of sunburn simply require "toughing it out." Pain and peeling of skin is the payment for clear days or high altitudes. Creams are available to help relieve some of the soreness and itching. Solarcaine is a good one.

Heat exhaustion is brought on by prolonged exposure to a hot environment, most often when the victim has been physically active and directly exposed to the elements. Under very hot conditions, the blood vessels dilate in order to radiate heat. This is the body's response to excessive heat build-up. Heat exhaustion is brought on when the blood vessels dilate to such a degree that there is not enough blood getting through to the vital organs, including the brain. Dehydration is also common in these circumstances, and will exacerbate the problem. Victims of heat exhaustion will recognize they are in difficulty. The problem is normally accompanied by faintness, dizziness, and nausea. In extreme cases, vomiting and unconsciousness can occur. When this happens it is important to ensure that the vomitus does not interfere with breathing. With heat exhaustion, the victim's temperature is not significantly above normal. Rest, fluids, and shade will soon relieve the problem. In my experience, most cases of heat exhaustion occur when someone new to camping insists that he doesn't need to wear a sun hat.

Heat stroke, also known as sun stroke, is far more serious than heat exhaustion. It occurs when, after prolonged exertion in a hot environment, the body's sweat glands tire and become less efficient at ridding the body of excess heat. Perspiration levels drop, and heat in the body core builds up very quickly. The actual onset of heat stroke is very rapid. Symptoms include confusion, deliriousness, unconsciousness, and a body temperature well above normal. Heat stroke requires immediate diagnosis and treatment. The body should be cooled immediately, either by soaking in water or by applying cold compresses over as much of the body as possible. It may help to massage limbs in order to encourage blood circulation. Without treatment, brain injury is possible.

SAFETY TIP

Heat stroke is more serious than heat exhaustion. With heat stroke, body temperature is well above normal and needs to be cooled immediately.

HYPOTHERMIA

Hypothermia is a condition in which the body's core temperature has cooled to the point where normal functioning cannot take place. In essence, body heat is being lost, usually through

Glacial streams should be forded with great care. Be sure to unhook your hip belt and loosen the shoulder straps.

direct exposure to the elements, faster than it can be generated. Among campers, hypothermia is a major cause of death. It can occur, for example, when an unanticipated storm catches you out ridge-walking, your canoe tips during the first outing in May, or severe winter weather finds you unprepared while cross-country skiing.

Like most other emergency care problems, hypothermia is best dealt with through prevention. This means being prepared and working within an established safety margin: carry a spare ski tip; have a change of clothes; wear protective raingear, hats and gloves; camp early rather than late; don't challenge the elements to the extreme.

The onset of hypothermia is subtle. Exposure in the early stages is not particularly noticeable. Victims will often simply try to keep moving in order to stay warm. Shivering, a mechanism the body uses to generate heat, is one of the best and most easily recognizable early signals of difficulty. If you or someone else in the party starts to shiver, consider the possible consequences of continuing to move on. If you are cold simply because you aren't moving, then fine, head out. If you are cold because you are worn out, and the weather conditions are worsening, then it's time to camp. If exposure is not terminated at this stage, it may never be, since the ability to make rational decisions is soon impaired. It doesn't take long for the body's shivering mechanism to fail since the effort isn't worth the gain. This is followed by failure of physical coordination; the victim will stumble, fall, or be unable to keep time with a regular canoe stroke. Soon, pulse and respiratory rates fall, and exhaustion accelerates. By this stage, the victim is rarely able to save himself. A rescuer who takes charge is the only hope.

SAFETY TIP

Shivering is an important signal which shouldn't be ignored.

Treatment for hypothermia begins by stopping exposure. Remove all wet clothes and surround the victim with warm, dry bedding or clothing. Warm drinks should be encouraged and, if possible, the victim should be kept awake. If the victim has slipped into semi-consciousness, the situation should be considered critical. Having someone slip into a sleeping bag with the victim will provide skin to skin contact and is an excellent way to transmit heat. Transporting an unconscious hypothermia victim carries special risks. For example, the myocardium becomes increasingly delicate and the slightest jarring of the body may result in the onset of life threatening arrhythmia.

Hypothermia victims experience a long slide into oblivion. The further down the slide you get, the steeper it becomes. Self rescue

SAFETY TIP

Hypothermia occurs most often in the fall and spring in relatively moderate weather conditions.

is only possible through prevention or early diagnosis. After the initial stages, the speed at which hypothermia accelerates, combined with its numbing effect on the brain, make self rescue all but impossible. Hypothermia occurs most often in relatively moderate temperatures, not, as one might first expect, in extremely cold conditions. A windy, rainy day with temperatures hovering just above the freezing mark is perfect for hypothermia. Heat will be conducted away from the body at a very fast rate, particularly if clothes are wet or body parts are exposed. In these circumstances, campers are often not as well prepared as they are when actual winter conditions exist.

Frostbite is a common winter problem. When exposed to cold weather, blood vessels near the surface of the skin will contract. This occurs naturally, and is a reaction designed to reduce the amount of heat loss from the body core. Under extreme conditions, blood vessels in the face, fingers, and toes may contract to the point where blood flow is virtually stopped. When that happens, the area is prone to freezing. Once freezing occurs in one area, then the condition spreads laterally across the skin surface as well as vertically into the tissue.

Preventing frostbite is most easily accomplished by making sure that bare skin is not exposed to severe winter weather. Unfortunately, the body does not always provide a warning when such conditions exist, and many people suffer frostbite without being aware of it until after the condition has spread. Using a "buddy" system, whereby members of the group watch each other for telltale signs, is a good early warning technique.

The ears, nose, chin, fingers, and toes are the most likely areas to suffer frostbite. The condition is diagnosed by the presence of white tissue with no feeling. Treatment is based on rapid and complete re-warming of the affected area. It is important that the treatment be complete. Partial re-warming, followed by re-freezing, will result in greater damage. This problem occurs in part because the surface layer of skin will thaw first, but the underlying layers are still frozen and will harm additional layers of tissue unless the entire area is completely thawed. Consequently, it is best to wait until you reach base camp, a lodge, or medical facility before beginning treatment. Obviously, the sooner the better.

Re-warming of frostbitten areas, even small and localized cases, is painful under the best of conditions. Blisters and dead skin are common after a day or two, and the appearance of frostbite on the mend will suggest damage that is out of proportion to the actual condition.

Body Temperature Table

Celsius	Fahrenheit	EXPERIENCE
37°	98.6°	Normal body functioning.
35°-36°	95°-97°	Chilliness; minor coordination problems.
33°-34°	91°-94°	Obvious coordination problems; coupled with difficulty in decision making; intense shivering.
30°-32°	85°-90°	Extreme coordination problems; shivering stops; drunken incoherence.
28°-29°	82°-84°	Difficult to find pulse; complete irrationality; muscular rigidity.
26°-27°	79°-81°	Unconsciousness.
25°	77°	Heart fibrillates; death occurs.

Snowblindness is sunburn to the surface of the eye. As with ordinary sunburn, the victim is not usually aware of the problem while the damage is being done. Snow blindness is best prevented by wearing glacier glasses or other eyeware that protect against strong sunlight and reflective surfaces. Under survival conditions, a mask made of bark or other material, with very tiny eye slits, may do the trick. Symptoms of snowblindness include painful itching, particularly when the eyes are blinked or moved. The victim will report a sensation similar to sand grating around in the eye sockets. Some victims will try to get the foreign objects out of the eyes before recognizing the problem. A dark and restful environment, along with time, will usually relieve the problem. Cold compresses over the eyes may alleviate some of the pain.

POISONING

Food poisoning should be a major concern to campers, not so much because of its frequency, but because of the severity. As with other medical problems, avoidance is much easier than the cure. Staphylococcal, salmonella, and botulism are three of the more common types of bacterial food poisoning to be aware of.

Staphylococcal poisoning is caused by eating food that has gone bad in warm weather. It is the food poisoning that people get when the hors d'oeuvres are left out for too long before the party. The bacteria multiply rapidly in meats and dairy products. Proper refrigeration avoids the problem. Symptoms of staphylo-

Learn to distinguish between poisonous and non-poisonous snakes.

coccal poisoning include vomiting, diarrhoea and cramps. The pain will be acute, to the point where shock is a possibility. Though there are relatively few deaths from this type of poisoning, medical attention should be sought as soon as practical.

Salmonella bacteria is transmitted by human and animal carriers, and may be found in meats, cheeses and other dairy products, fish, and vegetables. Contamination may take place at the source, through handling, or at the time of preparation. Salmonella is avoided by stressing cleanliness and purchasing quality foods from reputable suppliers. Symptoms of salmonella poisoning include cramps, vomiting, and diarrhoea. Prior to reaching medical facilities, treatment should include rest, and restoration of fluids lost through vomiting and diarrhoea.

Botulism is more serious than staphylococcal and salmonella poisoning. It results from improper canning. If you have any reason to suspect that canned foods are not as they should be, such as internal pressure deforming the lid before the can has been opened, don't risk eating them. Symptoms of botulism are delayed, beginning about 48 hours after the food has been ingested. Double vision, difficulty in breathing, low blood pressure, hoarseness, and inability to swallow are common manifestations. If untreated by medical authorities, botulism will likely result in death.

Much to the chagrin of those who like to sample nature in the raw, *edible plants* sometimes turn out to be not nearly as edible as first thought. Common sense dictates against eating anything unfamiliar. It's also wise to beware of others who claim to be able to identify edible plants. Beyond the obvious edibles, such as cattails, dandelions, and cedar bark, there is plenty of room for error, and the consequences can be critical. If you do venture into unfamiliar gastronomic territory, it is always a good idea to try a little, before indulging in quantity. It is also wise to save an example of the plant, to permit identification by an expert in order for medical authorities to determine an appropriate treatment. If the plant is unknown, then treatment will have to be based solely on symptoms until the stomach is pumped and the hard evidence analyzed.

Some of the more common poisonous plants include the well known poison ivy (*Rhus toxicodendron*), poison oak (*Rhus diversiloba*), poison sumach (*Rhus vernix*), pokeweed (*Phytolacca americana*), poison hemlock (*Conium macalatum*), water hemlock (*Cicuta maculata*), Jimson weed (*Datura stramonium*), and buttercup (*Ranunculus acris*).

The plant oil in poison ivy has a toxic effect on the skin of people who are sensitized to it. The result is a red, itchy swelling, that culminates in blisters. If you have been exposed to poison ivy, the best course is to wash the problem area with soap and lots of water. If a rash develops, keep the area clean and dry. The oil can be carried on clothing, making it possible for others who handle your clothes to suffer the effects. Poison oak and poison sumach cause similar rashes and are treated in the same way. Calamine lotion helps ease the itching.

The roots of pokeweed are similar to the roots of horseradish. However, eating pokeweed will result in vomiting, spasms, convulsions, and sometimes death. The fruit of the poison hemlock is the most toxic part of the plant. The roots of water hemlock are the most poisonous part of that plant. Ingestion of cicutoxin, found in water hemlock, will lead to violent convulsions, laboured breathing, frothing at the mouth, loss of sight, increased pulse, and great pain. Jimson weed is probably worse. Eating it in any quantity leads to headache, vertigo, thirst, nausea, loss of sight, convulsions and death. Being able to identify poisonous plants, with certainty, is strongly recommended for those who wish to sample nature's bounties directly from the field or forest.

Animal bites are problematic both because of the direct damage and associated blood loss as well as the fact that bacteria will often be introduced through the animal's saliva. To counteract this, a soap and water solution should be used to thoroughly wash the area, then sterile dressings applied to cover and protect.

Rabies is another problem related to animal bites. Unless vaccine is administered, this viral infection will almost certainly result in death. Therefore, rabies should be considered in the case of any and all animal bites. Household pets that have not been vaccinated, skunks, foxes, raccoons, wolves, and bats are common carriers. Birds and fish do not carry rabies. The rabies infection is transmitted via the animal's saliva into the wound at the time of the bite. If the bite does not break the skin, then infection is unlikely. However, a household pet could transmit the infection simply by licking a hand that has an open sore. Rabies must be treated before the symptoms occur, and the only way to determine for certain if the vaccine is necessary is to examine the animal. If the animal can be caught, a lab can do a rabies examination. If the animal cannot be caught, rabies will normally be assumed and the vaccine program started. The vaccine is administered through a serious of painful injections. As difficult as these are, most people chose injections over death.

CAMPING TIP

Not everyone is allergic to poison ivy, and the degree of sensitivity among those who are will vary.

Figure 7-6
Typical snake bite marks may show only a few of the teeth marks, and in some cases only one fang wll break the skin

Figure 7-7
Incisions should be made at right angles to the fang mark

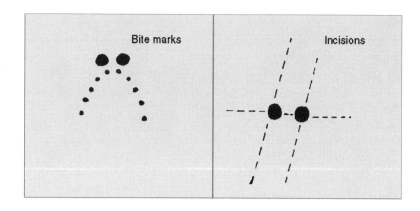

Snake bites are a problem only in certain geographic areas. For example, the Massasauga rattlesnake (*Sistrurus catenatus*) is typically found from the west, central United States up into the Georgian Bay area of Canada. However, this snake, like others, is very local in its orientation. Though you may be within the general range, the snake may not actually reside in your specific locale. Ask residents of the area, who are familiar with the outdoors, and you should have a pretty good idea whether or not poisonous snakes inhabit the area.

The Massasauga rattler is the only poisonous snake found in Canada. The United States has a much wider variety, including the Cottonmouth or Water Moccasin (*Agistrodun piscivorous*) which ranges from Virginia and Florida west through the Gulf States; the Copperhead (*Agcistroden contortix*), located from Massachusetts to northern Florida and west to Illinois; and the Coral Snake (*Micrurus fulvius*), found in South Carolina and Florida west through the Gulf States. There are fifteen species of rattlesnakes found in the US, ten of which live in the southwest.

It has been estimated that only one of eight adults die from an untreated rattlesnake bite. If the bite is treated, that number drops to one out of thirty. Copperheads rarely effect a fatal injury.

The bite of a poisonous snake will almost always result in a sharp burning pain. Swelling and bleeding occur within a few minutes, followed by faintness and nausea. At least one fang mark is usually visible, as well as teeth marks. If the bite was particularly solid, then both fangs may leave marks (see Fig. 7–6). If fang marks are not visible, the onset of symptoms will be the telling indicator as to whether or not poison was transmitted.

All the poisonous snakes located in North America are pit vipers, with the exception of the coral snake. Pit vipers tend to make fast strikes and then withdraw. Coral snakes, by contrast,

First Aid Kits

First aid kits will vary, depending on the length of trip, location, the first aid expertise of the participants, and any special medical problems among the group members. The following items are things an experienced leader may wish to carry on an extended trip.

- Assorted dressings
- Triangular bandage
- Butterfly bandages
- Roller bandages
- Elastic bandages
- Adhesive bandages

- Gauze dressings
- Adhesive tape
- Absorbent cotton
- Cotton-tipped applicators
- Antiseptic soap
- Moleskin
- Amonia inhalants
- Salt pills
- Tweezers
- Gravol
- Sutures
- Scissors
- Aspirin
- Safety pins
- Sunscreen lotion

- Isopropyl alcohol swabs
- Calamine lotion
- Scalpel
- Metal finger splints
- Painkillers
- Thread
- Thermometer
- First Aid Manual

These suggestions do not take into account special survival gear such as flares, fish hooks and line, special medication, or snake bite apparatus.

hold on and grind their fangs into the victim. Victims should be encouraged to relax, and their spirits cheered with the information that few people die from snake bites.

If medical attention and antivenin is not available within twenty to thirty minutes, the effects of the venom should be reduced by "bleeding" the area (see Fig. 7–7). An incision is made with a sterile razor blade across the fang marks, and then at right angles to the two marks. Avoid deep cuts. The incisions should bleed but not spurt blood. Apply a constrictive bandage between the body and the bite, assuming it has occurred on a limb, making sure that only veins are affected, not the arteries. It is important to be able to find the pulse below the bite. This ensures that the limb is still receiving fresh blood. The next step is to suck the wound with a snake bite suction cup, or your mouth, providing you do not have open sores. Evacuation to a facility with anti-venin should take place as soon as possible. Cold therapy—applying of very cold compresses to the wound—is not advised.

FOREIGN BODIES

Foreign bodies, such as drifting seeds, dust, or sand may easily become lodged in an eye. Irritation or inflammation will occur, and the natural reaction is to rub the eye. When the presence of a foreign body in the eye is suspected, try having the victim blink the eye several times in rapid succession, with his head facing down. That often helps bring the object out from under the lid and into the corner of the eye, where it is more easily removed. If this doesn't work, pull the lid up or down, and if the object is spotted, try and remove it with the corner of dampened, clean handkerchief or bandage. If this still doesn't work, rinse the eye with clean, lukewarm water. If the item appears embedded in the eye, seek medical assistance as soon as possible.

Foreign objects in the nose can usually be removed by strong sneezing. The ear is a particularly delicate area, discussed earlier in this chapter. Bugs and the like can often be removed from the ear canal by flushing with it lukewarm water. Swallowed objects are usually eliminated naturally, unless they are particularly large, or sharp in nature. In these cases, medical attention should be sought as soon as is practical.

Splinters are a common problem. The area should be cleaned and soaked in warm water to make the skin more malleable and less likely to be damaged during the removal process. If the splinter can be grasped with tweezers, work it out slowly. If, on the other hand, the splinter is broken off below the surface of the skin, it may be necessary to cut a portion of the skin along the length of the splinter, then apply pressure to bring the end of the splinter to the surface where it can be grasped with tweezers.

In the case of an embedded fish hook, it may be necessary to push the hook through until it surfaces, then cut the barb off, and remove the hook. Often, this is preferable to backing the hook out of the wound, and having the bard tear through skin. If medical help is nearby, it is a good idea to seek help since local anaesthetic can then be applied. With fish hooks, the possibility of infection is considerable.

DRESSINGS AND BANDAGES

Dressings are designed to protect the injury from infection and further damage, and to help control bleeding. Dressings must be kept in sterile packaging, or their value is severely hampered. Also, dressings must be applied in such a way that they remain sterile. Dirty hands, or exposing the dressing to contaminated

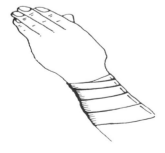

Figure 7-8
Spiral bandages are used on areas of uniform thickness

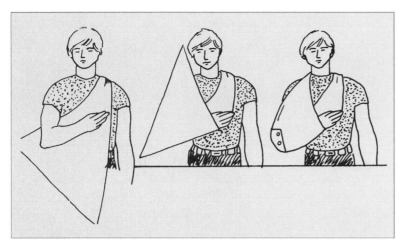

Figure 7-9
The arm sling supports the forearm and hand. It is one of the most common bandages.

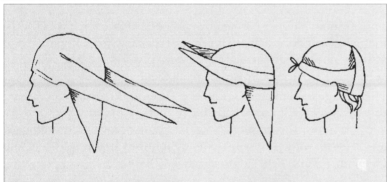

Figure 7-10
The scalp bandage covers and protects head wounds.

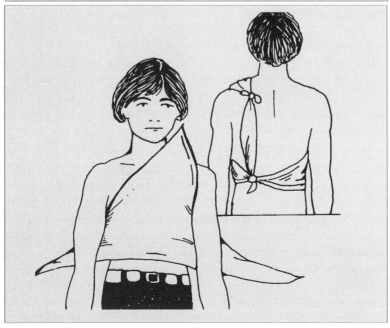

Figure 7-11
The chest bandage requires at least one large triangular bandage and one smaller bandage.

Figure 7-12
Butterfly bandages can be
made from adhesive tape.
These are useful for closing
wounds.

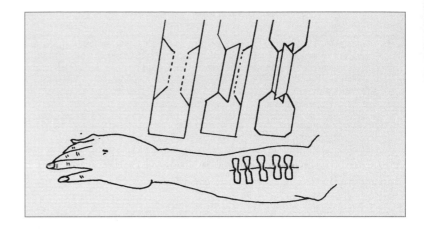

Figure 7-12
Butterfly bandages can be made from adhesive tape. These are useful for closing wounds.

objects, may hamper the healing process. However, it is obvious that in the outdoors, sterile items and spotless conditions are not always immediately available. When speed is the primary concern, use the cleanest material available.

Bandages are meant to hold dressings and splints in position, to act as slings, to assist in the reduction of swelling, and to support injured areas such as ankles. Bandaging is something of an art form, with almost as many delightful variations as origami (see Fig. 7-5 and Figs. 7-8 through 7-12).

TRANSPORTATION

Transporting the victim to medical facilities or, alternatively, bringing aid to the victim, is part and parcel of any serious first aid situation. The technique used and approach taken will depend in part on the extent of the injury, the nature of the injury, medical expertise available on-site, the distance to a medical facility, and the accessability of the location.

If the injury is not severe, it is usually easiest to transport the victim, no matter if the egress point is near or far. However, with more serious injuries, it is often best to bring medical aid to the scene, particularly if medical aid is not too distant. A critical question to be addressed when determining whether to transport or bring aid to the scene is whether or not transportation is likely to increase the severity of the injury. As discussed earlier in this chapter, transporting victims with neck or back injuries increases the risk of severe damage up to and including paralysis. In these cases, bringing aid to the scene is almost always preferred. On the other hand, there are locations where medical aid would not be accessible within a reasonable period of time. Transportation must then be carried out by the rescuers. In these situations, a knowledge of evacuation techniques is indispensable. Litters can be built out of wood or camping equipment such a as pack frames. A canoe can be used as a stable vehicle for transportation. Where complete immobilization is required, there are specific techniques for backboard use. These techniques can only be learned with considerable practice under the tutelage of a competent instructor.

SUMMARY

Wilderness emergency care is a broad field of study and opinions as to what constitutes appropriate care under what conditions change over time. No two situations are exactly the same and, as a result, no two treatments will be completely alike. Good training, coupled with practice and refresher courses will enable the rescuer to provide the most competent up-to-date medical care to accident victims. A book can only serve as a reference. Simulated practice under the guidance of an experienced teacher is required.

ADDITIONAL SOURCES

- *First Aid*, The Saint John Ambulance Society
- Henderson, J. (1978). *Emergency Medical Guide.* New York, McGraw Hill.
- Wilkerson, J. A. (1985). *Medicine for Mountaineering* (3rd Ed.). Seattle, The Mountaineers.
- Zydlo, S. M. & Hill, J. A. (Eds.). (1989). *The American Medical Association Handbook of First Aid and Medical Care.* New York: Random House.

When packed correctly, even
ridiculously large loads can be

8
Backpacking and Canoeing

Everyone lived on bear meat for a long time.
That's the way it goes: Monster one minute, food the
next.

Kiakshuk, Inuit Hunter and Author

Most campers, novice and experienced, tend to plan and
make their major trips during the summer, spring and
fall. In these seasons, backpacking and canoeing are the
two most popular types of extended, outdoor camping activities.
Accordingly, this chapter first focuses on backpacks: how they
are designed, how to select one, and how to pack one, and then
goes on to examine the various materials, processes, and designs
associated with canoe construction. The chapter concludes with
an overview of canoeing techniques.

BACKPACKING

If you are to enjoy backpacking, you must have two important
items: a correctly fitted and balanced backpack, and comfortable
footwear. Great food, lovely scenery, splendid companions are
wonderful additions to a backpacking trip, but all can be for
naught if a backpack is uncomfortable or when feet are rubbed
raw. Physical needs and comfort have to be achieved before a
trip can be enjoyed fully. This doesn't mean that there shouldn't
ever be sore muscles and cold, uncomfortable days; however, a
basic level of comfort is necessary for all but the most stoic of
campers. Backpacks come in a variety of shapes, sizes, and
designs. Each is suitable for a particular set of conditions and
body types. The trick is to sort out your needs, and find the
backpack that will most closely meet those needs.(The reader is
directed to Chapter Four for a discussion of hiking footwear.)

Sharing a trail snack with a friend.

EXTERNAL FRAME BACKPACKS

External frame backpacks are the most common packs used by hikers for overnight trips. The external frame provides a rigid support that coordinates and distributes weight. An external frame is the best design for very heavy loads, and it tends to be cooler since the pack doesn't actually rest against the back. The key questions to ask when considering an external frame backpack are: "does the frame fit my body and is the pack durable? "

Some external frames are straight, while others are curved, usually in the shape of an "S." The "S" shape is designed to follow the spine, for a contoured fit. Other frame designs such as the "hip wrap" and "figure 8" are not as common as the "S" shape, but they have certain advantages for some body types. Generally speaking, the packframe that rides closest to your body is the best. Some packframes have extensions on the bottom that allow you to stand them upright when unsupported. This can be helpful if it doesn't obstruct access to pocket areas or interfere with loading the pack.

Most backpack frames are made of aluminum. However, magnesium, plastic, and, very occasionally, wood, have been used by manufacturers. Strength is the key characteristic. Stand the frame on one corner and apply as much pressure as you can to the opposite corner. This will simulate the abuse your backpack will take when you swing the fully loaded pack off your shoulders and it bounces on bedrock. While applying full body weight to the frame, look closely to see if there are any signs of overstressing or weak welds. Some manufacturers guarantee their frames, but this will be of little comfort if the frame breaks on a trip. Most welded frames have little or no "give". Some "give" in the frame can be good. It indicates a degree of flexibility under pressure. Heliarc welding, used by some of the better frame manufacturers, is usually associated with a very strong frame. Some pack frames are adjustable, others come in a variety of sizes.

The frame of a loaded external frame backpack, should not touch your body. The only body contact points should be the straps and the horizontal webbing. This is why the horizontal crossbars must be curved out and away from the body. The frame webbing should be adjustable, porous, and wide enough to spread the pressure across your back. The shoulder straps should be fully adjustable. It helps if the straps are easy to adjust while you are wearing the pack. Above all, the straps must have a strong adjustment mechanism, one that will not slip under heavy loads, causing the pack to list to one side or the other.

Both the shoulder straps and the hip belt need to be well padded. Some hip belts are made of one continuous piece of material attached to several points on the backpack frame and fully encircling the backpacker. Others are two piece belts, with each piece attached to one side of the frame. The advantage of the one piece belt is that it surrounds the entire waist and upper hip area. This provides better distribution of the weight. A one-hand quick release system on the hip belt is helpful, especially if you fall into an icy stream or encounter a bear.

Gauging the fit of the frame in relation to your body is best done with a mirror or an experienced friend. Unfortunately, you can't always believe salespeople since some have never done any serious backpacking. The shoulder straps should come up and over the shoulder and go straight to the pack. The hip belt should come across the top of the hips. The primary purpose of the hip belt is to spread the weight across your hips whereas the primary purpose of the shoulder straps is to provide balance. Using the hip belt to carry most of the weight helps avoid compression of the spine. Shoulder straps will take some of the weight, but it should be possible to almost slip them off and carry the full weight via the hip belt. If the hip belt has to rise up from the pack to reach the hips, and the shoulder straps go from the shoulders up to the pack, then the pack is far too large. If, on the other hand, the hip belt is at the stomach and the shoulder straps fall down to the pack, then it is too small. A comfortable fit is very important.

The packsack itself is what most people spend their time fiddling and fussing over. The stitching should be checked to see if it is haphazard or neat and precise. How many stitches are there to the centimetre (inch)? Are the pressure points reinforced? Storm flaps may be desirable, though some manufacturers disagree. They argue that if you are going to use a waterproof pack cover—something that I highly recommend—then why bother with waterproofing the pack? Others argue that stormflaps and a waterproof coating will protect the pack contents in the event that your pack cover is damaged.

Most packs are top loading; however, front loading packs are available and some backpackers prefer them. A front loader allows for easy access to any part of the pack with a minimum of fuss. With a top loading pack, you have to take most things out in order to get to the items at the bottom. The better front loading packs will have compression straps running across the front in order to reduce the pressure on the zippers. Top loaders have the advantage of having no zippers on the main compartments.

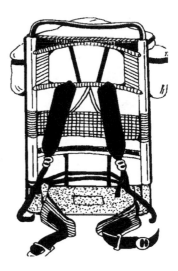

Figure 8-1
External Frame Backpack

EQUIPMENT TIP

Comfort is the most important characteristic of a backpack.

When the weather turns bad, effective rain gear is critical.

Choosing the right size backpack is difficult. It's important to remember that the frame size should correspond to body size, whereas the packsack size will be determined by the length and type of trips planned. If you plan weekend jaunts with the occasional four or five day trip thrown in, then you will not need a very large packsack. On the other hand, if serious expeditions of three to four weeks or more is your style, then you will be looking for an expedition capacity packsack. Small backpacks typically have a total volume of something in the neighbourhood of 55,000 cu.cm. (3,500 cu.in.); large backpacks will be 94,000 cu.cm. (6,000 cu.in.) and larger.

INTERNAL FRAME BACKPACKS

EQUIPMENT TIP

Internal frame backpacks are best suited for climbing and skiing.

Internal frame packs have become very popular during the last few years. They are a compromise between the external frame backpacks and soft packs. Internal frame backpacks bring the pack closer to your body and conventional wisdom argues that this makes them best for climbing and skiing activities. In these packs, internal stays are used to strengthen and shape the pack. These stays may be vertical or in the pattern of an "X." In some packs, these stays can be removed from the bag and adjusted, usually by simply bending them, to match the shape of your back. Some manufacturers have been experimenting with adjustable lumbar pads. Internal frame packs are a more specialized type of pack requiring greater expertise to pack and carry. Often they will have a variety of compression straps that permit overall adjustment of the bag size.

SOFT BACKPACKS

Soft backpacks, those with no frame whatsoever, are becoming rare, though they are still more common in Europe than in North America. Typically, soft packs are used by serious ski campers and mountaineers who need a completely flexible backpack. Similar in some respects to internal frame packs, soft packs normally have compression straps that allow the size and shape of the pack to be adjusted. In this way the pack can be modified in order to prevent equipment in a partially filled pack from bouncing around and throwing the hiker off balance. (The Duluth bag, a soft pack used for canoe tripping, is discussed later in this chapter.)

DAY PACKS

These are the nifty little sacks that campers carry on day outings while hiking, canoeing, cross-country skiing or snow-shoeing. Day packs are great for carrying trail food, maps, a ski tip replacement, rainwear and a variety of other little necessities. Frameless, the full weight of the day pack is carried with the shoulder straps. The waist strap simply prevents the pack from flopping around. Some day packs have a sternum strap (across the chest) to add additional stability. A wide range of day packs have flooded the market: some are large, while others are quite small; some are made of thick cordura, while others are coated nylon. Try several on before purchasing one, and be sure you fill it with at least some weight in order to get a real feel for how it will perform out on the trail. As with other packs, neat seams, waterproofing, ease of opening, quality buckles, storm-flaps and padding on the shoulder straps are things to look for.

BACKPACKS FOR CHILDREN

Suitable packs for children are very hard to find. If you locate one that fits, that factor alone may be the determining characteristic. When hiking with children, it's wise to have them carry at least some weight since that is the only way to get them accustomed to one of the important realities of hiking and, at the same time, make them full participants. In my experience, most kids will gladly volunteer to carry something.

If you are the least bit handy with wood and tools, I recommend that you consider building a wooden carrying frame as an alternative to investing in a pack that will be quickly outgrown. A piece of softwood, drilled with enough holes so that a sleeping

SAFETY TIP

When crossing a fast-flowing stream, release your pack's hip straps. If you fall, it will be much easier to get rid of your pack.

EQUIPMENT TIP

Children's backpacks shouldn't be loaded to more than 20-25% of their body weight.

Figure 8-2
A pack that rides high and close to the body allows for greater economy of effort.

bag and clothes can be tied to it, is not too difficult for almost anybody to make. Add shoulder straps, a plastic rain cover, and you have a packboard. It's important to get good straps since they will make a world of difference. Neoprene strips can be used to cushion the effect of the board on the shoulders and seat. As the child grows, simply change the position of the straps, or, if necessary, get a bigger board.

Care should be taken when loading a child's backpack. Adults may be able to carry 1/4 to 1/3 of their body weight; however, children, no matter how eager, should be restricted to the lower figure or even less. First and foremost, the trip should be an enjoyable experience.

CARRYING COMFORT

As stressed in the preceding paragraphs, comfort is the most important factor to consider when purchasing a backpack. There are many styles and types of backpacks, each of them suited for a particular purpose. If possible, borrow or rent several different types of backpacks before buying one. You may be able to do this through a store, a college course, or as a club member. By trying out someone else's pack, you will have a chance to narrow the field. When shopping for a backpack, don't be afraid to try on each one that appeals to you. Before the final purchase is made, bring your other equipment to the store to make sure it fits in and on the pack.

In order to carry a pack efficiently—this means using as little effort as possible—try to stand as straight as possible (see Fig. 8–2). Far more effort is expended when bent forward. The heaviest items in the pack should be as close as possible to an imaginary straight line running down through the body from the head to the feet, and as high as possible. Most frame packs tend to curve in at the upper back. Therefore, packing heavy items near the top brings the weight closer to the imaginary line. Heavy weights carried low and away from the body require you to compensate by leaning forward. An exception to this approach are situations where, for example, you are climbing a precarious route or a crossing tiny bridge. In these cases, heavy weight at the top of the pack may create a balance problem.

CANOEING

The art and enjoyment of wilderness travel by water is part of the Canadian heritage. Indians, Innuit and Voyageurs have left us techniques and traditions of water travel. The canoe, and to a lesser extent the kayak, provide many Canadians with an escape from urban areas, and a chance to experience a simpler, though in some ways more demanding, way of life.

CANOE MATERIALS AND CONSTRUCTION

Canoes are constructed in several different ways, with a host of different materials. In spite of their differences, the basic design is the same. This section describes the most popular canoe types, according to the materials from which they are constructed.

Wood and canvas canoes are very traditional. These canoes appeal to wilderness travellers who appreciate the balance, feel, and aesthetic beauty that only a wood canoe can provide. Wood and canvas canoes are constructed from strips of wood, usually cedar, that run from the bow to the stern. Placed 3–5 cm. (1–2 in.) apart, wooden ribs run at right angles to the strips. These ribs reinforce the canoe. The top of the sides of the canoe are finished with gunwales. The gunwales give the canoe its shape and also serve to hold the canvas in place. Canvas is stretched across the outside of the canoe in order to waterproof it. Thin coats of canvas filler are used to tighten and seal the canvas. The sides of the canoe are further strengthened and held in place by thwarts and

A good lifejacket is a canoeist's best friend.

seats. The keel, though not found on all wood and canvas canoes, is the thin piece of wood running along the outside bottom of the canoe. Most canoes have small decks on each end, the bow deck and the stern deck. Stembands, thin metal strips on the outside of each end of the canoe, protect the bow and the stern from minor bumps. If you look under the decks of a wood and canvas canoe you will see the inner stembands. These are strong strips of wood, likely ash, that reinforce the ends of the canoe. The wood and canvas canoe is constructed from the inside of the canoe working towards the outside, over a mould. Thus, the inner stembands and the inwales—these are the inside gunwales—are attached to a frame or mould, after which the ribs are steamed, bent over the mould, and then nailed to the inwales. The strips are added next, then the canoe is taken off the mould. The canoe is finished by adding the canvas, seats, decks, thwarts, and outwales (see Fig. 8–3).

Stripper canoes, another type of wood canoe, have become very popular during the last few years. Strippers are built by gluing and stapling thin strips of wood over a mould built in the shape of a canoe. When the basic canoe shape has been constructed, the new boat is removed from the mould, and is then fibreglassed, both inside and outside. Fancy designs are made by combining red and white cedar strips. Inwales, outwales, seats, thwarts, and decks are added towards the end of the construction.

The building of both wood and canvas canoes and stripper canoes is extremely labour intensive. For this reason many of these canoes are constructed in basements, garages, or even in backyards, by amateur builders who treat the work as a labour of love, not as a profit making venture. There are relatively few professional builders of wood canoes because the hefty prices have diminished demand. Wood and canvas canoes are very fragile. They need lots of tender, loving care.

Aluminum canoes became popular during the 1950s and 1960s. This popularity has sagged slightly in the 80s and 90s, largely because of increased competition and overall dampening of prices. However, outfitters still have a preference for aluminum canoes because of their durability. You can bash an aluminum canoe for years; it just keeps coming back for more. A drawback with aluminum canoes is the fact that they stick to rocks when white water canoeing. This may sound ridiculous if you have never experienced it, but aluminum tends to hang on rocks, whereas fibreglass and Royalex (discussed later) will slide off.

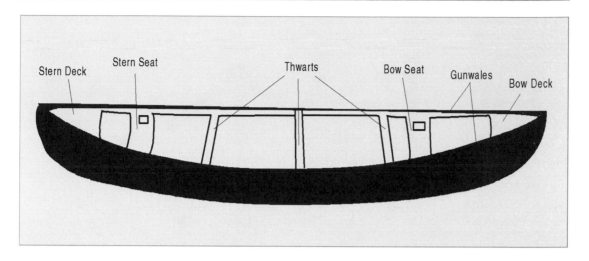

Figure 8-3
Canoe terms

The thickness and temper of the aluminum used in canoes varies considerably. Grumman manufactures very good aluminum canoes, including flatwater models and specially strengthened white water models. Grumman white water models have shoe keels, a short, flat, wide strip of aluminum, instead of the standard deep water keel. Alumicraft is another manufacturer of high quality aluminum canoes. Some aluminum canoes may come with a guarantee against puncture or "rip" damage. However, there is usually at least one qualification to these guarantees, such as "the canoe must be upright and occupied at the time of the damage." One of my canoeing partners had a brand new aluminum white water canoe on the river for less than two hours, following which an engagement with rocks and a waterfall reduced the canoe to scraps of metal. He sent for a refund, but was bluntly refused. I have heard canoeists lodge a variety of complaints against aluminum canoes, including the noise they make when hitting rocks, glare off the bow deck, and the fact that they can get quite cold when the water is chilly. Personally, after several thousand kilometres of travel in aluminum canoes, I can't say that I found these issues to be of great importance.

It's likely that there are more manufacturers of *fibreglass canoes* than any other single type. Fibreglass canoes are more quickly constructed than wood and canvas boats, and they don't require the capital investment inherent in the manufacture of aluminum canoes. Because there are so many fibreglass canoes on the market it is difficult to evaluate their construction technique and design.

Figure 8-4
More canoe terms

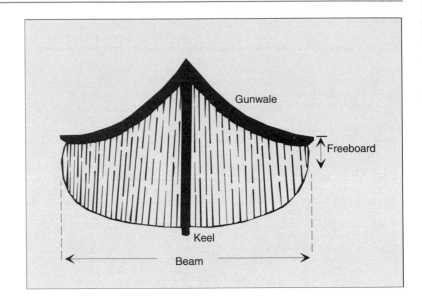

The "chopped glass process" is one of the most common techniques for working with fibreglass. In this technique, a combination of fibreglass threads and epoxy is blown into the mould with a "chopper gun." (Wood and canvas canoes are built around the outside of a mould, whereas fibreglass and other cloth canoes are built in a mould.) After the chopped glass sets in the mould, the canoe is popped out, then finished with decks, seats, thwarts, and flotation. The chopped glass technique produces non-resilient canoes that will not take the tough treatment and, in some cases, abuse that you expect a tripping canoe to handle. For this reason, chopped glass canoes are not recommended. In most cases they are quite inexpensive, have mediocre designs, and are built for the cottage market where they will be paddled out to the raft two or three times a summer.

If you are considering purchasing a fibreglass canoe, it should be a model that has been "laid up by hand." This means that fibreglass cloth has been laid in the mould and resin applied to the cloth. In this process, excess resin is skimmed out of the mould as several layers of cloth are established. The number of layers of cloth, the type of cloth and resin, and the skill of the craftsperson will affect the strength, weight, and durability of the final product. Now, here is where it becomes a bit confusing. Even after you rule out chopped glass construction, the variation in laminated hull canoes is substantial. First, there are different resins. Polyester is usually the least expensive, followed by vinylester and epoxy resins. And recently, polyester and

Making a few miles after the rain.

fibreglass cloth have been interwoven or otherwise combined to create proprietary layups. A proprietary layup is a combination of materials that is specific to a particular manufacturer. Nylon and fibreglass combinations have become particular favourites. The goal of the manufacturer is to create a light, tough, tear resistant canoe that is easy to construct. Competitive pricing is also important. There are many laminated hull canoes with different combinations of cloths and resins but, naturally, price is closely related to quality.

Since the late 70s, *Kevlar*™ cloth has been used by many high-tech canoe manufacturers. To the uninitiated, Kevlar looks very similar to fibreglass. However, its strength and high tear resistance, along with its light weight, make it far superior. Manufactured by Dupont, Kevlar is also used for the construction of such items as aircraft parts, flak jackets, and body armour. Some manufacturers combine Kevlar and nylon, while others combine Kevlar and graphite. The downside of Kevlar is its very high cost. A Kevlar canoe may cost twice as much as an ordinary hand-laid fibreglass canoe. Further, Kevlar is a difficult material to work with.

Royalex™ is a patented plastic material produced by Uniroyal. It became popular for canoe construction during the 1970s. Royalex is a sandwich construction of alternating layers of foam sheets and ABS (acrylonitrile-butadiene-styrene) bonded together, with a top and bottom layer of high strength vinyl. This construction has a "memory." When a Royalex canoe hits a rock or other hard object, the canoe will flex to absorb the shock, then

CANOEING TIP

Royalex canoes are very popular among white water wilderness canoeists.

Rubber bands cut from inner tubes have been used to fasten the paddles in place, which are th[en] used as a yoke. The life jacket provides comfortable cushioning.

return to its original state. (If stressed beyond the memory capability, it may, however, deform to a new shape.) Disadvantages of Royalex include its weight and price. Royalex canoes are extremely popular with wilderness white water canoeists. Although quite heavy, the durability of the material makes it extremely difficult to critically damage, something that is very appealing as you venture down a set of rapids in the high arctic. *Oltonar*™ is an ABS construction similar to Royalex. It is produced by Uniroyal for the Old Town Canoe Company.

Polyethylene, in many formulas, is another plastic used for canoe construction. One example is *Ram-X*™, a single sheet polyethylene produced by the Coleman Company. Although the Coleman hull design is not great, their canoes are manoeuvrable in white water, very strong, and cost far less than Royalex canoes. Unfortunately polyethylene canoes tend to weigh even more than Royalex canoes.

CANOE DESIGN

Boat design can't be fully addressed within the space of a paragraph or two; however, it isn't difficult to describe a few basic concepts that you can put to work when examining different canoes. First, and most important, is canoe length. Let me be blunt: *don't buy a short canoe!* The only advantages short canoes have are the ability to turn corners faster and the fact that you carry a few pounds less on a portage. Longer canoes have a greater carrying capacity and, assuming the same width, are faster and easier to paddle. Longer canoes also tend to track better, this means it's easier to keep them going in a straight line. I recommend a minimum canoe length of 16 feet, preferably 17 feet.

A common misconception is that wide canoes are more stable than narrow ones. This isn't necessarily so. In canoeing there are two types of stability: initial stability, which is the tendency of the boat to feel tippy; and final stability, which is the tendency for the boat to capsize. Wide hulls tend to have good initial stability, but poor final stability. Though this isn't true of all wide boats, most wide hulls are designed to favour initial stability at the expense of final stability. Narrow hulls tend to have greater final stability, trading off initial stability in order to minimize the likelihood of capsize. I have a 17' wood and canvas canoe that has a narrow, oval design. Whenever novices use this canoe, they get very excited because the slightest movement causes it to rock. They have difficulty believing the fact that this boat has very good final stability; it rocks a lot but it remains upright. The boat is easy to

CANOEING TIP

Wide canoes are not necessarily the most stable.

Canoe Comparisons

TYPE	LENGTH	WEIGHT	ADVANTAGES	DISADVANTAGES
Wood and Canvas	16'	74 lb.	Quiet; good performance; high aesthetic value.	Vulnerable to rocks and easy to damage; expensive; requires some maintenance.
Aluminium	17'	78 lb.	Durable; no maintenance required.	Noisy; conducts cold; sticks to rocks.
Fibreglass	16'	65 lb.	Easy to repair; light; relatively inexpensive; excellent designs to choose from.	Not as strong as aluminium, Kevlar, Royalex, or polyethylene.
Kevlar	16'	53 lb.	high tear resistance; very light; excellent designs to choose from.	Expensive.
Royalex	17'	80 lb.	Very durable; slips off rocks in white water.	Very heavy; expensive.
Polyethylene	17'	84 lb.	Very durable; slips off rocks in white water; less expensive than Royalex.	Mediocre designs; extremely heavy.

Weights and lengths will vary depending on the manufacturer and model.

paddle, relatively fast and, after you get used to it, a pleasure to own. Better to own a boat that is easy to paddle, will carry all your gear and still have plenty of freeboard (distance from the water to the top of the side of the canoe), than to own a boat that gives you a false sense of security and is slow to paddle.

Depth of the canoe is the third factor to consider. Along with length and width, depth contributes to carrying capacity. Generally, you want to have enough depth to give you the freeboard and carrying capacity you require, but not much more. If the canoe is deeper than you require, winds will tend to push the canoe, most often in the wrong direction at the worst of times, and it will be harder to find a comfortable paddling position.

The general shape of the canoe is very important. The end-to-end curve along the bottom of the boat is referred to as the *rocker*. If you sit the canoe on dry land and push down on the stern deck, a boat with a lot of rocker will come up at the bow. This is because only a small section of the middle of the canoe is on the ground. If the boat has little or no rocker, pushing on one end or the other will have little effect since the entire length of the canoe will be in contact with the ground. Boats with a lot of rocker turn faster. This makes them good for narrow rivers and white water paddling where sharp turns must be made. Boats with little or no rocker tend to track better.

Canoes with a sharp bow entry line track better with less initial water resistance than do canoes with blunt bows. The only purpose a blunt bow can serve is to act as a bumper. Some canoes widen out quite quickly, while others achieve their full width only at the middle of the canoe. In fact, in the case of racing boats, full width isn't achieved until aft of the mid-point. Generally, the slower the canoe widens, the easier it passes through the water. However, the cost is in carrying capacity and stability. The cross-sectional shape of the canoe is also very important. Variations run from flat bottom boats, which have high initial stability and virtually no final stability, to round bottom boats, which have great final stability but no initial stability.

Most high quality tripping canoes do not have keels, though aluminum canoes are an exception to this rule. Some canoeists argue that keels help the canoe track, but it is more likely that keels are simply a holdover from the days when they protected wood and canvas canoe bottoms from stray rocks.

Clearly, as with all other camping equipment, canoe choice is dependent on individual priorities. Decide what you plan to do with your canoe, select the appropriate type, and then go shopping. If you need a general recreation canoe for trips of three or four days twice a year, don't get drawn into purchasing a Kevlar boat, unless you think twenty pounds less weight is worth an extra $800. If you are a traditionalist, look carefully at wood and canvas canoes, both new and used. If a friend has an old aluminum canoe that is not in use, make an offer.

Finally, canoes should never be left unattended in water. Always take them out of the water and empty any standing water by flipping them over. Long term storage is best done by resting the weight of the canoe on its gunwales either by putting it upside down on sawhorses or by hanging it upside down from rafters. Any canoe worth buying is worth looking after.

On the water shortly after the ice goes out.

EMERGENCY REPAIRS

It is possible to do serious damage to any type of canoe, no matter how tough or indestructible the salesperson promised it would be. Therefore, if you are on an extended trip in a remote area, it is important to be able to effect basic emergency repairs.

The skin of wood and canvas canoes is fragile. However, ripped canvas, the result of a collision with a rock or other underwater obstruction, need not be as problematic as you might first think. Using a sharp knife, cut at right angles to the tear in order to make an "L" shape. If the initial tear is not a straight line, make your new cut in such a manner as to permit you to slip a patch under the canvas. However, before you slip the patch under, soak it in a strong fabric glue such as liquid cement. When the first patch dries, add a second, slightly larger patch over the entire rip. Larger tears should be sewn tight after the first patch is applied, but before the glue is dry. Obviously, you need to carry extra canvas and some glue in order to carry out this type of repair, though I have seen some canoeists use nylon combined with sap from a pine tree. Damage to the wood in a wood and canvas canoe is very difficult to repair in the field. You are probably best to simply patch the canvas as best you can and look after wood repairs when you return home.

If you paddle an aluminum canoe, dents are likely to be the most serious damage with which you will have to deal. Most dents can be fixed by placing a flat piece of wood over the convex side of the dent and striking the wood with a rock. If this doesn't work, try laying the damaged area of the canoe on sand and pounding the dent from the inside of the canoe. The sand will act as a mould. A rubber mallet is really helpful for this, but I have never seen anyone actually carry one on a trip. Leaks in an aluminum canoe tend to occur at rivets. Sand the rivet area with emery cloth and then apply a dab of regular epoxy glue. If you have managed to tear the skin open in an aluminum canoe, then you have inflicted serious damage. In these cases, use duct tape to patch the boat as best you can. No canoe trip should leave home without duct tape and epoxy glue, their uses are endless.

Most fibreglass canoe repairs can be handled with duct tape; however, if more extensive repairs are required, polyester cloth, resin and catalyst may be needed. The repair is effected by mixing the catalyst and resin, saturating the cloth and the surface of the canoe, then applying the patch and letting it set for as long as possible. If possible, try to match the resins used in manufacture with those used for repair. Though you may be loathe to carry cloth, resin, and catalyst, it will be worth its weight in gold if you have a serious accident in an isolated area. Kevlar canoes can be patched in the same way.

Royalex and polyethylene canoes are extremely difficult to damage. If you need to patch one of these canoes, you may also have to patch the paddlers. Duct tape is the best bet (for the canoe, not the canoeists). If duct tape fails, kevlar cloth patches may work.

CANOE PADDLES

There are many different paddle shapes and each has its devotees. I argue that length, strength, weight, grip, and balance are more important than shape.

In order to check the length of the paddle, hold it over your head with one hand on the grip and the other hand on the throat. The angle formed by your elbows should be 90°. If the angle is greater than 90° the shaft of the paddle is too long; if it is less than 90° the shaft is too short. If the paddle is too long or too short, it will be uncomfortable to work with. Remember, it is not the length of the blade that you are checking, it's the length of the shaft that is important.

A good paddle should last a long time, even if you subject it to regular abuse. I have a Clements softwood laminated paddle that has seen more than 3,500 very tough kilometres (2,000 miles). I tend to use my paddles to shove off from shore, stop the boat when I am too lazy to do it properly, and fend off rocks at the last minute. My Clements paddle has lots of fibreglass and epoxy over cracks and bruises, but it is still a fine paddle. If you buy a good paddle, it will last. If you buy a cheap paddle, it will likely break, just when you really need it.

Paddles are made from hardwoods and softwoods. My preference is for softwood paddles because they are lighter. Most softwood paddles are laminated to give them strength. I have heard some salespeople suggest that laminated paddles are weaker than single piece hardwood paddles. However, the truth is that a laminated paddle might break, but it will almost never break at or because of the lamination. I have a few hardwood paddles that I have carved. It is pleasure to paddle with them, provided I am not going more than 50 kilometres (30 miles).

The paddle grip and the balance of the paddle will be related to the style and shape. Choose a paddle that feels comfortable while paddling. Some people prefer the "T" grip that is common to racing and synthetic paddles, while others find this grip quite

CANOEING TIP

Shape may be the least important characteristic of a paddle.

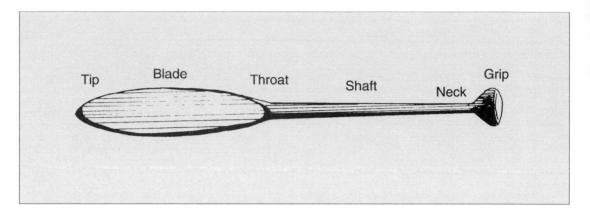

Tip   Blade   Throat   Shaft   Neck   Grip

Figure 8-5
Parts of a paddle

uncomfortable and opt for the standard palm grip. Blade widths vary from paddle to paddle. A wide blade requires considerable effort on each stroke, while a narrow blade may allow you to pull harder and more comfortably over a long haul.

Bent shaft paddles have become popular during the last few years. Initially these were used by racers, but some wilderness canoeists have adopted them. I recommend trying one out before you plunk down the cash. These paddles are quite expensive and require a different stroke action.

Paddles should never be left standing tip down in water. This will soon lead to cracks in the blades. Instead, paddles should be dried off and hung by the neck when not in use. If that is not possible, leave the paddle standing butt end down. Over time, paddles will acquire a salty flavour from the sweat off your hands. For this reason they should never be left where porcupines, who love gnawing on salty objects, can get to them. The same is true for leather pack straps and tumps.

CANOE PACKS AND WANNIGANS

The traditional canoe pack is a soft canvas bag with shoulder straps and a tumpline. The tumpline wraps around your forehead and takes pressure off your shoulders. The term Duluth bag appears to have become a generic name for this type of canoe pack. External frame packs are not used for canoeing because the frame makes it difficult to fit the pack between and under the canoe thwarts. Internal frame packs have a similar problem, though not as pronounced. By comparison, Duluth bags mould themselves to the shape of the canoe.

Wannigans are wooden boxes with tumps. Most wannigans do not have shoulder straps. Instead, the wannigan is carried entirely by the tump. Wannigans represent a tradeoff between discomfort and convenience. Though you may find wannigans difficult to carry, food and cooking gear can be carried in a very orderly fashion. Instead of having to open and empty a pack or two every time you want to make a snack or cook a meal, the wannigan lid flips off easily and most items can be quickly located. In my experience, wannigans make meal time a dream. I don't go canoe camping without one. Wannigan lids can be used as serving trays, food stored in a wannigan never gets crushed, and you even have a comfortable and handy seat. Most wannigans are designed with latches of some sort in order to prevent small animals from walking off with your food at night. There are very few commercially made wannigans, largely because it isn't too difficult to make your own. Softwood is best since the goal is to make it as light as possible. A nice size is 650 mm. x 450 mm. x 450 mm. (26 in. x 18 in. x 18 in.).

PERSONAL FLOTATION DEVICES

It is sheer stupidity to go canoeing without a good personal flotation device (PFD). Even on flat water for a short distance, life jackets should be worn, or at least should be within easy reach.

When shopping for a PFD don't go to the bargain basement store. You will never regret buying a quality PFD. The PFD should keep your head up and out of the water, even if you are unconscious. My PFD is thick and warm enough to be used as a vest when it gets cold. It also has a collar that will flip up and protect the back of my neck and head if I find myself bouncing down a set of rapids. Remember, your PFD may save your life, but only if you wear it.

CARRYING, LAUNCHING AND PORTAGING A CANOE

Many canoeists transport their canoes on the roof of a car or van. In order to do this safely, the roof racks must be strong. In some cases, roof racks that come as standard equipment, and inexpensive roof racks sold through department stores, are simply not strong enough to do the job. It's not so much the weight of the canoe, but strong winds and wind pressure generated by the speed of the vehicle that puts a great deal of stress on the roof rack. The last thing you want to see is your new canoe skidding down the asphalt at 100 km. (60 miles) per hour.

CANOEING TIP

Canoe trippers who use wannigans swear by them. And, they are very easy to construct.

Launching a canoe from shore is best done by two people. Have one person stand on each side and lift the canoe up by the gunwales. Then carry the canoe to the launch area, and ease one end into the water. As the canoe touches the water, ease it out further. It isn't a good idea to try and put the canoe in the water sideways, even from a dock.

Portaging is necessary when you have to carry the canoe from one water access point to another. Occasionally, you will see two people doubling up to carry a canoe. This is not recommended. It is almost impossible for two people to walk at the same gait over uneven ground without bumping, pulling, and pushing each other. Better to have one person carry the canoe for a short distance, then have the other person take over for a short distance, then revert back to the first person, and so on. If portaging seems like a lot of work, take a break. I used to work like a dog on portages in order to get everything across in one trip until I learned that there is lots to see and do while taking a break or walking back on a portage. Now, I don't go out of my way to take all the gear on one carry because, if I were to do so, I would miss getting a good look at the scenery.

CANOEING TIP

Tandem portaging of canoes is not recommended. It's better to carry solo and trade on and off with another person.

Although only one person should portage the canoe at any one time, it is easiest if two people prepare the canoe for portaging. This can be accomplished by two people swinging or lifting one end of the canoe up in the air upside down, leaving the other end on the ground. One person then holds the end of the canoe up in the air with arms extended. This is the *tepee position*. The second person, the one who is going to portage the canoe, gets under the canoe with shoulders beneath the centre thwart. This is close to the balance point of the canoe. When ready, the portager simply stands up straight and the person who is tepeeing the canoe gently releases it. The thwart will then rest on the shoulders of the portager. If you need to rest while travelling across the portage, look for a tree with a fork three to four metres (three to four yards) off the ground. If you slide the end of the canoe into the fork, or even across a branch, you can take a break while the tree holds the canoe in the teepee position. You then won't need two people to get the canoe back to a carrying position.

The canoe may be carried either stern first or bow first depending on personal preferences. If carried bow first, you will be slightly in front of the balance point and the front of the canoe will tend to rise. This makes it necessary to pull down as you grasp the gunwales. If carried stern first, you will have to push up

Some portages seem to be straight up.

Figure 8-6
Woods #100 Canoe Pack

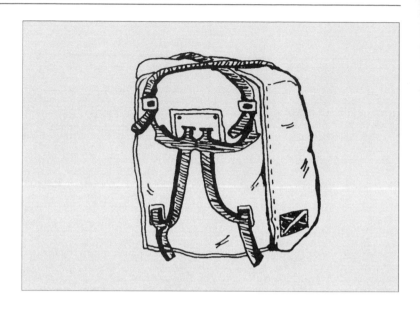

slightly on the gunwales. If the canoe has a built in yoke, as do many fibreglass models, you don't have a choice as to whether to carry the canoe bow or stern first. If you like to use a yoke, but the canoe is not equipped with one, a yoke can be fashioned with paddles (see Fig. 8-7). Lay two paddles running from bow to stern so that the blades of the paddles rest on the centre thwart while the shafts rest on the stern thwart (or bow thwart if you prefer to carry the canoe bow first). Spread the paddles so that your head will fit between the two blades. When carrying the canoe, the blades will rest on your shoulders. The paddles can be tied in this position with a few pieces of string, or sections of an old inner tube can be used like giant rubber bands to hold the paddles in place. If you are using the inner tube trick, slip circular pieces of an old inner tube—these should look like big thick rubber bands—over the grip of the paddle, around the stern thwart and over the grip again. Do the same for the blade of the paddle and the centre thwart. Once you have done both paddles, you should have a solid yoke. If you are using a yoke, make sure you leave enough room to get your head out of it if you suffer a fall. Whether using a yoke or not, most people find it useful to wrap a towel, blanket, or a life jacket around the shoulders in order to act as padding.

On occasion, you may find yourself alone, with no one to help tepee the canoe. Try putting the canoe on its side with the bottom resting against your legs. Grasp the centre thwart with your right hand near the gunwale. Take hold of the far gunwale with your

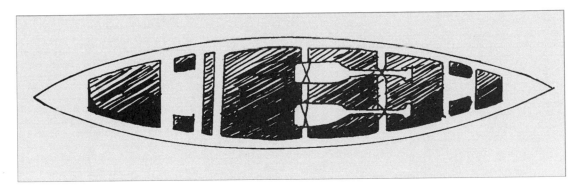

other hand, then roll the canoe up and over your head as you turn to your left. The centre thwart should end up resting on your shoulders. This manoeuvre takes a bit of practice, but in the end it requires more technique than brute strength.

Figure 8-7
Paddles lashed to act as a yoke.

CANOE TECHNIQUE

Getting into the canoe safely is a matter of common sense and practice. If there are two canoeists, one should steady the canoe while the other lays his paddle across the gunwales and steps into the middle of the canoe. While putting weight on the paddle, the first person into the canoe should walk down the centre of the boat until the correct spot is reached. The second person enters the canoe in the same fashion, while the person already onboard steadies the canoe and stays low.

When the canoe is paddled tandem (two canoeists), one person kneels in front of or sits on the bow seat while the other does the same at the stern seat. If there is a third paddler, he would kneel either in front of or behind the centre thwart depending on the balance of the canoe. For example, if the pack weight was evenly distributed and the person in the bow was very light, then the paddler in the middle (the midshipman) would sit in front of the centre thwart. Packs and wannigans should be placed in the canoe with great care. They go between the thwarts and should be packed as low in the canoe as possible. Normal practice includes lashing the packs into the canoe by looping one of the pack straps around a thwart or running a rope through the straps and tying it to the thwarts. If the canoe overturns, packs that have been lashed into the canoe don't drift off or slowly sink. Packs can be used to balance the canoe just as you might use the midshipman. When one person is paddling a canoe, the typical position is facing the stern, between the centre and bow thwarts.

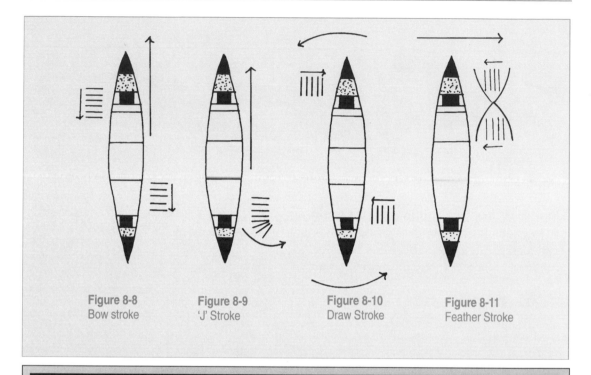

Figure 8-8
Bow stroke

Figure 8-9
'J' Stroke

Figure 8-10
Draw Stroke

Figure 8-11
Feather Stroke

Basic Canoe Strokes

In order to make the canoe go where you want it to go, you must master a few simple strokes. The short arrows indicate the direction of paddle thrust; the longer arrows indicate the canoe direction.

The *bow stroke* is the most basic. Simply reach forward with your paddle, dip it in the water, and draw it straight back (see Fig. 8–8). That's all there is to this stroke. A standard variation on the bow stroke is the reverse bow stroke or backwater stroke. Instead of pushing the water backward, you push it forward. If the bow stroke is practised by a paddler in the bow and a reverse bow stroke is practised by a paddler in the stern, the canoe will turn. This is the most simple method for two paddlers to turn the canoe over a short distance.

The *"J" stroke* is used to make the canoe go in a straight line (see Fig.8–9). The "J" stroke is practised by the stern paddler in tandem paddling and by solo canoeists. With the "J" stroke, the paddler starts with a normal bow stroke but turns the paddle just before reaching the termination point and then moves the paddle sideways at right angles to the canoe. The power surface of the paddle, which is the side that pushes the water, never changes.

The *draw stroke* moves the canoe sideways. The paddler reaches out from the canoe with the paddle, dips it into the water, and then pulls the paddle towards the canoe (see Fig.8–10). When the paddle reaches the side of the canoe, the paddler takes it out of the water and repeats the stroke.

The *figure 8 stroke* also moves the canoe sideways, but it's a little showier than the draw stroke (see Fig. 8–11). The paddle is pulled towards the canoe, slipped up sideways with downward pressure, pulled towards the canoe again, and then slipped up sideways with downward pressure to the starting position. The paddle never leaves the water and the two ends of the 8 are actually tiny draw strokes. The *feather stroke* is a variation where the paddle is simply moved through an arc at right angles to the canoe. Pressure on the power surface of the paddle is balanced by the pressure of the water coming off the paddle as it slips away from the trailing side. The power surface never changes.

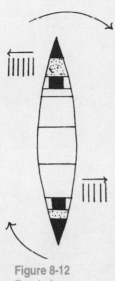

Figure 8-12
Pry stroke

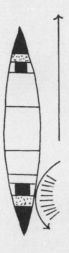

Figure 8-13
The 'C' Stroke pictured where
the solo canoeist sits behind
the bow seat facing the stern.

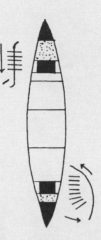

Figure 8-14
Indian Stroke

Basic Canoe Strokes

The *pry stroke* is simply the reverse of the draw stroke (see Fig. 8–12). The paddle is placed in the water, almost against the side of the canoe, then levered or pushed against the gunwale so that the power surface of the blade pushes water away from the boat. The canoeist then turns the paddle sideways and slips it back through the water to the start position and repeats the stroke.

The *"C" stroke*, used in heavy weather to keep the canoe tracking correctly, is normally practised by a solo canoeist or a bow pad-dler (see Fig. 8–13). The "C" stroke moves the canoe forward and prevents the bow from being blown downwind. It begins with a draw stroke done as far forward as possible, and, in a continuous movement, is followed by a "J" stroke with a very strong accent on the twist portion. If used by a bow paddler, the "J" part of the stroke is omitted. The "C" stroke is only used by the paddler on the windward side.

The *Indian stroke* is a "show" stroke (see Fig. 8–14). It can be combined with a bow stroke or a "J" stroke. At the end of the bow or "J" stroke, the pad-dle is turned sideways and slipped back to the start position while still in the water.

The bow, reverse bow, draw, pry and "J" are the primary strokes in canoe-ing. Most other strokes are combinations of these basic strokes. You need not know any other strokes in order to paddle with strength and certainty on flat water.

Running white water on the South Nahanni.

If Your Canoe Capsizes, Stay With It

As you practice and refine your canoeing technique, there is one important safety rule to keep in mind: *if your canoe capsizes, stay with it.* Every year many people drown after having abandoned their craft when it capsized. In many cases these people would have been saved had they stayed with their boat. Unless there is some immediate danger, you are almost certainly better off staying with the canoe, even if it is only a short distance from the shore.

RIVER TECHNIQUE

White water canoeing is very, very exciting. For many canoeists, white water is the *raison d'être.* This section briefly describes some white water canoeing techniques.

In order to control a canoe in fast flowing water, you must travel either faster or slower than the current. If you travel at the same speed as the current, and you are headed downstream, then you will have little or no control. Some canoeists opt to travel faster than the current. The problems with this approach are threefold: first, it is difficult to build up speed beyond the velocity of the current; second, every obstacle in the river approaches that much faster; and third, precision manoeuvring is difficult. For these reasons, most white water canoeists opt to slow the boat down, backpaddling in heavy water, unless the route is completely free of obstacles. By going slower, you have more time to scout the route and position the canoe appropriately.

As well as moving slowly, white water canoeists want to be able to move the canoe sideways in order to be positioned properly to shoot between and around rocks and other obstructions. By doing draws and prys, the bow paddler and the stern paddler can move the canoe across the current. However, in order to slow the boat down at the same time, the actual stroke often looks like a hybrid between back paddling and a pry or a draw. A common variation on the pry, usually practised by the bow paddler, is the *cross-bow draw.* In this stroke, the bow paddler reaches across the canoe, without changing hand position on the paddle, and pulls water towards the canoe. The reason for doing a cross-bow draw instead of a pry is the power in the stroke. Most paddlers do a much stronger cross-bow draw than a pry.

CANOEING TIP

Most white water canoeists opt to travel slower than the current.

Figure 8-15
While ferry gliding, the force of the current pushes the canoe downstream and across the river. Forward paddling minimizes the downstream movement, leaving only the sideways slippage. The short arrows indicate direction of paddle thrust.

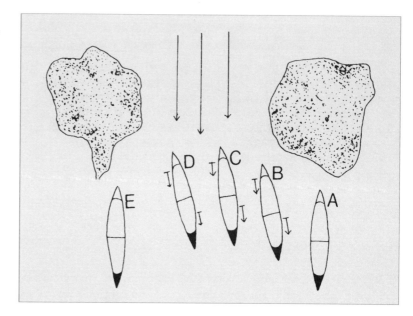

Figure 8-16
An eddy is formed by an obstruction in the river. Water tends to curl in behind the eddy, sometimes flowing back upstream.

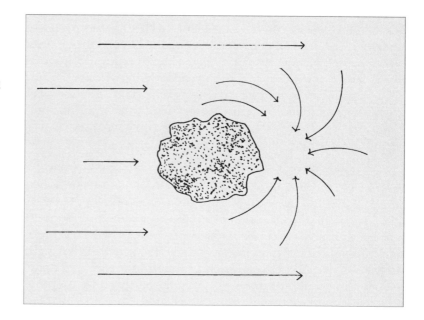

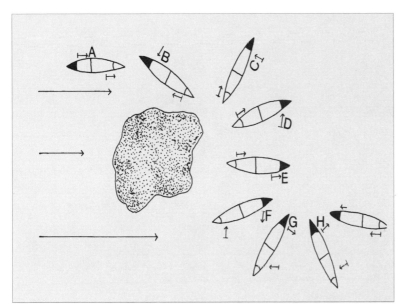

Figure 8-17
In order to pull into an eddy, the bow paddler reaches out and "draws" the bow into it. The stern paddler uses a draw stroke to swing the stern of the canoe around, minimizing the time during which the canoe is at right angles to the current. To move out of the eddy, the bow paddler does a strong draw or crossdraw which pulls the bow downstream. The stern paddler complements this with a strong pry or draw, forcing the canoe to pivot downstream.

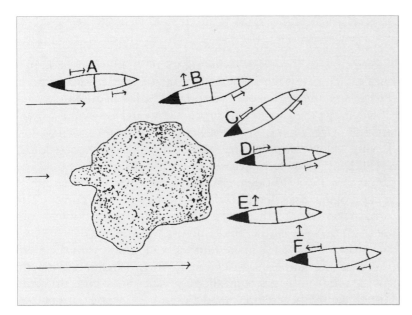

Figure 8-18
Moving into an eddy from a downstream position is a simple matter of ferry gliding into it at a slow speed. The angle of the canoe in position "B" and "C" makes use of the current's force to slip the canoe sideways and into the eddy.

Figure 8-19
When water flows around an obstruction a "V" is formed. This "V" faces upstream. If two parallel obstructions are present, the upstream "V"s create a downstream "V" . These downstream "V"s are like green lights. They are demarcations that signal where to go.

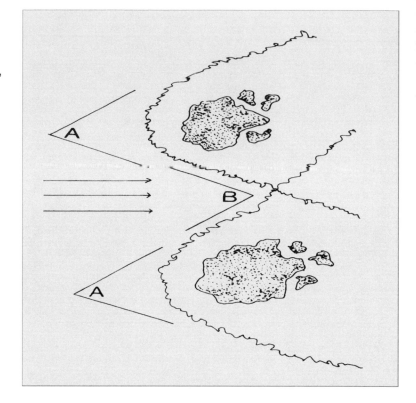

Inexperienced paddlers wanting to move from one side of a fast flowing river to the other might be tempted to simply point the canoe at the opposite shore and paddle for all they are worth. However, as they paddled, the canoe would be swept downstream. Ferry gliding involves slipping the canoe across fast flowing water while minimizing downstream movement (see Fig. 8–15). In order to ferry across a current, the paddlers hold the canoe at a 15 or 20 degree angle to the current. Thus, only a fraction of the canoe length is directly exposed to the current. The force of the water on the canoe will push it not only downstream but also, because of the angle, across the stream. By paddling forward, or backwards if the ferry is being done with the stern upstream, the canoeists counteract the downstream movement, leaving only the cross stream slippage. The canoe ends up being pushed across the stream. In practice, a very strong current may force the paddlers to lose some ground to the current, and the angle of the canoe in the current will depend on the speed of the river, the speed at which the canoeists want to slip across, and their paddling ability.

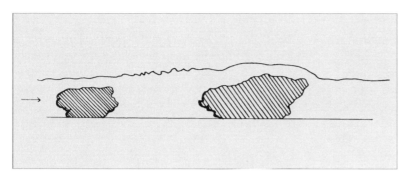

Figure 8-20
The deeper the obstruction, the further downstream will be the wave. Pillows are created when the obstruction is close to the surface.

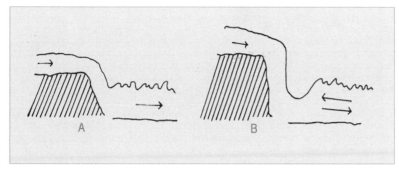

Figure 8-21
A—scalloped waves following a ledge
B—Hydraulic jump

Eddies are quiet spots in the river, often located behind rocks and other obstructions (see Fig. 8–16). Eddies are great spots to rest and check out the next set of rapids. An eddy is formed as the result of a current differential. Fast flowing water slows down when it nears slower moving or stationary objects such as rocks, the river bottom, or the river bank. The closer the water comes to the object, the greater the resistance. This resistance slows the water down and this is why water near the river bank is flowing slower than water in the middle of the river. In fast flowing rivers, the water near the river bank may even be flowing back upstream. Similarly, water flowing past a rock will be slowed down, and may even turn back upstream behind the rock.

Often, a canoe can be turned into an eddy fairly easily (see Figs. 8–17 and 8–18). When the canoe comes even with the rock, the bow paddler reaches into the quiet area behind the rock and draws hard. This stroke is repeated again and again in order to pull the bow into the eddy while the stern swings wide. Finally, the canoe comes to rest in the eddy, with the bow pointed upstream. To turn downstream out of the eddy, the bow paddler reaches out into the current and pulls the bow downstream. The stern paddler does a pry, draw, or bow stroke in order to help pivot the canoe.

Scalloped waves, standing waves, or haystacks if they are particularly large, are caused when fast water slows down as the river gets deeper (see Fig. 8-21). Deep water following a ledge will often slow the water down sufficiently for standing waves to be generated. Rocks and other obstructions often give rise to the same phenomenon. Provided they are not so large as to swamp the canoe, standing waves usually represent good safe deep water. There are two rules of thumb with regard to standing waves.

1. The further downstream the wave is from the obstruction, the deeper the obstruction.

2. A quiet spot in the middle of turbulence is often preceded by an obstruction.

Hydraulic jumps are similar to standing waves except for one very important fact: the water at the surface flows back upstream (see Fig. 8-21). This means that capsized paddlers can be trapped in the upstream water flow. The only way out of a strong hydraulic jump is at the side or underwater with the current. This type of wave is very dangerous. Pillows are slight bulges in the water surface. They usually indicate an obstruction close to the surface.

INTERNATIONAL RIVER CLASSIFICATION

At the two lowest grades, white water canoeing is challenging and exciting. I highly recommend it. Beyond grade 2, you need lots of skill, common sense, and practice. On wilderness trips, when you are a long way from help, exercising caution is a good practice. If you are ever in doubt, you might want to remember the old paddler's maxim—nobody ever drowned on a portage.

GRADE 1—Very Easy
This is the easiest rapid, suitable for novices in almost any type of canoe. Waves are small and regular. Safe routes are wide and obvious.

GRADE 2—Easy
These rapids are of medium difficulty. Though the passages are generally clear and fairly wide, ledges, protruding rocks, boulders, sweepers, and other visible objects may be present. Open boats may ship some water, so paddlers in this type of grade of rapid should be at the intermediate level. Novices in closed boats can handle these rapids with direction.

GRADE 3—Medium Difficulty

This is the limit for open canoes. Irregular waves and rocks, narrow passages requiring precise manoeuvring, and eddies will likely be present. These rapids are suitable for advanced paddlers in open canoes or intermediate paddlers in closed boats.

GRADE 4—Difficult

This grade is characterized by lengthy passages, narrow passages, strong eddies, and rough waves. Inspection is considered to be mandatory and often difficult. These rapids are suitable for advanced paddlers in closed boats.

GRADE 5—Very Difficult

These are extremely difficult rapids characterized by their length, violence, large drops, and few or no take-out or rest spots. Inspection is important and difficult. Expert white water paddlers might attempt these rapids.

GRADE 6—Extraordinarily Difficult

These rapids, characterized by the worst of Grade 5, border on the impossible. Only teams of experts with back-up support would attempt these rapids. Described as extremely dangerous, paddlers should be prepared for serious accidents and injury.

ADDITIONAL SOURCES

- Davidson, J. & Rugge, J. (1983). *The Complete Wilderness Paddler.* New York: Vintage.
- Fletcher, C. (1991) *The Complete Walker III.* New York: Knopf.
- Franks, C. (1977). *The Canoe and White Water.* Toronto: University of Toronto Press.
- Hart, J. (1984). *Walking Softly in the Wilderness.* San Francisco: Sierra Club.
- Mason, B. (1980). *Path of the Paddle.* Toronto: Van Nostrand.
- Mason, B. (1988). *Song of the Paddle.* Toronto: Key Porter Books.
- Moore, T. (1984). *Canoecraft.* Camden East, Ontario: Camden House Press.
- Stelmok, J. & Rollin, T. (1987). *The Wood & Canvas Canoe: A complete guide to its history, construction, restoration, and maintenance.* Camden East, Ontario: Old Bridge Press.

Lampwick snowshoe bindings are flexible and simple.

9
Snowshoeing and Cross-Country Skiing

The arctic expresses the sum of all wisdom: Silence.
Walter Bauer

There are far fewer campers in the bush during the winter than during the summer. This is easy to understand. Winter camping requires specialized equipment, additional preparation, and increased knowledge and skills. Winter camping is also more risky. Then why go winter camping? The answer is simple: winter conditions are spectacular, from the scenery to the physical sensations caused by –40 degree temperatures. And, in the same location where you might see three hundred people in the summer, you could be the only winter camper. You've got it all to yourself, and this adds immeasurably to the experience. Finally, the challenge of winter camping has tremendous appeal. To be able to travel in relative comfort and safety during the winter is, in and of itself, very satisfying.

I highly recommend going out in the winter. Start with some day trips, work up to an overnight or two, and soon you will find yourself out for three or fours days or longer. Beyond simple tramping on a thin blanket of the season's first snow are the greater pleasures of snowshoeing and cross-country skiing. In the beginning, snowshoeing is the best and easiest travel method for wilderness campers. However, after you develop your winter camping skills, then cross-country ski travel, with a pack, will be a suitable challenge.

SNOWSHOEING

Snowshoeing is the simplest and most convenient mode of wilderness travel for those campers who don't have a lot of winter travel experience. By spreading your body weight over a larger surface area, snowshoes reduce the tendency to sink in deep snow. The degree to which you will sink is influenced by the age, composition, surface of the snow, and the design of the snowshoe.

I remember my first experience in soft snow over a metre (3 feet) in depth. Every step I took, I sank to my waist. At the same time, a friend on snowshoes was walking circles around me, without sinking a single centimetre! I had to walk from a ploughed road to a cabin about three hundred metres (325 yards) in the bush. The trip took me almost twenty minutes and I was thoroughly soaked when I arrived at the cabin door. While it's true that you don't always need snowshoes when winter camping, there are times when you would be unable to travel without them. For this reason, you should not go winter camping without snowshoes or skis unless you are absolutely certain there is no chance of being caught in a heavy snowfall that could make travel without snowshoes or skis impossible.

There are three issues that the snowshoer must deal with: determining which method and materials are to be used for attaching the snowshoes to the feet; selecting appropriate footwear; and choosing the snowshoe type and design best suited for the area and conditions where you plan to go snowshoeing.

SNOWSHOES

Choosing the correct snowshoe shape is simply a matter of matching design and conditions. If you plan to travel through heavy bush, where the trees grow close together, you will want narrow snowshoes that are not too long. On the other hand, if you plan to travel through heavy drifts and across large lakes, it's a good idea to wear snowshoes that have turned up toes and long tails. Most winter travellers purchase snowshoes that are a compromise between these two extremes.

It's the snowshoe webbing that spreads your body weight across a large area of snow and prevents you from sinking. Without webbing, or with broken or torn webbing, the only extra support for your body weight would be the wooden frame. The frame will not support your weight; its purpose is simply to act as a structure to hold the webbing.

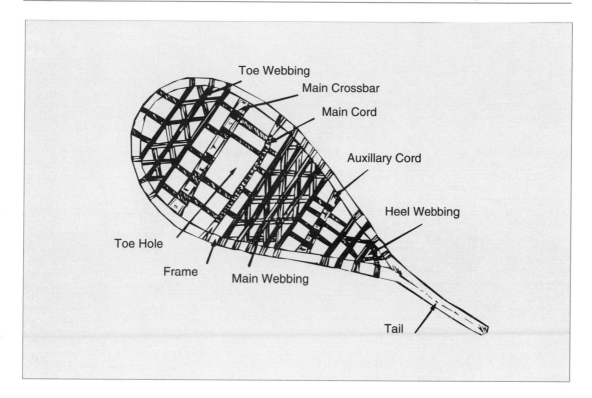

Toe Webbing
Main Crossbar
Main Cord
Auxillary Cord
Heel Webbing
Toe Hole
Frame
Main Webbing
Tail

If you snowshoe in very fine or soft snow, a close weave lace will be necessary in order to prevent sinking. If, however, the snow is hard and granular, a loose weave will suffice. Most snowshoes have crossbars. These add strength to the frame. Designs that exceed functional needs have resulted from specific materials at hand and isolated creativity. If your sole means of winter travel is by snowshoe, then, ultimately, the design will be specific to the environment at hand.

Figure 9-1
Basic Snowshoe Parts

Most snowshoes are coated with varnish to protect the wood and webbing from moisture. The varnish also helps prevent the webbing from stretching and acts as a repellant for rodents. After a season of heavy use, it's a good idea to re-varnish any parts of the snowshoe where the original varnish has worn off. Exceptions to this are snowshoes such as the Teslin, which are not varnished because they are designed and made to be worn in a very dry climate. Providing you use them only in dry conditions, Teslin and other unvarnished snowshoes will never need to be varnished. However, if you use them in places such as Ontario, Quebec, or the New England States, where the climate is anything but dry, you will quickly destroy them unless they are coated.

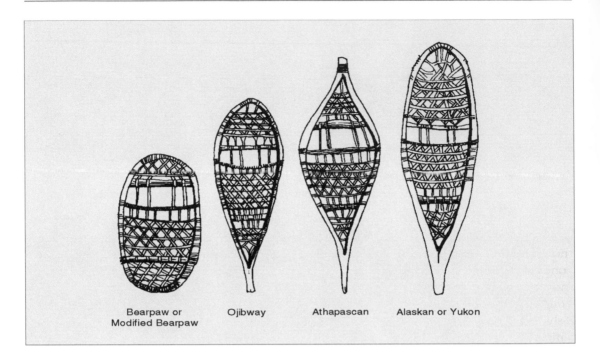

Bearpaw or   Ojibway   Athapascan   Alaskan or Yukon
Modified Bearpaw

Figure 9-2
Snowshoe types

Synthetic snowshoes are also uncoated. Obviously, plastic does not need to be protected the same way wood does. Though synthetic snowshoes are quite functional, they have no aesthetic appeal and often cost more than wooden snowshoes. I don't recommend synthetic snowshoes.

One of the best known snowshoe designs is the *Bearpaw* (see Fig. 9–2). This snowshoe is easy to construct and is an excellent design for working or travelling in heavy brush where constant turns are necessary. The Bearpaw is not a great snowshoe for open areas or for long distance travelling. It has been favoured by trappers for activities such as chopping wood or checking nearby traps or snares, where long distance travel doesn't come into play. The *Otter Tail* and *Ojibway* are slight modifications to the Bearpaw design. Their greater length to width ratio, and, in the case of the Ojibway, a true tail, keep the snowshoes aligned when travelling long distances along open trails. Long, narrow snowshoes with long tails and upturned pointed toes, such as the *Alaskan* or *Yukon*, are good for travelling long open lakes or across open country.

Most snowshoe lacing is made of rawhide. Today, most commercially made snowshoes use rawhide from cows, although some small operations use other animals. Some Teslin Indians are still making snowshoes with lacing from moose and caribou skins. Lacing designs will vary according to the specific weaver or manufacturer. I recommend carrying spare lacing on any serious outing since being stranded with a broken snowshoe can be life endangering. Hobby or craft stores that stock moccasin kits are good places to look for rawhide lacing. In an emergency, boot laces, parachute cord, or stuff sack cord will suffice. (See *Outdoor Canada,* Volume 6, No. 7, Sept/Oct 1978, for directions on making your own snowshoes.)

SNOWSHOE BINDINGS

Securing snowshoes to the boots, and keeping them attached, is for many novices the most difficult and frustrating part of snowshoeing. Many different types of bindings have come and gone. The most common snowshoe binding used by old-time snowshoers is the "Squaw Hitch." This binding is hand-tied from *lampwick* or *athletic wrap*. Lampwick can be purchased in old-fashioned hardware stores, the ones that stock parts for kerosene lamps. Athletic wrap is available from large athletic stores, though a local sports team would probably be happy to give you enough to do the job. Lampwick and athletic wrap are virtually the same. Both are natural fabrics, about 2.5 cm. (1 in.) wide, sold in rolls. You will need almost two meters of lampwick to try the Squaw Hitch bindings described in Figures 9–3 and 9–4. I strongly recommend the use of lampwick, rather than the commercial bindings described below. Lampwick is very inexpensive, easy to use, natural, and simple to replace.

Commercial producers have brought many different types of rawhide bindings to the market over the last ten to twenty years. Some of these work reasonably well, while others are next to useless. The biggest obstacle to overcome with snowshoe bindings is preventing the toe of the boot from sliding up to the crossbar. If the boot is flat across the top of the foot, then there is a tendency for the strap that goes over the toes to slide back towards the ankle. When moving quickly, this can happen in one stride and the front of the boot ends up being jammed either on top of or below the crossbar. The bottom of the boot, where it rests on the main cord (see Fig. 9–1), is meant to act like a hinge. You don't actually pick the snowshoe up when you walk, but rather drag it forward. If the toe of the boot becomes caught on top of or below the crossbar, the hinge action doesn't work, and novices often end up tripping. To prevent this, novices will sometimes tie the strap so tight that circulation to the toes is cut

Ski poles help snowshoers navigate steep hills.

Figure 9-3
Traditional Squaw Hitch made with lampwick.

Figure 9-4
This modified Squaw Hitch is based on a simple loop tied at "A." This loop is never untied. When the toe of the boot is put through the loop, the lampwick is simply wrapped around the ankle and tied at "B." This is one of the simplest and most comfortable ways to attach snowshoes to boots.

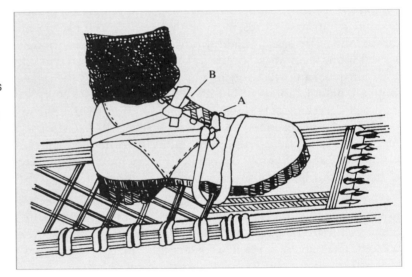

off. (Believe me, it's preferable to trip.) Leather bindings stretch when wet, with the result that it is very difficult to prevent the boot from slipping forward in the binding. Constant adjustments are required as the leather changes shape, and in cold weather this is no fun. One way to try and overcome this "slippage" is to attach the bindings to the snowshoes further back from the master cord. Normally, the binding is lashed to the corners of the main cord at the toe hole in order to maximize the hinge action. Although moving these attachment points back will reduce the

Take turns breaking trail and you will find the going is much easier.

effectiveness of the hinge, and put an increased strain on smaller cords, it can temporarily solve the "slippage" problem. Neoprene bindings do not suffer from the stretch problems usually encountered with leather harnesses, but they are very expensive. Snowshoe bindings are a case in point when newer is not necessarily better.

SNOWSHOE FOOTWEAR

Snowshoe footwear is quite varied. Mukluks, moccasins, snowmobile boots, lace-up hunting boots, and other types of footwear all have their adherents. The best approach is to try several different varieties of footwear and go with whatever works with your bindings while keeping your feet warm and comfortable. The boots should be flexible, and many snowshoers find it advantageous to have boots that slope down from the ankle to the toes. This will reduce the likelihood of the binding straps sliding from near the toes to the ankle area, as discussed in the last section. Breathable footwear is nice on cold days, but be sure that you won't end up with soggy feet when temperatures rise above the freezing mark. Flexibility, a low heel or no heel, and personal comfort are the objectives when snowshoeing.

SNOWSHOEING TIP

Snowshoe footwear should be flexible with flat soles.

SNOWSHOE TECHNIQUE

Snowshoeing technique is simple and very similar to walking. Place one foot in front of the other, then bring the back foot forward to a point where it becomes the front foot by *dragging*

Figure 9-5
Snowshoe pattern left by a
walking snowshoer.

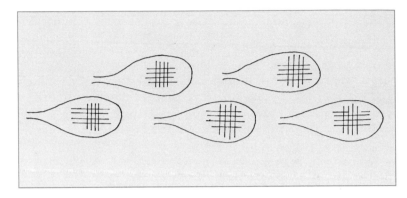

Figure 9-6
Pressure such as this will
unnecessarily stress the
snowshoes

the back snowshoe *over* the front snowshoe. Don't try and lift the snowshoes, unless the degree of sink makes it absolutely necessary. Most snowshoers do not find it necessary to spread their feet much further apart than they would when walking normally. In fact, the weighted foot normally sinks slightly in the snow leaving lots of room to slip the other foot forward across the top. Going up and down hills requires no more than half an hour of practice. Steep hills can be difficult, but creating switch-backs or sidestepping will help ease any problems. Downhill, the same is true. Ski poles can be used to good advantage while carrying a heavy pack on tough trails.

Carrying a pack while travelling on snowshoes is not terribly difficult. This is the reason why novice winter campers tend to travel on snowshoes rather than skis. Snowshoeing is a slower and more leisurely sport than skiing. As well, if the goal is to escape from snowmobilers, snowshoers often find that after climbing a few ridges and passing through a dense forest they will have left the skiers and snowmobilers far behind.

CROSS-COUNTRY SKIING

Originally, the snowshoe was used by the native people of North America, while in Europe and Asia the ski was the predominant non-mechanized means of winter travel. Except for a few transplanted Europeans and the Alpine ski enthusiasts, things pretty much stayed this way until the late 1960s, when the cross-country ski boom took hold. At that time, North Americans discovered that cross-country skiing can be exciting, dynamic, peaceful, and very beautiful. Nordic skiers enjoy the mental and physical harmony of physically demanding sports. As well, cross-country skiing is a good form of cardiovascular conditioning.

This section examines cross-country skis and skiing in terms of equipment, care of equipment, and technique. The focus in this section is on Nordic or traditional cross-country skiing; neither Alpine skiing nor ski skating is discussed.

SKIS

Cross-country skis vary in height, width, weight, flexibility, colour and the materials from which they are constructed. There are four broad categories of cross-country ski equipment: racing, light touring, touring, and mountain or Telemark skis. Each is designed for a specific type of skiing.

Racing skis are designed for groomed trails, either tracks or packed snow. Racing equipment is very light and, therefore, it can be easily damaged. Weight has been traded for strength. Light touring equipment is heavier than racing equipment, but it is still quite fragile. *Light touring skis* are designed primarily for use on groomed tracks. *Touring equipment* can be used on trails or off trails. This equipment is heavy when compared with either touring or light touring equipment. *Mountaineering* and *Telemark skis* are similar in weight to touring equipment, but are designed specifically for ski mountaineering, downhill Telemark skiing, and heavy brush and snow conditions found in the back-country.

There was a time when many stores sold light touring equipment, passing it off as suitable for most conditions. In fact, the general skier who is skiing off prepared tracks is far better served by a touring ski than by light touring equipment. A touring ski has the width and strength necessary for off-trail skiing. The additional width provides stability in varied snow and trail conditions, and the increased strength reduces the likelihood of breaking under heavy stress, as when a tip gets caught under a tree root. Stability and strength are important for off-track skiing.

SKIING TIP
Off-track skiers are best served by touring equipment.

Types of Skis

TYPE	APPROX. WIDTH AT WAIST	APPROX WEIGHT	PURPOSE	BOOTS AND POLES
Racing	43-47 mm.	1.1 kg. (2.3 lbs.)	Very light skis for use on prepared courses; easily damaged if used for touring.	Boots are lightweight and cut below the ankle. Poles are lightweight carbon fibre, fibreglass, boron or aramid fibre with small 7-8 cm. (2.8-3 in.) assymmetrical baskets.
Light Touring	49-50 mm.	1.5 kg. (3.3 lbs.)	Light skis for use on prepared tracks and trails.	Boots are medium weight, cut above the ankle. Poles are aluminium alloy or fibreglass with round or asymmetrical 10 cm.(4 in.) baskets.
Touring	52-55 mm.	2.6 kg. (5.8 lbs.)	For general ski use including packed snow and off-track skiing in light or heavy snow.	Boots are cut above the ankle and are similar to, but lighter than, hiking boots. Poles are similar to those used in light touring, but with slightly larger baskets, 14 cm. (5.5 in.).
Mountain Skis	60-60+ mm.	2.8 kg (6.1 lbs.)	Heavy, rugged ski for use in downhill runs, ski mountaineering, and unpacked heavy snow.	Boots may be like ski touring or mountaineering boots. Poles are fibreglass or aluminium alloy with heavy shafts and baskets, 13 cm. (5.2 in.) and over.

Cross-country-skis are constructed of wood, metal, or synthetic fibres. Although skis are sometimes fabricated with a combination of materials, they are normally classified according to the material that provides the structural strength. Therefore, even though a wood ski may have fibreglass on its tip and tail, it is still described as a wood ski because the wood is the material that provides the structural strength.

These days, *synthetic fibre skis* dominate the market. This is a significant change from the early 70s, when wood skis were in vogue. This change occurred in part because of the increased costs of producing wood skis. Although the wood in wood skis

Injection Moulded Skis

Wooden skis are disappearing mainly because of labour costs. Synthetic skis are less expensive than wooden skis, but most require labour intensive production. One type of synthetic ski construction that minimizes labour is the injection moulded approach, of which there are two types. In the first type, the core is moulded, with the structural and outer layers added later. In the second type, the outside and structural layers are placed inside the mould, then foam is injected through a hole in the side of the mould. The foam is created when its two constituent parts are brought together, at which time it expands and traps carbon dioxide in cells. The smaller the cells, the stronger the foam. With core moulding, the cells at the outside of the ski are smaller than the cells in the middle. This works to the advantage of the skier in that the core ends up being strongest around its perimeter, something akin to having a protective shell.

Injection moulded skis are one way manufacturers are trying to control high labour costs.

is less expensive than the synthetic fibre in synthetic skis, the cost of production, and the labour in particular, has killed the mass market for wooden skis. The beauty of wood skis, with their hickory bases and lignostone (compressed beech) edges, is for all intents and purposes gone. If you have an old pair in your garage, I recommend keeping them. Wood skis are very good at holding wax and there is a special joy in skiing on natural fibres. It isn't likely you will ever buy another pair of wood skis. Metal skis are rare. Although quite durable, they often don't hold wax very well.

Synthetic ski construction is based on two somewhat different approaches. First is the *sandwich construction technique*. In this approach, layers of synthetic fibre are laminated one on top of the other, similar to the way plywood is made. The strongest layers are placed on the top and the bottom. The advantages to the sandwich construction method include the ability to finely control the materials and processes, a highly regulated curing process, and precision control over the degree of flex and stiffness in the final product. The big disadvantage to the sandwich construction approach is its tendency to delaminate over time and under stress. This requires careful construction processes and a preoccupation with the bonding resins used between the layers. The second approach to ski construction is the *box method*, also

On a bright winter day, you may n[ot] realize it's −30°. So, no matter wh[at] the weather, be sure to keep an active lookout for early signs of frostbite.

know as monobloc, torsion box, and torsion cell construction. With this technique, there are a host of different variations, including wrapping, spinning, and laying or forming cloth or cloth fibres around a ski core. The box technique lacks the precision and fine tuning that is part of sandwich construction; however, the box method is usually free of delamination problems.

Synthetic fibre skis are built around a core which may comprise more than 80% of the total volume of the ski. Core materials include wood, foam plastic, and aluminum honeycomb. The choice of core material will affect the weight, strength, warp resistance, ease of construction, cost, and likelihood of delamination. Wood is a popular core material because it is available in many different densities, doesn't break easily across the grain, and is easy to work with. Foam plastic is also available in different densities and is easy to work with. However, most of the lighter foams tend to be brittle and they lack the bonding qualities that minimize delamination or sheering. Some plastic cores will be wrapped in wood to increase overall strength and potency of the bonding. This is sometimes referred to as "double-box" construction. Aluminum honeycomb cores are strong, stiff, and light. They are also very expensive.

After you have decided what type of skis you want to purchase, and for most readers of this book it is safe to assume these would be touring skis for mixed conditions and off-track skiing, the next question you face is whether to buy waxable or waxless skis. Waxless ski technology developed in the early 70s as a response to the difficulties inherent in ski waxing. The purpose of wax is prevent the ski from sliding backwards; waxless skis must achieve this same goal.

Waxless ski bases have been manufactured in three different forms—patterned bases, mohair strips, and active-type bases. In the case of patterned skis, there are positive bases and negative bases. Positive bases are those where the pattern rises up out of the base of the ski. These tend to grip best on hard snow, but will by definition impede the glide of the ski. Negative bases are patterns cut into the base of the ski. They don't work as well on hard snow, but will have little effect on the glide. Patterned or mechanical bases are designed to bite into the snow and hold it. If the snow is prone to shearing, which is common in cold and loose snow conditions, these bases will not work well. Patterned bases differ according to the slope of the pattern, the depth of the patter, and the total gripping edge. Mohair strips, a very different

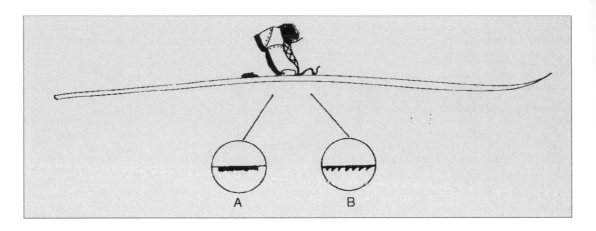

Figure 9-7
Waxless skis use different base surfaces to help the ski grip the snow. Mohair strips ("A") are composed of tiny hairs that dig into the snow if the ski starts to slide backwards. Patterned scales ("B") dig into the snow when pressure is put on the ski. Waxless skis tend to work best under changeable conditions when the temperature is at or near the freezing point.

type of waxless base, were quite popular during the 70s, but have since fallen out of favour. This is somewhat surprising since most ski-mountaineers describe their climbing skins, which are similar in design function to mohair strips, as very effective. The mohairs stand up and bite into the snow if the ski moves backward, but flatten during the gliding phase. Active bases are the result of combining materials with different thermal coefficients. This means that the structure of the base will subtlety change shape according to temperature in order to minimize backward movement of the ski. Active bases have a reputation for impeding the glide phase so it is important that the insert, which is the gripping part of the base, be properly located and the ski camber be precisely matched to the skier.

On the whole, waxless bases work best when temperatures are at or near freezing. In very cold temperatures, when the snow is loose and prone to shearing, waxless bases tend to function very poorly. If you hate the thought of waxing and tend to ski only when the weather is moderate, then waxless bases may be the best choice. Waxless skis seldom outperform waxable skis, but they make life a whole heck of a lot easier.

Choosing the appropriate *ski length* is fairly easy. The skier should be able to touch the tip of the ski with the palm or wrist when standing beside the extended ski. Convention also has it that skiers new to the sport, skiers very light for their height, and ski mountaineers or telemark skiers, may be better served by skis that are 5 to 10 centimetres shorter than normal. Heavy skiers or very powerful skiers may choose skis that are 5 centimetres longer than the standard length.

Ski and Pole Lengths

SKIER'S HEIGHT	APPROX. SKI LENGTH	APPROX. POLE LENGTH
130 cm. (4 ft. 4 in.)	160 cm.	110 cm.
140 cm. (4 ft. 8 in.)	170 cm.	115 cm.
150 cm. (5 ft.)	180 cm.	120 cm.
155 cm. (5 ft. 2 in.)	185 cm.	120 cm.
160 cm. (5 ft. 4 in.)	190 cm.	125 cm.
165 cm. (5 ft. 6 in.)	195 cm.	125 cm.
170 cm. (5 ft. 8 in.)	200 cm.	130 cm.
175 cm. (5 ft. 10 in.)	205 cm.	135 cm.
180 cm. (6 ft.)	210 cm.	140 cm.
185 cm. (6 ft. 2 in.)	215 cm.	145 cm.
190 cm. (6 ft. 4 in.)	220 cm.	150 cm.
195 cm. (6 ft. 6 in.)	225 cm.	155 cm.

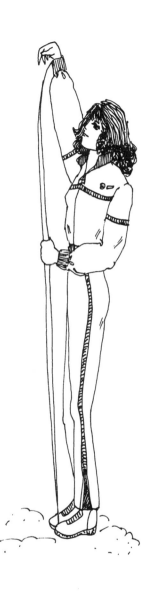

Figure 9-8
For most skiers, the ski length should reach to the wrist or palm.

The *camber* or camber stiffness of the ski is very important. This is what allows the skier's kick to flatten the ski base out in order for it to grip the snow. If you lay a ski on the ground, you will see that only the tip and tail touch. As you place your weight on the ski, more and more of the ski base comes into contact with the ground. When you push down on the ski, using a kicking action as you would when actually skiing, the entire ski base should contact the ground. If the ski is too stiff, not all the base will contact the ground; if the ski isn't stiff enough, the entire base will contact the ground before you exert full pressure. It is important that your skis have the right amount of camber for your weight and skiing ability. Not all skis of a given length will have the same camber. Manufacturers will produce a given length of ski with a range of cambers in order to meet the needs of different skier weights and abilities. The paper test is a tried and true method for checking the camber. It involves placing a piece of paper under the skis, then standing on them with your weight evenly distributed at the balance points. The paper, when pulled, should move back and forth with some resistance. When weight is shifted to one ski, this should lock the paper in place. If the paper can still be moved, the skis are too stiff. If the paper cannot be moved with your weight on both skis, the skis are not stiff enough. If you are a particularly strong skier, you should choose stiffer skis. Heavy skiers may not be able to find skis that are stiff enough and may have to use longer skis to get the right camber.

Even though the ski camber may match your weight and skiing ability, there are other things you should inspect before buying. Check for twist and warp by holding the pair of skis together and sighting from tip to tail. The ski bases should touch over their entire width without pressure. If the bases touch only on one side, look for another pair. If the bases do touch over their entire width, pull the skis together to overcome the camber, and check to see that the mid-points of the skis meet evenly. If one is slightly offset from the other, look for another pair. Finally, don't forget to see if the serial numbers match. You want to buy a true pair.

SKI BOOTS

SKIING TIP

For cross-country skiing to be enjoyable, the boots must be comfortable and warm.

In the same way that there are different types of skis, there are different types of boots: racing, light touring, touring, and Telemark or mountaineering ski boots. Boots vary in size and weight as do the skis, but all are quite flexible with the possible exception of Telemark or mountaineering ski boots. Racing boots are comparable to very light track shoes. Like the skis they are designed for, these boots are constructed to minimize weight, at the expense of strength. By comparison, light touring boots have more substance, though they still don't normally cover the ankle. Touring boots cover the ankle and provide the support required for off-track skiing. Touring boots will also likely have some insulation for protection in cold weather skiing. Mountaineering ski boots are much sturdier and, in fact, may be quite similar to older downhill ski boots. Some skiers prefer the lightness of light touring boots, and combine them with gaiters and touring skis for off-track skiing.

Ski Boots are constructed of leather, rubber or synthetics. Leather boots tend to be stronger; this means added support in the upper part of the boot. Rubber is sometimes used just for the soles of ski boots, though there have been some comprehensive rubber ski boots on the market. Some synthetic boots have been known to have flexibility problems under extremely cold conditions. Leather boots breathe nicely, but take a long time to dry out. Boots with rubber or vinyl uppers are waterproof, but breathability may be a problem. The amount of insulation will vary according to the style of the boot. Most cross-country ski boot insulation is synthetic fleece (see Chapter 2).

Equivalent Boot Sizes

Men	Women	European
4 - 4½	5½ - 6	37
5 - 5½	6½ - 7	38
6 - 6½	7½ - 8	39
7 - 7½	8 - 8½	40
8 - 8½	9	41
8½ - 9	9½ - 10	42
9½		43
10		44
10½		45
11½ - 12		46

Note that manufacturer's sizing may differ.

The fit of the boot is probably the most important single factor for an enjoyable cross-country skiing experience. Take your ski socks to the store when trying on ski boots, and don't be hurried by sales staff. The fit should be snug with just enough room to wiggle your toes. Many skiers use two pair of socks, one light and one heavy. With the laces removed, you should be able to fit two fingers between your heel and the back of the boot when your toes are resting against the front of the boot. Boot selection must be made in conjunction with a decision on bindings (see next section). As most cross-country ski boots are measured in European sizes, the boot size chart at the top of this page may be useful.

Racing

Light touring

BINDINGS

The most common bindings used for cross-country skiing are *toe-bindings*. Within this type, there are two very different kinds: boot-flex and binding-flex. As the name suggests, boot-flex bindings rely on the boot to flex as the skier moves through the ski motion, whereas the binding-flex system incorporates a hinge in the binding itself. The boot-flex system is the more common. The boot is held in the binding either by a series of pins and an overlapping bail that presses down on the front piece of the boot, or simply by a bail that clamps down on a "snout" or extended portion of the boot. Both these systems work well, providing the skier with a good, stable connection. The binding-flex system is newer. Its major advantage lies in the fact that the flex can be

Touring

Figure 9-9
Ski boots

adjusted for different conditions and skier abilities. This means greater ski control. With the binding-flex system, the boot is attached to the binding by means of a latch system. It is more difficult to walk in these boots.

Cable bindings continue to be used for ski mountaineering, some forms of wilderness skiing, and with some Telemark skis. These bindings permit the skier to use heavy boots, and they hold the heel in place for downhill runs.

Some stores will mount the bindings as part of a package price or they will pre-drill the holes so that all you do is screw the bindings on. This saves the cost of labour. However, you may find that mounting your own bindings from scratch is not difficult. First determine the balance point of the ski and mark it, then set the binding on the ski so that the front lever or pin sockets are over the balance point. Then mark the front screw hole and drill it out using a slightly smaller bit than the actual screw size. After putting the first screw in, mount the boot and swing the harness so that the boot is aligned on the ski. Finish by marking the remaining holes, drilling them out, and attaching the screws. Heel plates are designed to fit on the ski under the heel of the boot. They prevent snow from balling up underfoot while skiing.

SKI POLES

SKIING TIP

Ski poles should be armpit high when wearing low heels.

A ski pole should fit snugly under the armpit when resting on the surface of the snow. To measure a pole when you are in a store, just rest the pole on the floor, and it should fit into your armpit while wearing low heels. Some skiers will prefer a slightly longer or shorter pole, but this can only be determined through experience. Small (about 10 cm. or 4 in.), asymmetrical baskets are best for prepared tracks, while larger baskets are better for deep, untracked snow. Check the straps and grips while wearing the gloves or mitts that you intend to wear while skiing. Comfort is the key rule.

Poles shafts are commonly made from aluminum alloy, fibreglass, carbon fibre, or other high-strength alloy. Cane poles, which were very popular for several decades, are now quite rare. Generally, the more expensive the pole, the lighter and stronger it will be. Some skiers find aluminum poles very cold.

SKI PACKAGES

Ski packages tend to be a good deal for the consumer and the retailer. Typically, the retail price on a grouping of equipment— skis, boots, bindings, and poles—is less than if the individual

Many animals are easier to spot in winter than in summer.

picces weie bought separately. The ski store will match equipment of similar quality and purpose, giving the customer a break on the price in return for purchasing the entire package. Often, installation will be included in the package.

SKI WAXING

The principles of waxing are quite straightforward. Waxing simply prepares the undersurface of the ski so that the ski will resist sliding backwards when the skier's full weight and kick forces that part of the ski into contact with the snow.

Snow is hexagonal in shape, and it is the tiny points on each snowflake hexagon that are critical for ski waxing. Depending on the temperature and the age of the snow, the angularity and strength of the snowflakes will vary. Basically though, the snowflake points are supposed to stick into the wax and, at least in theory, hold the ski firm and in place until forward motion is initiated by the skier. At that time, the fine points of the snow break off and the wax smooths out, providing the required gliding surface. During the forward movement, friction helps produce a tiny film of water on which the ski glides. If the wax is too hard, the tiny points on the snowflakes will be unable to stick into it. Then the ski will slide forward beautifully, and slide backwards almost equally well. If the wax is too soft, the points of the snowflake will continue to stick into the ski even when strong forward motion is initiated. This results in the snow balling up under the ski and preventing a good glide. *In cold weather the*

SKIING TIP

Keep your ski wax cold and it will be much easier to apply.

Figure 9-10
Heating the base of wood skis with a torch opens up the pores to admit tar. A torch can also be used to assist in the removal of old wax.

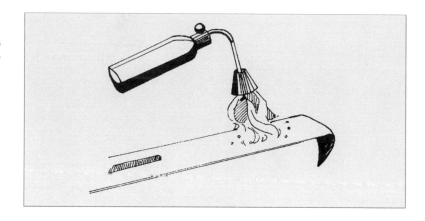

snow is usually very hard and angular, requiring a hard wax; in warm weather the snow is soft and less angular, therefore a softer wax is needed. In addition, moisture content, the age of the snow, air temperature, snow temperature, and even barometric pressure may affect the composition of the snow crystals.

Wax should always be kept cold since this will make it easier and less messy to apply. When corking wax on the ski, always run the cork from the tip to the tail. After applying wax, the skis should stand with their bases exposed to the air so that the wax has a chance to harden before you start skiing. If after a few minutes of skiing, the snow is balling up underfoot, the wax is too soft. This means you will have to scrape it off and try again. If, on the other hand, the ski keeps slipping backwards, add a softer wax just under the foot, then try again. A soft wax can be put over a hard wax, but hard wax cannot be put on a soft wax. As a result, many skiers prefer to err on the hard wax side. A base wax, sometimes called a running wax, is sometimes applied before any other wax. It will provide a better binding surface for the later waxes.

CARE OF SKI EQUIPMENT

Equipment care is common sense. The nicer you are to your skis, boots and poles, the longer they will last. Stand your skis in the snow with the tips up when stopped on the trail, and be sure to clean all the snow and ice off them at the end of the day. If the skis are carried on the top of a car or van for the journey home, be sure to wipe any road salt or other debris off the skis and bindings before storing them. Wet boots should be dried naturally, without applying strong heat.

Figure 9-11
Diagonal stride

At the end of the season, bindings should be carefully cleaned, and a little oil added to the moving parts. Screws should be checked to be sure that they are tight, and leather boots should be treated with a good conditioner. Skis are best stored by hanging them upside down by their tips and tails from garage rafters or pipes. Skis should not be left strapped together nor stored in a dry area. If you are still using wood skis, they should be hot tarred at least once a year in order to keep them healthy (see page 230 for instructions).

SKI TECHNIQUE

Ski technique is, for the most part, an example of an easy subject made difficult through the explosion of literature and instruction. Traditional cross-country skiing has a standard movement called the *diagonal stride*. For most people, the diagonal stride comes quite naturally. It is similar to walking: when one leg moves forward, the opposite arm goes with it. Your feet slide forward over the snow; they are not lifted.

A simple way to start your skiing career is as follows: Go to a park or farm, wherever you intend to ski, and walk on your skis without poles for 100 metres or so in a straight line, then turn around and walk back in the same track lines. Next time, try to glide on the forward ski, instead of shuffling as you did while walking. Turn around and return using the same technique. The third time, throw your opposite arm forward as you enter each of the glide phases. Don't get so heavy handed that you are thrown off balance, but try to get enough arm motion so that you begin

Still Have Those Old Wood Skis?

Wood skis require special preparation and cleaning. When they are first purchased, wood skis have a preservative on the base. This soon wears off and, in any event, is not usually as good as a hot tar treatment. A good hot tar treatment is recommended at least once a year, either at the beginning or the end of the season, depending on the condition of your skis. If you finish the season with a worn and slightly waterlogged pair of wood skis, then don't wait until the fall to do your hot tarring. If, on the other hand, the skis still look good at the end of the season, you may hold off tarring the skis until the fall.

Ski tar is different than road tar, and it comes in two types—hot and cold. Hot tarring is preferred since it will last considerably longer and do a better job. Before applying hot tar, smooth the running surface of the ski with steel wool in order to remove old preservatives and to clean the base. Then heat the base with a blowtorch to open up the wood, and brush on the tar (see Fig. 9–10). Immediately run the blowtorch over the base again in order to keep the pores open so that the tar sinks into the wood. After a few minutes, clean the excess tar of the ski base with a rag, applying heat as necessary.

Left   Right

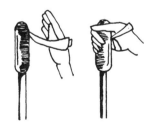

Figure 9-12
The hand goes up through the strap.

to feel a rhythm. Add poles and you will find the whole routine easy. It's a good idea to spend some time skiing without poles in order to develop and reinforce the kick/glide motion. Otherwise you may fall into the trap of relying on your arm strength rather than learning how to kick.

To grasp the poles properly, your hands should go up through the straps (see Fig. 9–12). The lower strap, as determined by how it exits from the handle, should be on the thumb side of your hand while skiing. In the beginning you may find it easier to go up a hill sideways (sidestepping) or by walking with your ski tips spread far apart and the tails close together (herringbone). When you fall, it is easier to get up if your skis are downhill from your body. Double poling, skate turns and kick turns are techniques developed over time.

Cross-country ski technique is learned by doing. So get out and try it. Lessons are helpful for correcting faults and they make your skiing more efficient.

SKI ACCESSORIES

On any ski trip into the bush, it is advisable to carry an extra ski tip. Your ski tips are quite vulnerable and travelling off-trail without a spare could endanger your safety. A map, compass, trail food, matches, and other day hiking gear are also important. Always ask yourself what physical and mental state you would be in if the worst happened. The worst could be a broken leg, a broken ski, or a storm that forces you to make camp. Are you prepared to spend a night in an emergency shelter?

A day pack to carry light items such as a ski tip and trail food is highly recommended. Ski camping backpacks, for overnight trips, are usually internal frame or soft packs since external frames interfere with the natural motion in cross-country skiing. (See Chapter Eight for a discussion on backpacks.)

Cross-country ski clothing, like Alpine ski clothing, has suffered from a tendency to become flashy and expensive. I say "suffered" because this trend has made the clothing quite expensive. In spite of this propensity, many skiers have a good time while wearing combinations of hand-me-downs and what is available around the house. The layer method of dressing is particularly appropriate for skiing. Clothes must be loose and roomy. Cross-country skiing involves consistent rhythmic movement with lots of bending and stretching: tight clothing is out. Select your clothing and equipment carefully but don't get seduced by the maze of technical detail and esoteric information presented by some manufacturers and specialist stores. Above all, have fun.

ADDITIONAL SOURCES

- Brady, M. (1987). *Cross-Country Ski Gear* (2nd Ed.). Seattle: The Mountaineers.

- Jackson, J. (1985/86, Winter). A Close Look at Waxless Technology. *Explore, 23.* 44–45.

- Osgood, W. & Hurley, L. (1983). *The Snowshoe Book* (3rd Ed.). Brattleboro, Vermont: The Stephen Greene Press.

- Prater, G. (1988). *Snowshoeing* (3rd Ed.). Seattle: The Mountaineers.

- Rees, O. (1975). *Cross-Country Skiing*, Toronto: Copp Clark.

Looking upstream towards Pulpit Rock on the South Nahanni River.

10
Selected North American Routes

Oh, how good it is to be
Foot loose and heart free!
        Robert Service (from *The Rover*)

The chapter highlights a few outstanding hiking, cycling, canoeing, snowshoeing, and cross-country routes that are particularly special for their history, geography, wildlife, or beauty. These areas vary from easy day hiking to extended wilderness camping; from north to south and east to west. The fact that many routes are within the boundaries of national parks is not mere chance. National parks are designed to preserve wild, rugged and interesting tracts—exactly the kind of areas that attract those of us who enjoy the outdoors. The following descriptions are very brief. In the case of wilderness routes, the reader is cautioned that these descriptions are mere overviews designed to introduce and tantalize. It is the responsibility of each trip participant, and leaders in particular, to ensure that adequate research provides the party with sufficient information to allow for a safe and rewarding outdoor experience.

The Witless Bay Bird Sanctuary is a good place to spot puffins.

For more information contact:

Newfoundland Department of Tourism
P.O. Box 8730
St. John's, Newfoundland
A1B 4K2
1–800–563–6353 or
(709) 729–2830

or

Hostelling Association of
Newfoundland and Labrador
P.O. Box 1815
St. John's, Newfoundland
A1C 5P9
(709) 739–5866

AVALON PENINSULA, NEWFOUNDLAND —
Bicycling

Newfoundland is rich in wilderness areas, and the people are truly a delight to meet. One of the best ways to explore Newfoundland, and the Avalon Peninsula in particular, is by bicycle.

Newfoundland can be reached by plane or ferry from North Sydney, Nova Scotia. The ferries travel to Port aux Basques on the west coast (an eight hour trip) and Argentia on the Avalon (an eighteen hour trip). Bicycle trips out of Argentia provide cyclists with a variety of options, easily examined by looking at a provincial road map. Highway 91 west through Colinet will give an idea of the scenic possibilities of the island. Or, for the more adventurous, the oval route following Highways 90, 10 and 13 rings the Avalon Wilderness Area. Newfoundland towns tend to be independent outposts where the people have been making a living from the sea for generations. Bicycling along the Avalon route, cyclists will see town after town nestled in tiny coves. There is a tendency to fly right through these towns, and use the momentum to climb the next hill; but, each town is full of characters with great stories that make every one of them well worth visiting. Supplies can be bought locally, except in the interior. Provincial parks offer good overnight spots for cyclists, and there is a hostel system in Newfoundland that relies in part on the use of private homes.

If travelling south on Highway 10, visit the Witless Bay Bird Sanctuary, home and breeding grounds to thousands of gulls, puffins, guillemots, and countless other sea birds. It is possible to rent a dory, for a reasonable fee, complete with a local guide to take you out and around the islands.

Although it isn't actually a "wilderness" trip, bicycling the Avalon is an exciting and interesting camping experience. Traffic is very light, the pace is unhurried, and the people are great. The inland part of the peninsula and the main body of Newfoundland are wild, rugged areas with a wide variety of hiking and canoe routes.

GROS MORNE & THE CALLAGHAN TRAIL, NEWFOUNDLAND — Hiking, Snowshoeing & Cross-Country Skiing

Enjoying the view of the water from the top of a small knoll.

Gros Morne National Park, home of the James Callaghan Trail, is set amid the Long Range Mountains of Newfoundland's north-western peninsula. Most of the nearly 2,000 square kilometres (780 square miles) is rugged and remote. Backpackers going out for more than a day hike should be well experienced. The park is accessible by car from Port aux Basques, which can be reached via the Canadian National ferry service from North Sydney, Nova Scotia.

The park staff have developed a series of short trails that vary in length and topography. A small pamphlet describing them is available at the visitors' centre. One popular track is the James Callaghan Trail that leads to the top of the 806 meter (2,620 feet) Gros Morne Mountain. It starts out in boreal forest, rises to arctic alpine habitat, and, at the top, includes a tremendous view of the Long Range Mountains and Bonne Bay. Each of the short trails can be hiked in one day or less, and it's worth considering spending several days hiking a few of them since each has been built in order to show off unique features of the park. More adventurous campers should check at the visitors' centre regarding longer routes.

Some skiers argue that Newfoundland, and Gros Morne in particular, contains some of the best cross-country skiing in eastern Canada. The finest skiing in Gros Morne is on the western side of the Long Range Mountains, where annual snowfall can exceed 6 metres (20 feet). Ski touring along the summit plateau is exciting, and Telemarking down the slopes, with the ocean spread out below, is a memorable experience. Skiers should be experienced, and a good topographical map, compass, and the ability to use them, are prerequisites.

The park contains sheer cliffs that fall into the sea, rocky but shallow headlands near some of the deep fjords, thick boreal forest, treeless barrens, wet meadows, and chemically ridden volcanic rocks that support a minimum of vegetation. This is a wilderness of contrasts that has been home to three pre-European cultures: the Maritime Archaic Indians, Dorset Eskimos, and Beothuk Indians. The extinction of the Beothuks in the early 1880s is a sad comment on our present culture.

Moose and rabbit are the two mammals most often seen by park visitors, but lynx, bear and a small version of the woodland caribou are found in the interior. Hikers or skiers who go in search of wildlife may have to pass through the narrow band of unusually stunted white spruce and balsam fir that appear wherever the coastline lacks protection from the open sea. The wind has whipped these trees into a thick mat of interwoven vegetation called *krummholz*. Known locally as *tuckamore*, this barrier may at first seem impenetrable, but persevere and you will eventually find a route through it.

Backcountry permits are required for overnight trips, and supplies can be obtained locally in the small communities adjacent to the park. Newfoundland is a unique part of Canada with fascinating people and exciting wilderness areas.

For more information contact:

Superintendent
Gros Morne National Park
P.O. Box 130
Rocky Harbour, Newfoundland
A0K 4N0
(709) 458–2417

AUYUITTUQ NATIONAL PARK, NORTH WEST TERRITORIES — Hiking and Mountaineering

Auyuittuq is an Inuit word meaning "the place that does not melt". In 1972 this park was created as the first national park to encompass territory above the Arctic Circle. It was established to help preserve a small part of Canada's unique and spectacular arctic wilderness. Access is by jet from Montreal to Iqaluit (formerly Frobisher Bay), and then by regular flight to Pangnirtung. From this village, near the mouth of the fjord, travel to Overlord on the park border can be arranged either by snowmobile or sled early in the season or by boat later on.

Crossing the arctic circle in Auyuituq National Park.

The park encompasses an area of over 21,000 square kilometres (8,000 square miles) and includes the Penny Ice Cap and Pangnirtung Pass. Naturalists, hikers and climbers are attracted to the park, with visitors arriving from as far away as New Zealand and South Africa. Rugged terrain and demanding weather conditions require a high degree of expertise among all who venture to this park. Most visitors bring in their own supplies; however, there are Hudson's Bay stores at both Iqaluit, which is a full scale town, and Pangnirtung, which is a much smaller settlement with a limited range of supplies. Pangnirtung also sports a small motel, nursing station, post office, cooperative store, hotel, and police station. Guides and boats or snowmobiles are available for hire.

Although a few mountaineers arrive to explore the peaks of the central Cumberland Peninsula, the majority of visitors are hikers who plan to trek through the Pangnirtung Pass. This pass is up to 1.5 kilometres (.9 miles) deep and winds of 100 kilometres (60 miles) per hour are not unknown. One of the most common itineraries is to travel on foot from Overlord up the east side of the pass, around Summit and Glacier Lakes, then return south on the western side. Travelling the entire length of the pass will take you to the north Pangnirtung Fjord. From this point a boat can be hired (arrangements should be made in advance) to take you to Broughton Island. There is scheduled air service from Broughton Island back to Iqaluit. The loop from Pangnirtung around Glacier Lake and back to the town is just over 100 kilometres (60 miles). It is recommended that you allow at least five days to cover this distance, exclusive of rest days and side trips.

Lemmings, arctic fox, arctic hare and snowy owls are common to the area, with polar bear and caribou being less common. The ringed seal is the most often seen marine animal, but beluga whales and Atlantic walrus are also sighted.

All arrangements should be made ahead of time, all participants should be experienced and in good condition, and it is
important to notify the park office in Pangnirtung or Broughton
Island regarding travel plans. Campers must be totally self-suffi-
cient. The number of visitors entering the park each year is
relatively small.

For more information contact:

The Superintendent
Auyuittuq National Park
Pangnirtung, N.W.T.
X0A 0R0
(819) 473–8828

ALLAGASH WILDERNESS WATERWAY, MAINE — Canoeing

The Allagash Waterway is a 146 kilometre (92 mile) stretch of wilderness in northern Maine. It is often described as the finest combination of wilderness lakes and white water canoeing in the eastern United States. The route is protected and administered by the State of Maine. Camping permits are required.

Deer are very common in northern Maine.

Until fairly recently, the Allagash River was used to float logs downstream, and horses were used to pull barges upstream, bringing supplies to the logging camps. When the barges were emptied, the horses were loaded on to them for a quick ride back downstream. The logging continues and, though there is a buffer zone of about 150 to 250 metres (165 to 275 yards) between the river and logging operations, paddlers will hear the sounds of chain saws and heavy equipment. Originally, the logging companies actively opposed any sort of designated wilderness area.

There is relatively little public road access into the northern Maine and the Allagash area. Though logging roads exist, these are privately controlled and arrangements to use them should be made in advance.

Moose, deer, raccoons, and mink are common; black bears may also be seen. In addition, there are many relics from early logging days. Near the shore of Chamberlain Lake is an old paddle-wheeler that used to tow log booms. Abandoned to its fate, this boat is slowly rotting in the harsh Maine climate. Back from the shore of Eagle Lake, still on tracks, are two old steam locomotives forsaken during the Depression.

The most common departure point for those who plan to canoe the entire length of the waterway is Telos Landing on Telos Lake. Telos Landing can be reached via the logging roads from Millinocket and Patten. During July and August, weekends on Allagash are very crowded, this is particularly evident in the vicinity of Telos. In recent years, more than 10,000 canoeists paddle the Allagash each season. As a result, the best time to travel the river is from mid September through October, even though the lower water levels will likely create some difficulties. Black fly season is June.

USGS topographic maps provide the necessary detail to prepare paddlers for the Allagash. The maps required for this trip include Chesuncook, Telos Lake, Allagash Lake, Churchill Lake, Umsakis Lake, Round Pond, Allagash Falls, and Allagash. (For information on ordering USGS maps see Chapter 4.)

The first third of the trip is lake paddling, then the river takes over. A portage service is available below Churchill Dam for the 15 kilometre (9 mile) Chase Rapids, though many choose to pole, walk, line, and portage this section where necessary. In high water you may be able to tackle the Class II rapids. However, your approach to Chase Rapids will be dictated by the time of year and your temperament. There are also short portages around Lock Dam and Allagash Falls. The most difficult rapids are located below West Twin Brook. These rapids can reach Class III if the water level is particularly high. You can end the trip at the town of Allagash. The best side trip is up the Allagash Stream into Allagash Lake. No motorized watercraft or airplanes are permitted in this area.

The trip requires seven days, but you can take more time and investigate any of the adjoining bays and lakes in the area. Travel permits can be obtained at Telos Landing.

For information on accessing private roads in the Allagash area contact:

North Maine Woods
Landowners Association
Box 552
Presque Isle, Maine 04769

or

Paper Industry Information
Office
133 State St.
Augusta, Maine 04330
(207) 622–3166

For route information contact:

State Park and Recreation
Commission
State Office Building
Augusta, Maine 04330

or read

AMC River Guide: Maine.

TUCKERMAN RAVINE TRAIL & MOUNT WASHINGTON, NEW HAMPSHIRE — Hiking & Skiing

Whiteouts, like this one, are common on Mount Washington.

The White Mountains of New Hampshire offer some of the best hiking trips in the northeastern United States. The trails vary from easy day hiking to extended hut-to-hut treks. This description focuses on one relatively short hike, the Tuckerman Ravine Trail to the summit of Mount Washington.

At 1,917 metres (6,288 feet), Mount Washington is the highest summit in the Presidential Range. It is well known for extreme weather conditions. The recorded temperature at the summit has never risen above 22° Celsius (71° Fahrenheit), and annual snowfall averages 452 cm. (178 inches) per year. Winds of 100 kilometres (60 miles) per hour are common, and in 1934 the weather station at the summit recorded a wind speed of 367 kilometres (231 miles) per hour—a record for the planet! This is not a mountain to be trifled with. One minute you may be hiking in beautiful weather, and the next you may be engulfed by a severe storm. Be prepared for snow throughout the year.

There are three ways to reach the top of Mount Washington: the automobile road, a cog railway line, and Tuckerman Trail. The automobile route is a toll road, open in good weather during the summer. It appeals to tourists who want to see the view from the summit (usually not very good) and buy a "This car climbed Mount Washington" bumper sticker. The cog railroad was built in 1869. It climbs an average grade of 25% over its 6 kilometre (3½ mile) length. It also appeals to the summer tourist trade. Recently, the owner and operator of the railroad has been experimenting with a rotary plough in order to offer transportation to the top during the winter season.

The Tuckerman Ravine Trail is well marked and easy to follow. It begins on the east side of the mountain at Pinkham Notch, located on New Hampshire's Route 16 south of Gorham. The first section of the path follows an old fire trail, crosses the Cutler River, then begins to climb the mountain via two long switchbacks. Following the switchbacks, the path continues west at a steady grade, reaching the Herman Lake camping shelters at kilometre 4 (mile 2.4). These shelters are operated by the Appalachian Mountain Club (AMC). The trail begins again just beyond the buildings, stays to the right of the stream, and climbs up and into Tuckerman Ravine, the sight of a glacial cirque. Hikers should continue to the headwall, then turn right and ascend a steep slope littered with rock debris. A snow arch, located to the left, sometimes forms in this area. *Avoid the arch, and, under no conditions, walk under it.* At least one death has occurred when a hiker ventured close and a section of the arch fell. If the arch extends across the entire trail, hikers should backtrack and ascend via the Lion Head Trail. At the top of the slope, the trail turns left, and shortly thereafter, after passing under a cliff, it runs west up a grassy slope. After reaching the plateau, the trail then turns right and follows cairns and painted rocks to a point where it joins the automobile road near the summit. The total distance is 6.6 kilometres (4.1 miles). Hiking time is estimated at 4½ hours.

Since the 1930s, the headwall area of Tuckerman Ravine has attracted skiers. Many of them reached the top of the mountain on the train, then skied all the way down to Pinkham Notch. Nowadays, most skiers hike into the ravine via Tuckerman Trail. Purists argue that if the winter train starts operating again, it will bring inexperienced, marginal skiers to an area known for severe weather and extreme skiing. The result could be a disaster. Others argue that skiers have been using the area for decades, and have a right to use any means available to enjoy their sport. Whatever the result of this debate, skiing Tuckerman is only a good idea if you are a very strong skier equipped with the proper gear. Though many skiers use regular downhill equipment, mountaineering or telemark equipment is preferable. The best skiing is usually after April 1st. In mid-April, the area attracts several thousand skiers, many of whom attempt the 215 metre (700 foot) headwall, often described as the steepest regularly skied slope in the United States. When skiing the headwall, care should be taken to avoid the crevasses. The ski-out from the ravine follows the John Shelbourne ski trail, which ends near Pinkham Notch. Skiing on the hiking path is not permitted because of the danger to those on foot.

For White Mountain trail descriptions read:

AMC White Mountain Trail Guide **or** *AMC Guide to Mount Washington & the Presidential Range*; both are by Eugene Daniell.

For information on conditions in the Tuckerman area phone:

Androscoggin Ranger Station (603) 466–2713

APPALACHIAN TRAIL, EASTERN UNITED STATES — Hiking

This trail, begun in 1921, is one of the world's paramount hiking tracks. The Appalachian Trail covers a total distance of 3,120 kilometres (2,015 miles), and runs from Springer Mountain in northern Georgia to Mount Katahdin in Maine. Over its distance the trail winds and weaves through parts of 14 states: Georgia, North Carolina, Tennessee, Virginia, West Virginia, Maryland, Pennsylvania, New Jersey, New York, Connecticut, Massachusetts, Vermont, New Hampshire, and Maine.

Enjoying the view on the Tennessee/North Carolina border.

The concept of a hiking trail that would range through the Appalachian Mountains of the eastern United States originated with Benton MacKaye in the early part of the 20th century. Encouraged by friends, he wrote an article titled "An Appalachian Trail, A Project in Regional Planning" for the American Institute of Architects' *Journal*. Published in 1921, this article generated support for the planning and development of the trail. The Bear Mountain section, located in the Palisades Interstate Park of New York and New Jersey, opened in 1923. The final section of the trail was completed in 1937. The Appalachian Trail Conference was founded in 1925 as a nonprofit, educational organization to represent the interests of the Appalachian Trail. Along with its member clubs, and federal and state agencies, the Conference continues to financially support and physically develop the trail, as well as publish a variety of guidebooks and other literature pertaining to the trail.

The southernmost section of the trail runs for 255 kilometres (160 miles) from Springer Mountain to Fontana Dam at the edge of Great Smoky Mountains National Park. Typical Georgia and North Carolina highland vegetation is found in this area, and, though the occasional moonshiner may still haunt the hills, you are more likely to run into soldiers on manoeuvres from Fort Benning.

For many Appalachian hikers, the Smokies are the best part of the trail. If you are planning to hike only one section of the Appalachians, the Smokies would be a good choice. This section of the trail is a mere 115 kilometres (70 miles) in length; however, there are about 1,000 kilometres (600 miles) of side trails and assorted paths within the National Park. Through the Smokies, the Appalachian Trail pretty much follows the Tennessee/North Carolina border. Intense green canopies loom overhead, and more than 1,200 varieties of flowering plants, 350 types of mosses, and 2,000 kinds of fungi spring from the dark soil. In the highland areas, the foliage is supported by more than 250 centimetres (100 inches) of precipitation each year, so don't forget your rain gear. Most hikers climb Clingmans Dome to the summit. At 2025 metres (6,643 feet) it is the highest peak on the Appalachian Trail.

On much of the Appalachian Trail, overnight camping is permitted only in shelters. In the Smokies, these shelters provide some protection from the bears. It has been estimated that there are as many as 350 black bears within the park boundaries, and many have become semi-tame as a result of visitor handouts—a foolish practice. The shelters are built with strong wire fencing on the open side in order to discourage bears.

North of the Smokies an 800 kilometre (500 mile) section of the trail runs in a northeast direction to Shenandoah National Park. This part of the trail passes through four national forests: the Cherokee National Forest in Tennessee, the Pisgah National Forest in North Carolina, the Jefferson National Forest in Virginia, and the George Washington National Forest also in Virginia. A highlight of this section of the trail is Roan Mountain, which at 1,916 metres (6,286 feet) is one of the highest peaks on the trail.

In northern Virginia, a 160 kilometre (100 mile) section of the trail crisscrosses Shenandoah National Park's Skyline Drive 25 times. Situated in the Blue Ridge mountains, this is one of the most heavily travelled sections of the trail. A variety of side trails leads to lookout points, streams, caves, and waterfalls. Some of these trails have been specifically designed for travel by horse. North of Shenandoah, the path follows ridges and rocky ground into Maryland, passing near Harpers Ferry, then continues north to South Mountain on the Maryland/Pennsylvania border. The Pennsylvania section of the trail is one of contrasts, including open farmlands, high ridges, state game lands, and several notable crests.

After crossing into New Jersey, the trail continues in a northeast direction until it reaches the New York border. At that point it turns southeast into New York State, dips due south briefly back into New Jersey, then finally turns northeast once more and enters Palisades Interstate Park. After crossing the Hudson River via the Bear Mountain Bridge, the trail runs through a series of state forests in Connecticut and Massachusetts, finally reaching the Vermont border at the Green Mountain National Forest. At this juncture, the Appalachian Trail and the Long Trail of the Green Mountain Club merge for a distance of almost 160 kilometres (95 miles). The stretch through the Green Mountains runs on a north-south axis, following which the trail turns northeast once again, crossing the Vermont/New Hampshire border, and entering the White Mountain National Forest in northern New Hampshire. The Green Mountain National Forest and the White Mountain National Forest are two of the most beautiful and more difficult sections of the trail. The weather in the White Mountain area, and Mount Washington in particular (see the Tuckerman Ravine and White Mountain section in this chapter), can be extremely severe.

The final section of the trail stretches for 460 kilometres (270 miles), from the New Hampshire state line deep into the heart of Maine. Swamps, lakes, streams, bogs, and deep forests typify this isolated section of the trail. The small town of Monson is the last supply point before Baxter State Park, where the trail ends at Mount Katahdin. A well supplied hiker in good condition will take about ten days to travel this 200 kilometre (120 mile) section of the trail. Self-sufficiency is required. Climbing and descending Katahdin requires one good day.

The Appalachian Trail Conference estimates that as many as 2,000 people set off each year to hike the entire trail, but only 150 accomplish their objective. Many start at Springer Mountain, and quit when they reach the first town, twenty miles north. These hikers give up because they are ill-prepared for the rugged terrain, are in poor physical shape, and lack the required equipment. Examining maps and day dreaming in the comfort of your living room is a far cry from the physically and mentally challenging conditions that are part and parcel of long distance hiking. Unless you are prepared to dedicate the better part of a year to planning and carrying out a "thru-hike," it's best to pick a pleasant section of the trail and enjoy an easy, relaxed pace.

For more information contact:

The Appalachian Trail Conference
Washington & Jackson Streets
P.O. Box 807
Harpers Ferry, West Virginia 25425
(304) 535–6331

Bald Cypress trees along the canoe route in Okefenokee.

OKEFENOKEE NATIONAL WILDLIFE REFUGE, GEORGIA AND FLORIDA — Canoeing

The Okefenokee swamp and wilderness area, established in 1937, covers approximately 1,760 square kilometres (680 square miles) of southeastern Georgia and northeastern Florida. Though not large when compared with many other parks, the Okefenokee is an extremely unusual wilderness area. Bounded by civilization, the refuge has survived as a unique ecosystem where nature remains pretty much in balance.

Some 250,000 years ago, the shoreline of the Atlantic Ocean was 120 kilometres (75 miles) further inland than the present day coast of Georgia. Tides, currents and surf action created a narrow sandbar along the coast, stretching north to south for a distance of 65 kilometres (40 miles). Over time, as this sandbar took shape, a shallow lagoon was created. When the ocean retreated, the lagoon evolved into the body of water that currently exists. The result is a swamp which, at more than 30 metres (100 feet) above sea level, is higher than most of the land that surrounds it. The greater part of this swamp drains to the west, into the Suwannee River and then to the Gulf of Mexico. Water in the east part of the swamp drains into the St. Marys River and flows down to the Atlantic Ocean. The swamp is refueled with spring water and rain.

The peat bed islands in the Okefenokee developed as dead and decaying plant material was separated from the bottom of the swamp by trapped gases. Considerable vegetation has developed on the peat beds, which, because they lack solid bases, tremble and quake as you walk on them. The peat bogs gave rise to the Indian name Okefenokee, meaning "trembling earth." Approximately 70 land masses, large and stable enough to be called islands, as well as 60 lakes of different sizes are in the refuge.

The Okefenokee is home to a wide variety of wildlife and plants. Over 200 species of birds have been spotted in the swamp, along with 40 species of mammals, 50 species of reptiles, and 30 species of amphibians. The largest mammal in the area is the black bear. Bladderwort, pitcher plants, and sun dew, all of which are carnivorous, are among some of the more interesting plants found in the Okefenokee.

The Okefenokee is cared for by the Department of the Interior through the Fish and Wildlife Service. Part of the caretaker role has involved mapping canoe trails through the swamp and building overnight platform shelters for canoeists wanting to spend a few uninterrupted days in the interior. The trails are colour coded, making the routefinding quite straightforward, and the shelters are lean-to affairs, usually equipped with chemical toilets. The coffee coloured water is quite drinkable. If this sounds too neat and orderly, not to mention too sanitary, for a wilderness experience, consider the alligators, the thousands of roosting birds, the jungle-like canopies created by the cypress trees, the broad meadows of sedge and lilies, and the poisonous snakes. Make no mistake, the Okefenokee, particularly at night, is a disquieting experience. As the sun sets, the crickets and other insects begin their chorus, then the birds start to "talk," making a racket that continues for hours. But the alligators, and the sounds they make while snapping up an unwary turtle or bird, really let you know this isn't a typical northern river. The best time to canoe the Okefenokee is in March or April; October and November are second best. During June and July the mosquitoes and rain make the area less attractive.

The designated canoe trips within the refuge range from two to five days in length. Camping is only permitted at specified sites and permits are required. Canoeists are advised to stay clear of the alligators. Contrary to some opinions, alligators are extremely fast. There will likely be times when you have to step into the water in order to push clear of plants or mud; it's wise to look around very carefully before leaving the canoe. Snakes, are another problem. The Okefenokce is home to 37 species of snakes, including representatives from three of the four poisonous snake groups. The cottonmouth,or water moccasin, is the most numerous. It has a reputation for being grouchy and fast. Other poisonous snakes include the pygmy rattlesnake, the canebrake, the eastern diamondback, and the coral snake. Even the nonvenomous snakes, such as the eastern coachwhip, can inflict painful bites. Alligator snapping turtles are found throughout the park.

Talk of alligators, snakes, and other beasts is not meant to dissuade you from canoeing the Okefenokee. Be enthusiastic, but wary. In fact, few canoeists experience any serious difficulties. This area represents a singular canoeing experience. The sights and sounds of the Okefenokee, like any extraordinary adventure, are hard to forget.

For more information write:

Okefenokee National Wildlife Refuge
RT. 2, Box 338
Folkston, Georgia 31537
(912) 496–3331

or read:

The Okefenokee Swamp by Franklin Russell.

A tough looking crew at High Falls on the Dumoine River.

KIPAWA DISTRICT AND LA VERENDRYE PARK, QUEBEC — Canoeing

This central-western area of Quebec has a maze of interconnected lakes and rivers that make it very popular among residents of Quebec, Ontario, New York and Pennsylvania. The most common access point is at the town of Kipawa, about 70 kilometres (40 miles) northwest of North Bay, Ontario. Although reasonably isolated, this area is of moderate difficulty for most campers. The major problem is the blackflies, which are abundant early in the season. There are no supply points in the interior, so extensive provisions must be carried or arrangements made to have food flown to a preselected location. This second option can be organized through the Kipawa Air Service in the town of Kipawa.

The many lakes in Kipawa and La Verendrye allow for numerous canoe route combinations. One nice route is through the Kipawa, Pommeroy, Short Cut, Taylor, Cigarette, Watson and Grassy Lakes chain. You can then backtrack to Watson and Lac des Loupes, travel south on the Kipawa River to Lac Sairs, and return to Kipawa via Booth and Grindstone. This would require a minimum of 15–18 good travelling days. Moose are plentiful, the fishing is great, and the scenery grand.

For those who want something more challenging, it is possible to continue east past Grassy, to Lac Dumoine. Then, the Dumoine River can be used as an exit route to Stonecliffe on the Ottawa River. The Dumoine is a challenging white water river, and all canoeists should be skilled. If you take this route, you might also want to consider a short diversion north on Lac Dumoine and into La Verendrye Park via Lac Antiquois. Moose are very plentiful just south of the Lac Antiquois portage, and the fishing in Antiquois is tremendous. The journey from Kipawa to Stonecliffe, complete with rest days and side trips to places such as Antiquois, will require approximately 25–28 days. The western area of Kipawa is fairly well travelled, and the Dumoine River has become quite busy in recent years.

MISSINAIBI RIVER, ONTARIO — Canoeing

The Missinaibi River is one of the finest, easily accessible, white water, wilderness canoeing experiences available. It includes excellent opportunities to see wildlife, interesting geological formations, and archaeological dig sites. The river starts about 90 air kilometres (55 miles) north of Chapleau. Entry points include: Highway 651 at Dog Lake via car; Missinaibi Station on Dog Lake via railway; and Missinaibi Lake Provincial Park via the access road from Chapleau. Some canoeists start at the mouth of the Michipecoten River on Lake Superior and travel the entire route from Lake Superior to James Bay, while others take the C.N.R. to Peterbell and enter at this point. The Peterbell entry point excludes Missinaibi Lake which, in my opinion, is a high point of the trip. Canoeists with limited time may choose to restrict their canoeing to the northern portion of the river, from Mattice to Moose River Crossing or Moosonee.

Thunderhouse Falls on the Missinaibi River.

The Missinaibi River requires a high degree of skill. Parts of the river are quite isolated, the trip is a long one, and the rapids are challenging. From Dog Lake to Moosonee is about 640 kilometres (380 miles). This trip can require as much as four weeks, in part because there is so much to see. Limited reprovisioning can take place at Mattice (where Highway 11 crosses the river). Alternatively, you may want to travel the 30 kilometres (18 miles) from Mattice to Hearst, where you can fully reprovision.

Assuming you start at Dog Lake, the route runs east through Crooked Lake (which is quite straight) into Lake Missinaibi. The portage between Dog and Crooked marks the divide between the Atlantic and Arctic watersheds. Some of the best examples of Indian pictographs ever found are located at Fairy Point on Lake Missinaibi. Look for them on the sheer rock that faces the setting sun. Whitefish Falls has pictographs and good fishing. Lake trout are abundant. The Lake Missinaibi provincial campground supervisor may be able to tell you where government archaeologists are digging. If reports are available, they make for interesting reading. Between the provincial campground and New Brunswick House, the lake narrows and becomes quite shallow. This is the southern boundary of the Chapleau Game Reserve, where there has been no authorized hunting for over 50 years and, as a result, moose seem to take a very casual view towards canoeists. Early in the morning this may be one of the best spots in Canada to photograph moose in their natural habitat. A herd of elk lives in the vicinity of New Brunswick House, but it is unlikely you will catch a glimpse of them since, unlike the moose, they seem to be very wary of humans.

At the end of Missinaibi Lake, the river takes over. All the rapids, and there are many, should be carefully checked before running. Between Lake Missinaibi and Mattice there are two possible exit points in the event of an emergency. The first is the C.N.R. line at Peterbell. Peterbell is a defunct logging town, and, at most, boasts a few fishermen. The second exit is two kilometres (1.25 miles) upstream from the junction of the Brunswick River, where the Spruce Falls Pulp and Paper Company built a logging road. Downstream from Mattice there is a road which runs parallel to the river for about 14 kilometres (9 miles), following which the next exit point is Moose River Crossing.

North of Mattice the river increases in size and changes in character, becoming wide (200 metres or 215 yards) and shallow. Thunderhouse Falls, about 30 kilometres (18 miles) north of Mattice, marks the beginning of the transformation from the Canadian shield to the Hudson Bay lowlands. A major geological fault sends the 200 meter (215 yards) wide river through a three metre (10 foot) gap. There are three falls at this location, and a large rock pillar (Conjuring House) sacred to the Cree. Kettles are common. Stone Rapids and Hell's Gate follow in quick succession. These obstructions are avoided by taking the 4 kilometre (2.5 mile) portage on the east side of the river, or two slightly shorter portages if you want to paddle the flat water that separates them. The Stone Rapids and Hell's Gate portage is relatively straight and wide.

Fishing for walleye in Hell's Gate can be very productive. At the end of the portage, paddle over to the west side, and walk part way back up the rapid, then cast into the pools formed by indentations in the rock. I recommend a Mepp's #3, or a leech if you prefer live bait. Below Long Rapids the river attains a width of up to two kilometres (1.2 miles) and becomes quite shallow. Watch for the strong riffle immediately below the junction with the Moose River, and be very wary of white water located just above the junction with the Kwatoboahegan River. From this point it is just a few hours paddling time to Moosonee.

For further information see:

Wild Rivers: James Bay and Hudson Bay. (1977). Ottawa: Parks Canada.

For a route description, contact:

Mithril Wilderness Programs
61 Bessborough Drive
Toronto, Ontario
M4G 3H8

ALBANY RIVER AND JAMES BAY, ONTARIO — Canoeing

The stretch of James Bay coast between Fort Albany and Moosonee can be warm and inviting on a pleasant summer afternoon, or harsh, frigid, and very cruel when the weather turns bad. Canoeists are attracted to this area for its isolation, sweeping scenery, tens of thousands of shorebirds, beluga whales, seals, tundra-like tidal flats, and challenge.

In order to get to Fort Albany, which is the jumping off point for the trip along the coast, most canoeists begin near the town of Hearst on Highway 11. Approximately 45 kilometres (27 miles) west of Hearst, there is a small access road that runs north from Highway 11 to the Kabinakagami River. This is the spot where the boats go in the water. The Kabinakagami flows north to join the Kenogami River, which in turn joins the Albany River. The Albany flows east to Fort Albany, which is just a short distance from James Bay. This river section of the trip can take up to two weeks. Woodland caribou and occasional white water are the highlights. Some canoeists begin the trip as far west as Savant Lake, and follow the Albany for its entire length; however, this will add another ten to fourteen days to the trip.

Waiting for the tide to come in on James Bay.

The trip down the Bay should be attempted only by highly experienced canoeists. In good weather, this section can be paddled in as little as five days, but bad weather could easily stretch this out for ten to fourteen days. Almost every conceivable canoeing predicament is a possibility, with the biggest single concern being the tide. High tide occurs every twelve and one half hours, and because the bay is very shallow, with tidal flats running two kilometres (1.2 miles) or more out into the bay, it is usually very difficult to get to dry ground except at high tide. Slogging equipment across the tidal flats is very laborious; you sink in the mud up to your knees. Further, salt water paddling requires fresh water to be carried for the duration of the trip. The top maps show that fresh water river outlets are at a premium, and rarely in locations that make them easy to access.

When you depart from Fort Albany, it is worth considering a long day of paddling in order to make your first camp at Nomansland Point. This tiny spit of land juts out into the bay and acts as a container for a number of small, saline ponds. Through to the late summer, small delicate wildflowers grace the landscape and berries are everywhere. In the late summer, migrating shorebirds arrive in huge numbers. Indian hunting camps dot the shoreline, but most are uninhabited except for the occasional dog that has been left to forage for itself over the summer months. Cockispenny Point, Halfway Point, Longridge Point, and North Point provide the best possibilities for campsites on this section of the Bay. Halfway Point is a particularly good spot since it is only a short walk south from the point to the mouth of a fresh water river where your water jugs can be replenished. Sandhill Cranes and Hudsonian Godwits may be spotted in this area. Immediately south of North Point there is a Goose Hunting Camp that has been used by the Canadian Wildlife Services as a bird observation and banding station. If the station is active, and the banders have time to show you what they're doing, it is quite interesting.

The Bay portion of this route is rarely travelled for obvious reasons, and it is important to emphasize that weather conditions will make an incredible difference in your trip. If a gentle northwest wind persists, then it is feasible to sail down the bay using a rain poncho or a piece of plastic; however, freak rain and hail storms can force you to remain camped for days. If you are out on the Bay and a storm hits, exposure will be your major concern. The water will often be a meter (3 feet) or less in depth, but the nearest solid ground may be two kilometres (1.2 miles) across the tidal flats. Experienced canoeists have died on this section of the trip, some by drowning and others from exposure.

POINT PELEE NATIONAL PARK, ONTARIO —
Hiking

Point Pelee National Park, known worldwide as a preeminent bird watching area, is the most southerly part of mainland Canada. Pelee's unique habitat is home to many unusual species of plants, amphibians, insects and mammals, making it a mecca for professional and amateur naturalists. Pelee, particularly in the spring, is an exceptional experience.

By road, Pelee is about one hour from Windsor and four hours from Toronto. Although Pelee is far from being a wilderness area, its unusual flora and abundance of bird life more than make up for the lack of isolation. The park includes a variety of trails, an interpretive centre, and, during the summer, a natural gas powered mini-train takes visitors to the southern tip. Camping is not permitted in the park except by groups or organizations that book well in advance; however, there are many places that offer accommodation just outside the park. Most people who visit Pelee are interested in day hiking and often start at 5 a.m. since it is the first four to five hours of daylight that often prove to be the most productive when looking for birds.

Day hiking routes vary according to personal tastes. Be sure to get a copy of the park map at the entry point, and don't be afraid to ask questions of staff or other visitors. Many birders start out very early at the tip since this is where the latest migrants will be, though other birders prefer the marsh walks. A pair of binoculars or a spotting scope is essential, and the first two weeks in May are the best for warbler migration.

Birds are the major attraction at Point Pelee.

For more information contact:

The Superintendent
Point Pelee National Park
Leamington, Ontario
N8H 3V4
(519) 326–3204

Checking the park map on Isle Royale.

ISLE ROYALE NATIONAL PARK, LAKE SUPERIOR — Hiking and Canoeing

This 544 square kilometre (210 square mile) island tucked into the northwestern corner of Lake Superior is home to some outstanding hiking and canoeing routes. The park was created in 1940 and is part of Michigan, though it's closer to Minnesota. Just 70 kilometres (44 miles) in length and averaging less than 5 kilometres (3 miles) in width, Isle Royale has remained quite isolated. In part, this is because there are no public roads, and the only way to get to the island is by ferry or float plane.

Ferries leave from Grand Portage in northeastern Minnesota and from Houghton and Copper Harbour in Michigan. These take anywhere from 2½ to 6 hours each way, depending on where you leave from and where you want to get off. The main entry point for the park is at Rock Harbour on the southeastern coast. This is where you can check out the hotel, pick up a few last minute supplies, get your camping permit, and rent a canoe.

The Greenstone Ridge Trail, at 65 kilometres (40 miles) in length, is the longest in the park. It is well marked, runs from one end of the island to the other, is fairly level, and is easily accessible from Rock Island. North of this is the Minong Trail. It joins with the Greenstone Ridge Trail, and the two make for an interesting and challenging loop hike. The Minong Trail is relatively isolated and harder to follow. It appeals to hikers who want some solitude. Other trails branch off from these two trails, leading to quiet, out of the way places. There are a total of 285 kilometres (180 miles) of hiking trails on the island.

The best canoe route begins at McCargoe Cove on the north side of the island and follows a series of rivers, portages, and small lakes until it reaches Siskiwit Lake, the largest on the island. From here, canoeists can paddle south and east to Chippewa Harbour, then turn north to rejoin the original route at Lake Ritchie. The scenery is delightful and the solitude enchanting.

There are two important cautions with regard to Isle Royale. The first relates to paddling the perimeter of the island. Lake Superior is a notoriously nasty lake. Storms, heavy waves, and cold water are frequent and unforgiving. Anyone planning to kayak or canoe on open water should be well prepared and highly experienced. The second problem relates to the park water. Tapeworm parasites make the water unfit for human consumption without first boiling or filtering it. Though the park is a true wilderness area, the water is undrinkable without first being treated.

Lake Superior, the largest freshwater body of water in the world, buffers the island's climate, so that temperatures tend to be cooler in the summer and warmer in the winter than those experienced on the mainland. The island lies within the transition zone between boreal and northern hardwood forests. Near the shoreline, white spruce, white birch, and aspen are common. Away from the water, at higher elevations, sugar maple and yellow birch are found. Mammals on the island include wolves, fox, moose, beaver, otters, and hares. Estimated at 1,400, the moose population on Isle Royale is considerable. Both the moose and their predators the wolves have been the subject of major research projects. The moose arrived on the island at the turn of the century, while the wolf came across the ice in the late 1940's. Most of the moose on the island eventually fall prey to the wolves.

Isle Royale closes in the winter, with the last ferry run in mid-October. Whereas most national parks measure the length of stay for the average visitor in terms of hours, at Isle Royale the typical hiker or canoeist lingers for four days. And with 15,000 visitors each year, low impact camping is a must. There is lots to see and do. The charm, beauty, and isolation of Isle Royale are very attractive.

For more information contact:

National Park Service
87 N. Ripley Street
Houghton, Michigan 49931
(906) 482–0986

or read:

Isle Royale National Park by
Jim DuFresne

Winter in the BWCA/Quetico is a pristine experience.

BOUNDARY WATERS CANOE AREA (BWCA), MINNESOTA, & QUETICO PROVINCIAL PARK, ONTARIO — Canoeing & Winter Camping

The Boundary Waters Canoe Area (BWCA) in northeastern Minnesota adjoins Quetico Provincial Park in western Ontario. It has been described as the biggest designated wilderness tract in North America, outside Alaska. The BWCA includes the northern part of Superior National Forest, and, combined with Quetico, ranges over more than 1,215,000 hectares (3 million acres)

Within the BWCA and Quetico wilderness, there are hundreds of good sized lakes, many joined by rivers or short portages. And, the entire area sits on the Canadian Shield, one of the few places in the world where the earth's original crust lies exposed. This means rocky outcroppings for great campsites and clear, clean, cool, deep lakes.

Temperatures in the BWCA and Quetico areas range from summer highs of 40° Celsius (104° Fahrenheit), to winter lows of –40° Celsius (–40° Fahrenheit). In spite of warm daytime temperatures during July and August, the thermometer will often dip below freezing at night. This means canoeists must pack warm sleeping bags and extra clothing, even during mid-summer.

From the Minnesota side, access to the BWCA is from the towns of Ely, Grand Marais, Crane Lake, and Tofte. These can be reached by road from Duluth. In Ontario, access to Quetico is from the town of Atikokan, which can be reached by road from Fort Francis or Thunder Bay. Atikokan also has daily scheduled air service.

Although described in much of the literature as a wilderness area, the BWCA and Quetico park system is better characterized as a heavily used outdoor recreation area, with good canoeing and hiking, and great winter camping. Each year, park visitors number in the tens of thousands. Many are day guests, but a sizeable number spend a week or more in the interior. In order to cope with the traffic, quota systems, restrictions on group size, and permits have been instituted. A "pack it in and pack it out" policy is in effect, and stoves are encouraged. During July and August the parks are crowded. In May, June and September, the canoeing is just as good, and the crowds have disappeared. Better still are the winter months. For snowshoeing and cross-country skiing, the BWCA and Quetico areas are superb.

Canoe routes are numerous and, with the aid of a BWCA or Quetico map, anyone with limited canoeing experience can chart out a good route, including plenty of alternatives in the event that the trip itinerary requires modification. Alternately, if you plan to rent equipment from one of the many guiding and outfitting services, they will sketch out a route designed to dovetail with your interests and expertise. They will also arrange for the necessary permits and give you good advice on everything from campsite locations to fishing holes.

Winter routes are a little trickier, largely because of the greater challenges inherent in winter camping. Before entering either the BWCA or Quetico area in winter, you should be proficient in all facets of cold weather camping. In the winter when the crowds are gone you needn't go long distances for an isolated and challenging outdoor experience, but winter visitors need to be accordingly more experienced and cautious. The shorter canoe routes, near the major departure sites, make for good cross-country skiing and snowshoeing routes.

For more information contact:

Parks & Recreation Areas
Ministry of Natural Resources
Whitney Block
Toronto, Ontario M7A 1W3
(416) 965–3081

or

BWCA, Superior National Forest
P.O. Box 338
Federal Building
Duluth, Minnesota 55801
(218) 720–5440

Arctic terns are commonly seen on northern rivers.

For more information see:

Wild Rivers: Saskatchewan.
(1974). Ottawa: Parks Canada.

UPPER CHURCHILL RIVER, SASKATCHEWAN —
Canoeing

The journey from Lac Ile-a-la-Crosse to Sandy Bay retraces one of the main voyageur routes. For this reason, the trip attracts many canoeists, particularly those with an interest in fur trade history.

By car, Ile-a-la-Crosse can be reached by travelling north from either Prince Albert or North Battleford, both in Saskatchewan, for about 400 kilometres (240 miles). If you want to leave your car in Prince Albert or North Battleford, a float plane can be chartered to fly you to Ile-a-la-Crosse, but at considerable cost. The area is isolated and, in the event of an emergency, there is only one exit other than the termination point—where Highway 102 crosses the river near Missinipe. The trip terminates either at Sandy Bay or Pelican Narrows, approximately 650 kilometres (390 miles) downstream. Both Sandy Bay and Pelican Narrows are accessible by car via Highway 135, which is normally approached from either Prince Albert or, in Manitoba, The Pas.

The river is not too difficult; but the 30 odd portages, long distance and isolation require experience and independence. The trip typically takes from 24 to 28 days. Most provisions should be carried since major reprovisioning at the isolated settlements may not be possible. You may be able to arrange for limited supplies to be available through the Hudson's Bay Company, but it is important to make these arrangements well in advance.

The trip starts off in a northerly direction, but at the end of Lac Ile-a-la-Crosse the river turns east and runs to the Manitoba border. Initially, the area is sandy and good campsites are difficult to find; however, near Drum Rapids, the river enters shield country and good campsites are easier to locate. Much of the trip is through a series of what appear to be small interconnected lakes rather than a river, with rapids at most narrow points. Amateur and professional historians argue that this part of the country is little changed since explorers such as Frobisher, Thompson and Pond explored it.

Pictographs can be seen at McDonald Bay near the main body of Snake Lake, and downriver from Silent Rapids. Alexander MacKenzie referred to these rapids in his journal as the rapid "qui ne parle point"!

This entire area provides good habitat for moose, caribou and lynx, as well as Bald and Golden Eagles. Travel on this river system is not crowded, and some say voyageur songs still echo near the rapids and on the portages.

HANBURY AND THELON RIVERS, NORTH WEST TERRITORIES — Canoeing

This is a spectacular barrenground river trip. It incorporates incredible wildlife, challenging white water, outstanding fishing, ferocious bugs, and sensational scenery. The area is completely isolated, so canoeists must be highly experienced and fully outfitted. There are no early exit points.

Muskox are easy to spot along the Hanbury and Thelon rivers.

The usual starting point for this trip is Sifton Lake. The easiest way to get to this lake is to charter a plane out of Yellowknife, approximately 415 kilometres (250 miles) to the west. A Twin Otter, will carry up to three canoes, six canoeists, and gear: the distance from Sifton Lake to the termination of the trip at the town of Baker Lake is approximately 870 kilometres (522 miles). The trip takes three to four weeks, depending on the weather.

The first section runs from Sifton Lake, down the Hanbury River, to the Thelon River. This seven day paddle includes a 5 kilometre (3 mile) portage around Dickson Canyon and the opportunity to see muskoxen. The second section begins at the Hanbury/Thelon junction, and ends at Beverly Lake. It takes about six or seven days to paddle this fast flowing 320 kilometre stretch (190 miles). Caribou, muskoxen, wolves, grizzly bear, and fox are common. The third section includes three large lakes: Beverly, Aberdeen, and Shultz. In good weather, this section may require five or six days; in bad weather, two weeks. The final section runs from the end of Shultz Lake down the Thelon to Baker Lake, a distance of close to 100 kilometres (60 miles). If necessary, this section can be run in one long day. Take care if you choose to shoot the Aleksektok Rapids, and watch for the many unmarked rapids in the lower part of the river.

For a route description, contact:

Mithril Wilderness Programs
61 Bessborough Drive
Toronto, Ontario
M4G 3H8

Food and accommodation can be obtained in Baker Lake, and there is a regularly air service to Winnipeg via Churchill. Arrangements can be made through the Hudson's Bay store for canoes to be shipped to Churchill and then taken by train to Winnipeg.

This is a very challenging canoe trip. Spray covers are recommended, as are stoves, bug hats and bug jackets. Preparation for this trip should include reading Hanbury's *Sport and Travel in the Northland of Canada*, Christian's *Unflinching*, and Whalley's *The Legend of John Hornby*.

Bison should be given a wide berth.

For more information contact:

The Superintendent
Wood Buffalo National Park
Fort Smith, N.W.T.
X0E 0P0
(403) 872–2349

WOOD BUFFALO NATIONAL PARK, ALBERTA & NORTH WEST TERRITORIES — Hiking / Cycling

Wood Buffalo, Canada's largest national park, straddles the border of Alberta and the Northwest Territories. Most people reach the park by driving the Mackenzie Highway north from Edmonton to Hay River, and then taking Highway #5 east and south to Fort Smith. All necessary supplies can be purchased in Fort Smith—a lovely town.

There are several good reasons for visiting Wood Buffalo; chief among these is the chance to see free-roaming wood bison. The bison are often spotted along the roads, especially on the park road south of Fort Smith. The campground at Pine Lake is an excellent spot from which to take day trips, but, if you are driving, bear in mind that the only available gas is in Fort Smith and the park road circuit can use close to a tankful.

Other features of this park include sinkholes associated with karst topography. Pine Lake, the result of several sinkholes that have joined together, is more than 20 meters (22 yards) deep. Over 200 species of birds have been reported in the park, including Whooping Crane.

Several good hiking routes are located within the park, and rangers at Fort Smith are very helpful with regard to current information and suggestions. Rangers ask that you check with them and get a backcountry permit if you plan to leave the modest day trails. A short trail runs from the loop road into the Rainbow Lakes, where fishing is said to be reasonably good. This trip could be a pleasant day or overnight excursion. Because there is very little pavement anywhere in this part of the Territories, mountain bikes, along with spare parts and patch kits, are recommended for those who want to do some cycling.

One cautionary note: *bison are very unpredictable*. Given a head start, a slow car can probably outdistance a bison, but hikers and cyclists should stay as far away from the bison as possible.

Wood Buffalo Park has a steady stream of visitors but is in no way overcrowded. Many of the people coming to the park are residents of the territories; there are few outsiders relative to the size of the park. Currently there is considerable debate surrounding the bison, with some groups arguing that the herd should be destroyed because it carries infectious diseases that can be transmitted to cattle.

LONGS PEAK, ROCKY MOUNTAIN NATIONAL PARK, COLORADO — Hiking

Over half a million visitors hike the trails of Rocky Mountain National Park each year. Drawn by the spectacular scenery and unspoiled reaches, few are disappointed by what they find. Near the centre of the preserve, at 4,346 metres (14,255 feet), is Longs Peak, the highest mountain in the park. The view from the top is spectacular.

The view from Longs Peak.

Longs Peak is not an easy climb; however, five year olds have climbed it as well as many others well into their 70s. Preparation, a good night's sleep, a strong desire to reach the top, and a bit of luck will see you to the summit. More than 20 deaths have occurred in this area, so caution is important.

The trail begins at the Longs Peak Ranger Station. The climb up and down takes anywhere from 10 to 16 hours, so most hikers begin very early in the morning, often climbing by flashlight for the first few hours. The first part of the trail is quite steep, and the stands of lodgepole and limber pines make for an interesting contrast. After crossing Alpine Brook, the trail continues towards the treeline and then divides. The left trail runs alongside Mills Moraine toward Chasm Lake. This is an excellent location to get some stunning photographs, but it isn't on the direct route to the summit. The right-hand trail is the one to take. It runs back across Alpine Brook, then turns left (west) up to Jims Grove, a haven for limber pines about 5 kilometres (3 miles) from the start of the trail.

From Jims Grove the trail is quite steep, finally joining with the North Longs Peak Trail. At this point the route turns south and follows a series of switchbacks to the Boulder Field. In the past, climbers hiked from here up the north face of Longs via a series of wire cables bolted to the rocks. These have since been removed, and hikers now travel a more circuitous but safer route through the Keyhole. This narrow gap between Longs Peak and Storm Peak is overhung by granite ledges that create a keyhole silhouette. Just before the Keyhole there is a stone hut.

After passing through the Keyhole, the trail leads down into the Trough, a semi-vertical gully filled with loose stones. Below the Trough, and after following a narrow ledge, hikers climb a smooth slab of granite, appropriately named Homestretch, to the summit. In good weather it is worth spending several hours at the top of the mountain. If, however, there are storm clouds anywhere on the horizon, it is best to start down as soon as possible. There is a cairn at the summit, and most climbers sign their names on the register.

Colonel Stephen Long first documented the peak in 1820, and it was subsequently named after him. In 1868 W. N. Byers was the first to climb Longs Peak. Longs is a spectacular day hike requiring good physical and mental preparation. Be sure to take some trail food; you can fill your water bottle along the route. Warm clothing and storm gear are strongly recommended. Summer is the best time, though the hike can be carried out by experienced climbers when there is snow on the ground.

For more information read:

Rocky Mountain National Park Hiking Trails by Kent and Donna Dannen and *Facts About Longs Peak* by Harold Dunning.

BOW LAKE TO BOW HUT, ALBERTA — Hiking, Snowshoeing & Skiing

The trail to Bow Hut is located off the Banff-Jasper Highway about 40 kilometres (25 miles) north of Lake Louise. This trail is an excellent outing for day hikers in the summer and experienced cross-country skiers in the winter. During the winter the route ranks very high in degree of difficulty because of the risk of avalanche. All skiers should check with a park warden before attempting to ski this trail.

The Bow Lake to Bow Hut trail is characterized by easy accessibility, short length and very pretty scenery, especially above the tree line. The trail begins at Num-ti-jak Lodge, runs across or around the lake—depending on the season—in a west-south-west direction, then makes a gradual turn to the left as it runs uphill through a softwood forest. Above the tree line is avalanche country. Once into the basin, continue until very close to the basin wall, then turn to the right (northwest) and continue to Bow Hut. Although the route is only about 5 kilometres (3 miles) in length, it will take a good skier up to four hours to reach the hut. It isn't necessary to finish the entire route; so if in doubt, call it a day.

As with most of the Banff/Jasper routes, this trail connects with others. Experienced and equipped hikers or skiers could continue to either the Balfour Hut or the Peter Whyte Hut.

Sheep are a common sighting in the Canadian Rockies.

For more information read:

Ski Trails in the Canadian Rockies by Rick Kunelius.

If bad weather strikes, you should be prepared and able to build a snow cave.

For more information read:

The Canadian Rockies Trail Guide (4th Ed.) by Brian Patton and Bart Robinson.

The Jasper/Banff parks system is a natural envelope for hundreds of interconnected hiking trails, and there are several good guide books describing most of these routes. This brief description, and the previous one of the Bow Lake to Bow Hut route, are meant to highlight two easily accessible and yet spectacular routes. But don't forget that the entire area is a wealth of hiking trails varying in degree of difficulty from simple to demanding.

VALLEY OF A THOUSAND FALLS, BRITISH COLUMBIA — Hiking

The Valley of a Thousand Falls trail is located in Mount Robson Provincial Park, bordering on the west side of Jasper National Park. To reach the provincial park, travel northwest on Highway 16 (the Yellowhead Highway) from Jasper to the Alberta/B.C. border. Approximately 60 kilometres (36 miles) inside the park is a service station near the provincial campground. A dirt road running north from the service station for 2.5 kilometres (1.5 miles) will take you to the parking lot at the start of the trail.

Hikers should be experienced, confident with a map and compass, and in good shape. The trail is almost 38 kilometres (22 miles) roundtrip to Berg Lake. It is a relaxed three day hike or a challenging two day trip. All provisions must be carried.

The route follows the Robson River up a gradual climb to Kenney Lake at kilometre 5 (mile 3). The forest growth tends to be very thick and lush since Mount Robson acts as a barrier to clouds and forces the moisture out of them. Shortly after passing the Whitehorn Warden cabin at kilometre 10.5 (mile 6.3), hikers ascend through the Valley of a Thousand Falls. The steep climb is surrounded by sheer walls. Three major waterfalls, and a host of smaller ones, drop down these walls. At kilometre 14.5 (mile 8.7) the trail levels off and rejoins the Robson River. This is a good spot to camp since the remainder of the trail to Berg Lake offers very little in the way of good sites. On a good day the summit of Mount Robson can be seen looming over Berg Lake; however, the area is known for heavy rainfall. The return trip, although it follows the same route, provides hikers with a new perspective. At 3,954 meters (12,972 feet), Mount Robson is the highest point in the Canadian Rockies. Although well travelled, spectacular scenery makes this trip worthwhile.

SIERRA HIGH ROUTE, CALIFORNIA
— Hiking

The Sierra Nevada area of eastern California is a vast wilderness of lakes and mountains. There are few roads, and the contrast with the urban smog of western California is striking. High in the Sierra Nevadas the air is fresh, the water clear, and the relative isolation invigorating. This area, stretching virtually unimpeded from north of Bakersfield through Yosemite has many hiking trails. Hikers can choose from simple and short day hikes through to expeditions requiring a season or more. This description focuses on a high route trail that begins in King's Canyon, about six hours drive north of Los Angeles, and ends at Twin Lakes, just northwest of Yosemite. It is easy to combine the Sierra High Route and the John Muir Trail, or hike only a small section of any of the trails in this area; therefore, individual approaches to the area can and should be dictated by personal preferences for rigour, height, distance, and time on the trail.

Using a water purifier.

King's Canyon is about six hours drive north from Los Angeles. From Fresno, take Highway #180 east for 80 kilometres (50 miles) into Sequoia National Forest, then north and east directly into King's Canyon National Park. The trailhead for the Sierra High Route begins near the end of King's Canyon Highway, at an elevation of 1,525 metres (5,000 feet). The route runs north and northwest for 325 kilometres (195 miles), generally parallel to the John Muir Trail. The first 16 kilometres (10 miles) is tough, as the Sierra High Route climbs more than 1,600 vertical metres (5,200 feet). The highest elevation on the trip is reached at Frozen Lake Pass near kilometre 40 (mile 25). At Mather Pass, kilometre 50 (mile 30), the route turns northwest, headed for Leconte Canyon and Dusy Basin. Near this point there are two exit roads that lead to Highway 395 on the east side of the trail. From the trailhead to Dusy Basin and the exit road is a solid six to seven days of hiking.

In Leconte Canyon the trail dips to about 2,600 metres (8,500 feet), but soon climbs back to 3,660 metres (12,000 feet) at Muir Pass. This is followed by Snow-Tongue Pass and Feather Pass. The distance from Leconte Canyon to Feather Pass is approximately 50 kilometres (30 miles), representing about five days hiking at these altitudes. Northeast of Feather Pass is Pine Creek Road, which is a short distance to Bishop, California. This is a good place to resupply or break the trip.

Twenty-five kilometres (15 miles) beyond Feather Pass is Mono Creek, a favourite spot for fishing. Unfortunately, this area's easy access is betrayed by evidence of garbage and other indications of popularity. Forty kilometres (25 miles) further is Mammoth Crest, where the High Sierra and John Muir Trails join together to traverse the spine of the Sierras. A downhill section follows, ending at Devil's Postpile National Monument. With the exception of the trailhead and termination points, this is the lowest point on the High Sierra Route.

The Ritter Range is a two to three day traverse through red and black metamorphic rock. The route then turns south for a short distance, before reaching Lyell Fork Crossing. First aid assistance is available here. From Lyell Fork to Tuolomne Meadows at the Tioga High Pass Highway is 32 kilometres (20 miles). Hot showers and fresh supplies are a welcome sight for all but the toughest backpackers.

The final section of the Sierra High Route, from the Tioga Highway to Twin Lakes, takes about a week. From Twin Lakes to the town of Bridgeport is 22 kilometres (13 miles) along a paved road.

Permits are now required for overnight travel in the Sierras; it is to be hoped that this will have a positive effect on the very fragile environment. The travel season in the High Sierras is from the beginning of July through the first half of October. Streams are crystal clear, but *giardia* is common; therefore, all water must be either filtered or boiled. Campsites should be at least 50 metres (160 feet) away from water and a "pack it in and pack it out" policy is in effect.

Hiking the entire High Sierra Route as described here will take a full month with additional time required for resupply detours.

For information on overnight travel permits, contact one of the following:

National Forest Service
Sequoia/King's Canyon
Three Rivers, California 93271
(209) 565–3306

National Forest Service
798 North Main Street
Bishop, California 93514
(619) 872–0308

National Forest Service
P.O. Box 595
Bridgeport, California 93517
(619) 932–7070.

For further information on routes in the Sierra Nevadas, read:

Timberline Country by Steve Roper or "Trail in the Clouds" also by Steve Roper.

SOUTH NAHANNI RIVER, NORTH WEST TERRITORIES — Canoeing

The South Nahanni River has a reputation as one of the best canoe routes for combining challenging white water, spectacular scenery, abundant wildlife and unique geological formations. It is nestled in the southwest corner of the Northwest Territories and runs from near the Yukon border southeast to the Liard River. Canoeists can reach the moose ponds at the headwaters by chartered aircraft from Watson Lake in the Yukon, or Fort Simpson or Fort Liard in the Northwest Territories.

The South Nahanni is an extremely challenging river route, and only very experienced canoeists normally consider this trip. Mountain storms can cause the river to rise as much as 1 vertical metre (three feet) overnight, so it's important to be careful where you camp. The time required to complete the river will vary according to the starting point; however, if you plan to do the full length of the river, from the moose ponds to the Liard River, allow a minimum of 18 days. Many canoeists run the river in 14–16 days, but this allows little time to observe sheep, hike some of the canyons, and explore hot springs. The South Nahanni is approximately 560 kilometres (335 miles) in length. About 300 kilometres (180 miles) is within Nahanni National Park.

Preparing to run the canyon below Virginia Falls.

All provisions must be carried, and canoeists must be self sufficient and well prepared to deal with any emergencies. The distance on the Liard River from Nahanni Butte to Fort Simpson is an additional 180 kilometres (100 miles), and includes the Beaver Dam Rapids, a tortuous run of spectacular white water (runnable, at least under some conditions, along the right hand side).

Over thirty species of mammals have been spotted within the park, including black bear, moose and beaver. Dall sheep, grizzlies, caribou and mule deer are less common. The lower section of the river includes Virginia Falls, a spectacular drop of almost 90 meters (300 feet). Further downstream is Hell's Gate, also known as Figure Eight Rapids. This rapid is described at length by Patterson in *Dangerous River*. Patterson's memories of early exploration on the river are very interesting, though they are taken with a grain of salt by experienced Nahanni canoeists.

Below the Flat River, the South Nahanni plunges through a canyon 1 thousand meters (1,100 yards) deep and 19 kilometres (12 miles) long. This is followed by two more canyons, the last of which is the site of several hot springs. Camping here, many canoeists set aside a few days to explore the limestone formations that have created caves and oxbows now located more than 400 meters (1,300 ft.) above the present river level. The park will provide a brief route description on request, but it is important that canoeists understand that the Nahanni is unpredictable and isolated. Considerable skill is required.

For more information contact:

The Superintendent
Nahanni National Park
Postal Bag 300
Fort Simpson, N.W.T.
X0E 0N0
(403) 695–2443

PACIFIC RIM NATIONAL PARK, BRITISH COLUMBIA — Hiking

This Vancouver Island park incorporates three different areas. The Long Beach section, reached by travelling west on Highway #4 from Port Alberni, attracts most visitors. The Broken Group Islands section is at the entrance to Barkley Sound, and can be reached by boat from Ucluelet, Bamfield and Port Alberni. The third section, the West Coast Trail, runs from Bamfield southwest to Port Renfrew. Both of these towns can be reached by road.

The West Coast Trail is a backpacker's delight, combining isolation and rugged beauty. The trail, first developed in 1907, was intended to run south from Bamfield to Carmanak Lighthouse. Known as the Lifesaving Trail, it was built to provide access to the area in order to improve navigational aids and furnish a rescue route for shipwreck victims. In 1973 Parks Canada began rebuilding the trail, which had gone without maintenance since World War II. Currently, the 72 kilometre (43 mile) route is in reasonably good condition. Rainfall is very high in this area, with Bamfield recording an average of 270 centimetres (108 inches) per year. (This creates thick lush vegetation that provides the backdrop for waterfalls, sea caves, and tidal pools.)

Hikers should be in very good condition. The trail is long and rough, and weather conditions will almost certainly be erratic. No reprovisioning can be guaranteed along the route, though it may be possible to buy fish and crabs from natives. Count on at least eight days travelling time. Indians will provide ferry service across the Gordon River and Nitinat Narrows. These rivers cannot be waded safely.

A variety of short trails are located in the Long Beach section. These range from .5 to 2.5 kilometres (.3 to 1.5 miles) in length. Though these trails are not wilderness areas, the beaches are quite attractive to shell collectors, birders, naturalists, and sun lovers. In summer grey whales and sea lions may be spotted offshore.

Most people visit the Broken Group Islands to see wildlife. Mussels, starfish, crabs and limpets can be spotted while beachcombing. All travellers planning overnight excursions should check with the park warden prior to departure.

Hiking the West Coast Trail.

For more information contact:

The Superintendent
Pacific Rim National Park
P.O. Box 280
Ucluelet, B.C. V0R 3A0
(604) 726–7721

For information specific to the West Coast Trail read:

The West Coast Trail (6th Ed.) by T. Leadem.

Victims of the slide were buried in the cemetery at Dyea.

Further information:

Tickets or other arrangements for the train or bus trip out of Bennet should be arranged either in Skagway or Whitehorse.

Preparation for the trip should include reading Berton's *Klondike: The Last Great Gold Rush 1896–99* and Satterfield's *Chilkoot Pass: Then and Now.* Parks Canada has a small pamphlet titled *The Historic Chilkoot Trail Guide* that is an excellent stick map outline of the trail.

CHILKOOT TRAIL, ALASKA AND BRITISH COLUMBIA — Hiking

The Chilkoot Trail developed as a gold rush route following the discovery of '96. Access is from Skagway, which can be reached by ferry from Prince Rupert, Vancouver or Seattle. The actual trailhead is reached by taking a taxi or bus from Skagway to the bridge across the Taiga River at Dyea. The trail is 53 kilometres (32 miles) long and many underestimate its difficulty.

Hikers must be in good condition and experienced in dealing with bad weather under cold and exposed conditions. A few people literally race across the trail in three days; however, five days is more typical. All provisions must be carried, and return is by train (if it's running) or road from Bennett to Skagway or Whitehorse. A stove is essential since open fires are not permitted, and you may wish to pack as much as you can in the way of supplies since prices in Skagway and Whitehorse are much higher than in southern Canada or the United States.

The most interesting aspect of the Chilkoot Trial is its history. Be sure to visit the town cemetery in Skagway (where the remains of Soapy Smith are located) and the slide cemetery at Dyea. On the trail itself you will see some of the thousands of cast-aside articles and remnants left behind by weary goldrush hopefuls.

The trail begins 13.5 kilometres (8 miles) from Skagway, near the town of Dyea. To visit the slide cemetery, continue past the bridge for several kilometres and watch for the cemetery on the left side of the road. The driver who takes you out from Skagway can sometimes be coaxed to go all the way to the cemetery.

The first kilometre of the trail is very steep, but it flattens out a bit after you gain some height. The shelter at Canyon City is a good spot to make first camp. Sheep Camp is the site of a second shelter where most hikers camp for the night in order to prepare for the summit climb. The U.S. Forest Service, which controls this area of the trail, does not permit camping between Sheep Camp and the summit. The final trek leading up to the summit has been immortalized in pictures by A. E. Hegg. These depict a struggling line of men plodding up a 35 slope, loaded with packs and baggage of all types. This climb is enough to test the mettle of modern day pioneers. The trail which started out in a rainforest, leaves the tree line behind shortly past Sheep Camp. By contrast, once you get past the summit snowfields, the Canadian side is largely scrubby pine forest.

This is a well travelled trail, but the scenery and history make the journey a once-in-a-lifetime experience.

DENALI NATIONAL PARK AND RESERVE, ALASKA — Hiking

Many argue that Denali National Park & Preserve is the quintessential nature park, equalling or possibly even bettering the great game reserves in southern Africa. The wildlife, scenery, mountains, and vast wilderness draw hikers, mountain climbers, photographers, and naturalists from around the world.

Caribou are common in Denali.

Denali is accessible from Anchorage or Fairbanks, both of which can be reached by road or regularly scheduled air service. In addition, Anchorage is a stopover port for many of the cruise ships and ferries that sail the west coast of Canada and Alaska. If you don't have a vehicle, you can travel to the park by the Alaska Railroad from Anchorage or Fairbanks.

Denali is home to almost three dozen species of mammals, including caribou, moose, grizzly and black bears, dall sheep, wolves, fox, lynx, weasels, ground squirrels, marmots, and beavers. Bird life is highly varied, including wheatears from Africa, terns from Antarctica, and jaegers from the oceans in the southern hemisphere. In total, more than 150 species of birds have been identified within the park boundaries. On the south side of the park is Mount McKinley, part of the Alaska range. At 6,194 metres (20,320 feet), McKinley is the highest peak in North America.

There is one road into the park. It begins at Highway #3, near the park gate, and winds, twists, climbs, and dips in a westerly direction for almost 140 kilometres (84 miles). Beyond the first 22 kilometres (15 miles), this road is not open to public traffic during the summer; instead, you are required to take a shuttle bus into the interior. Alongside the road there are five organized campgrounds, ranging from spacious sites designed for vehicle camping through to very rudimentary sites designed for backpackers. I recommend booking a campsite at one of the more remote campgrounds, and taking day trips until you get an overall feeling for the park.

The bus ride is magnificent. It begins in coniferous forests, runs through the Teklanika Valley, climbs up Sable and Polychrome Passes, then heads across the tundra towards Wonder Lake. The various habitats through which the road wanders support moose, sheep, grizzly bears, and caribou. The shuttle bus trip takes about 11 hours to make the round trip from the park gate to Wonder Lake and back again. However, not all buses are scheduled for the entire distance.

All the buses make regular stops in order to view scenery and wildlife, and the driver will pull over whenever you spot something interesting. The drivers are in contact with each other via radio, so they generally know where the wildlife is located. If you get off the bus to hike for a bit, simply return to the road when ready and flag the next bus.

Even if you are camping at one of the designated camping areas, Denali is a wilderness experience. Be sure you have warm clothing, lots of food, and, if leaving sight of the road, a map and compass. No supplies are available beyond the park gates, and the weather can change in a matter of minutes. What may appear to be a warm sunny bus ride, can change dramatically as soon as you leave the bus, even for a short hike.

Denali is well known for grizzly bears. While hiking, extreme caution is appropriate. I recommend a "bear bell" or some other trinket or device that will announce your approach. Once you are in the upper reaches of the park, where the sheep are most often seen, bears are of less concern, though you should be cautious about disturbing any wild animal.

If the weather is clear, and this is not always the case since the park has a reputation for extreme weather conditions, Mount McKinley can be seen from a number of different vantage points along the road and in the backcountry. The classic view is from Wonder Lake, where the bus turns around to begin the journey back to the park entrance. Although McKinley is the highest peak in North America, it is not a technically difficult climb. In fact, many intermediate level climbers, in good condition and with adequate equipment, reach the summit each year.

Backcountry permits are available at the information centre just inside the park. Be prepared to have equipment checked, and expect to answer questions about previous hiking experience. The park personnel are not going to issue a permit unless they are confident that you can look after yourself. Permits are available on a first-come-first-served basis, and there are quotas. The backcountry of Denali is one of the last great wilderness areas and travelling it is an incomparable experience.

For further information contact:

The Superintendent
Denali National Park & Preserve
P.O. Box 9, Denali Park
Alaska 99755
(907) 683–2294

NOATAK RIVER, ALASKA — Canoeing & Hiking

The Noatak River in northwestern Alaska runs above the arctic circle for its entire 675 kilometre (425 mile) length. Born in the Schwatka Mountains of the Brooks Range, it winds its way westward, before turning south and emptying into Kotzebue Sound at Hatham Inlet on Alaska's west coast. The Noatak flows through the Gates of the Arctic National Park and the Noatak National Preserve.

Look for Dall Sheep on the rocky slopes near the headwaters of the Noatak.

There are several features that make this river particularly attractive. First, the rapids are Class I and Class II, making it a challenging but not overpowering experience for less than expert canoeists. In fact, the Noatak is sometimes described as a river suitable for a family canoe trip with kids (assuming they have a sense of adventure). Second, the scenery is spectacular: mountains, barrens, isolated stands of stunted trees, canyons, and broad plains combine to create a dramatic picture of the north. Like many northern rivers, the Noatak winds its way down a broad alluvial plain, becoming increasingly braided as it nears the ocean.

Foxes are the most commonly seen mammal, though it is also likely that you will see wolves, sheep, grizzlies, caribou, and, on the lower river, moose. Peregrine falcons, a delightful sighting, are also common.

Most canoeists fly from Fairbanks to Bettles, then charter a plane for the 160 kilometre (100 mile) trip to the river. Matchurak Lake, Pingo Lake, and 12 Mile Slough are the three most common starting points. Flying over the Arrigetch Peaks is quite an experience, particularly in a Beaver or single-engine Otter that has to work hard to gain the altitude required to clear the mountain tops.

It's worth spending some time hiking the headwaters area before getting too far downstream. This is the place to look for Dall sheep and caribou. Hiking continues to be good as the valley widens and the hills rise. Make camp on a gravel bar and climb the nearest slope. The views are spectacular. Areas of special interest include Kogruk Creek, where a short hike upstream leads to hot springs, and Igning Creek, noted for its population of grizzlies. The Aglungak Hills are very pretty, even when the weather is on the wet side, a common occurrence in the arctic. Noatak Canyon, another very scenic spot on the river, poses no great difficulty for canoeists in spite of its forbidding cliffs and narrow entrance.

The river is comprised of four fairly distinctive sections. First is the headwaters to Lake Matcharak, characterized by alpine tundra and depths ranging from 7 centimetres (3 inches) to 1 metre (3 feet). The second section is a wide basin with high brush and a stream width of 25 to 75 metres (80 to 250 feet). In the third section the valley is narrower, with standing waves up to one metre (3 feet). This section finishes with the Noatak Canyon. The final section includes birch and spruce lowlands, and the river becomes increasingly braided. There are about 13 kilometres (8 miles) of Class II white water below Douglas Creek.

Most canoeists end their trip at the town of Noatak. Arrangements can be made to fly from here to Kotzebue, where regularly scheduled aircraft depart for Fairbanks and Anchorage. All in all, the most difficult aspect of the Noatak is getting in and out of the area; the river itself is quite straightforward. The USGS maps for this trip include Survey Pass, Ambler River, Howard Pass, Misheguk Mountain, Baird Mountain, and Noatak. (For information on ordering USGS maps see Chapter 4.)

The Noatak is a relatively well travelled arctic river, and you will likely see two or three other groups enjoying the route. The arctic canoeing season is short, and this means that most paddlers begin and end their trips within a few days of each other. However, in spite of the fact that yours isn't likely to be the only trip on the river, the Noatak is pristine and isolated when compared to any river south of the 48th parallel. If you are looking for a family trip in the arctic, or a great experience for novice to intermediate canoeists, the Noatak is a river worth considering. Plan on fifteen days paddling time, and then add a few extra days for hiking, fishing and photography.

For more information, contact:

Gates of the Arctic National Park
P.O. Box 74680
Fairbanks, Alaska 99701
(907) 456–0281

or

Noatak National Preserve
P.O. Box 1029
Kotzebue, Alaska 99752
(907) 442–3760

and read

Alaska Paddling Guide by Jack Mosby and David Dapkus.

SUGGESTED READINGS

- *AMC River Guide: Maine.* (1986). Boston: The Appalachian Mountain Club.

- Berton, P. (1977). *Klondike: The Last Great Gold Rush 1896–1899* (Rev. Ed.). Toronto: McClelland and Stewart.

- Christian, E. (1938). *Unflinching: A Diary of Tragic Adventure.* New York: Funk & Wagnalls.

- Daniell, E. (1987). *AMC Guide to Mount Washington & the Presidential Range* (4th Ed.). Boston: The Appalachian Mountain Club.

- Daniell, E. (Ed.). (1987). *AMC White Mountain Guide: A Guide to the Trails in the Mountains of New Hampshire and Adjacent Parts of Maine* (24th Ed.). Boston: The Appalachian Mountain Club.

- Dannen, K, & Dannen, D. (1978). *Rocky Mountain National Park Hiking Trails.* Charlotte, North Carolina: East Woods Press Books.

- Deer, D. (Ed.) (1977). *Best Hiking Trails in the United States.* Matteson, Illinois: Great Lakes Press.

- DuFresne, J. (1984). *Isle Royale National Park: Foot Trails and Water Routes.* Seattle: The Mountaineers.

- Dunning, H. (1970). *Facts About Longs Peak.* Boulder, Colorado: Johnson Publishing Company.

- Fisher, R. (1971). *The Appalachian Trail.* Washington: National Geographic Society.

- Fisher, R. (1977). *Still Waters, White Waters: Exploring America's Rivers and Lakes.* Washington: National Geographic Society.

- Hanbury, D. (1904). *Sport and Travel in the Northland of Canada.* New York: Macmillan.

- Horwood, D. & Parkin, T. (1989). *Islands for Discovery: An Outdoor Guide to B.C.'s Queen Charlotte Islands.* Victoria: Orca Publishing.

- Katz, E. (1991). *The Complete Guide to Walking in Canada.* Toronto: Doubleday.

- Kunelius, R. (1977). *Ski Trails in the Canadian Rockies.* Banff, Alberta: Summerthought Ltd.

- Leadem, T. (Ed.). (1987). *The West Coast Trail* (6th Ed.). Vancouver: Douglas & McIntyre

- Mosby, J. & Dupkus, D. (1986). *Alaska Paddling Guide.* Anchorage: JR Enterprises.

- Patterson, R. (1973) *The Dangerous River,* Sidney, British Columbia: Grey's Publishing Limited. (Originally published in 1954 by William Sloane Associates.)

- Patton, B. & Robinson, B. (1991). *The Canadian Rockies Trail Guide* (4th Ed.). Banff, Alberta: Summerthought Ltd.

- Pyle, S. (1979). *Canoeing & Rafting: The Complete Where-To-Go Guide to America's Best Tame and Wild Rivers.* New York: William Morrow.

- Robertson, D. (1984). *The Best Hiking in Ontario.* Edmonton: Hurtig Press.

- Roper, S. (1982). *Timberline Country: The Sierra High Route.* San Francisco: Sierra Club Books.

- Roper, S. (1990, February). Trail in the Clouds. *Backpacker, 18* (1), pp. 22–33.

- Russell, F. (1973). *The Okefenokee Swamp.* New York: Time-Life Books.

- Satterfield, A. (1974). *Chilkoot Pass: Then and Now* (Rev. Ed.). Anchorage: Alaska Northwest Publishing Company.

- Whalley, G. (1962). *The Legend of John Hornby.* Toronto: Macmillan.

- *Wild Rivers: James Bay and Hudson Bay.* (1977). Ottawa: Parks Canada.

- *Wild Rivers: Saskatchewan.* (1974). Ottawa: Parks Canada.

Appendix A

The following is a list of the food carried on a five day hike in the Yukon Territory by four people.

BREAKFAST—totals 2.5 kilograms

Familia was made of the following ingredients and quantities. This provided all of the breakfasts.

- 4 cups rolled oats
- 4 cups tritacayle
- 4 cups wheat flakes
- 2 cups sunflower seeds
- 4 cups raisins
- 2 cups chopped peanuts
- 1 cup sesame seeds
- 6 cups powdered milk

This was divided into two portions, with 1 cup of banana chips added to the first and 1 cup of candied lemon and orange rind added to the second. To serve, add boiling water to 2/3 cup of the mixture and let sit for three minutes.

LUNCH— totals 11.4 kilograms

The following items were used to make different lunches according to weather, tastes and interests.

- 170 gm. tea
- 56 gm. coffee
- 540 gm. hot chocolate
- 738 gm. flour (for bannock)
- 710 gm. (8 pkgs.) soup
- 142 gm. pepper, salt, garlic, ginger
- 300 gm. cashews
- 426 gm. peanut oil
- 284 gm. carrots
- 908 gm. German rye bread
- 200 gm. baked crust

- 3010 gm. margarine (squeeze Parkay)
- 800 gm. cheese
- 370 gm. honey
- 483 gm. peanut butter
- 2272 gm. (23 pkgs.) assorted juice

DINNER—totals 6.082 kilograms

The following dinners were carried. Some intermingling was done.

#1 Stew

- 227 gm. noodles plus bay leaves
- 454 gm. corned beef (tinned)
- 227 gm. tomato paste
- 114 gm. soup base

#2 Salami & Eggs

- 795 gm. salami
- 454 gm. eggs
- 57 gm. green beans (F.D.)
- 171 gm. pudding (dried)

#3 Bacon & Eggs

- 570 gm. bacon
- 454 gm. eggs
- 710 gm. potatoes

#4 Pasta Meal

- 200 gm. macaroni shells
- 85 gm. diced beef (F.D.)
- 171 gm. pudding (dried)

Dinner Meals—continued.

#5 Chinese Meal

- 370 gm. veg. (dry kale, lily leaves, mustard greens)
- 85 gm. peas (F.D.)
- 370 gm. rice
- 114 gm. beef
- 170 gm. noodles
- 227 gm. soy sauce, mustard, plum sauce
- 57 gm. mushrooms (dried)

EXTRAS & ACCESSORIES—total 1.533 kilograms

- 426 gm. brown sugar
- 113 gm. raisins
- 227 gm. banana chips (F.D.)
- 113 gm. coconut (F.D.)
- 200 gm. apricots (F.D.)
- 227 gm. pears (F.D.)
- 227 gm. apples (F.D.)

F.D. denotes freeze-dried.
Meal #5 takes a long time to prepare.

It is interesting to note that the lightest meal is the pasta, and the heaviest is the one involving whole potatoes. This menu has several superior points: breakfasts are fast, easy to prepare, and high in nutritive value; lunches allow complete freedom of choice, therefore allowing for greater taste appeal; the high quantities of fresh eggs provide the essential amino acids in appropriate proportions. Total weight is 21.524 kilograms or 5.381 kilograms per person or 1.076 kilograms per person per day.

Menu compliments of Jack Gryfe, Bill Lorimer, Roger Nightingale and Gerry Weisberg.

Appendix B

Clothing & Equipment for a Six Day Arctic Summer Hike Through a Mountain Pass

CLOTHING

1. watch cap
2. sun hat
3. rain pants
4. rain jacket with hood
5. mountain parka with hood (wind proof)
6. wool oversweater (loose, long and roomy)
7. wool innersweater (turtleneck)
8. wool long underwear
9. wool shirt
10. wool pants
11. chamois or flannel shirt
12. wool socks
13. gloves (nylon)
14. wool mitts
15. cotton underwear (boxer style)
16. belt or suspenders
17. cotton 'T' shirt
18. shorts (wool or heavy cordura)
19. sneakers
20. hiking boots
21. large bandanna or small towel
22. vest

PERSONAL EQUIPMENT

1. sleeping bag and liner
2. sleeping pad
3. pack
4. nylon cord, thread, tacks
5. knife, fork, spoon, cup, plate (according to your menu)
6. toothbrush, comb, toiletries
7. soap, shampoo, flashlight
8. insect repellent
9. bear bell, lip balm, glacier cream, sunglasses
10. water bottle
11. compass and top map
12. whistle
13. American Express Card

GROUP EQUIPMENT

1. tent and fly
2. stove, fuel bottle and fuel
3. repair equipment (tape, needles, thread, tacks,clevis pins, locking rings, screwdriver, rip-stop tape)
4. first aid kit
5. cooking gear (frying pan, pliers,, grill, pots, choregirl, plastic flipper)
6. candle
7. toilet paper
8. matches

Appendix C

Answer all parts, using "N/A" if not applicable to you.
If necessary, use the back of this form.

Name	Phone No.
Address	Health Ins. No.
	Height
Date of Birth	Weight

In case of illness, notify:

Name	Relationship
Address	Phone No.

Is allergy identification worn? Yes___No___	If yes, what type

List all drug and food allergies and any drugs which should not be administered:

Will you be taking any drugs or special medications with you on the trip?	Yes___No___

If so, note all details including the name of the medication, purpose, history and dosages:

List all other diseases you are immunized against:

Please note any conditions or history such as diabetes, heart disease, asthma, cancer, epilepsy, etc., that may be useful to the trip leaders in the course of regular operations or in the event of an emergency:

Are contact lenses normally worn Yes___No___	Additional information is attached Yes___No___

TO THE BEST OF MY KNOWLEDGE, THE ABOVE INFORMATION IS CORRECT AND COMPLETE, AND I AM IN GOOD HEALTH AND HAVE NOT BEEN EXPOSED TO ANY INFECTIOUS DISEASE(S) IN THE PAST FOUR WEEKS. IF I BECOME EXPOSED TO ANY INFECTIOUS DISEASE BETWEEN NOW AND THE TIME OF DEPARTURE, I UNDERSTAND THAT THE TRIP LEADER MUST BE NOTIFIED IN WRITING.

Date	Signature

Appendix D

Map of Clear Lake Based On Map Drawing Exercise in Chapter 4

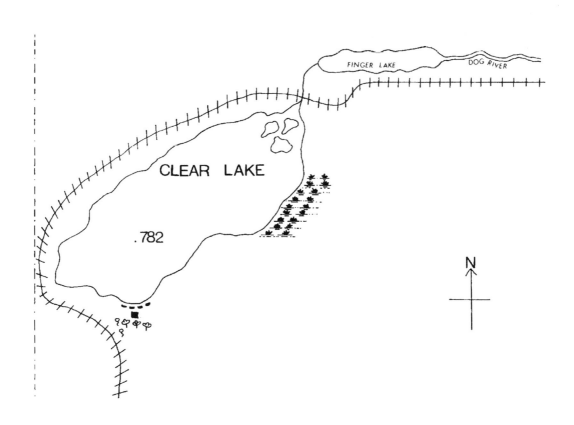

Index